Belated Modernity
and Aesthetic Culture

Theory and History of Literature
Edited by Wlad Godzich and Jochen Schulte-Sasse

For other books in the series, see p. 209.

Belated Modernity
and Aesthetic Culture
Inventing National
Literature

Gregory Jusdanis

Theory and History of Literature, Volume 81

University of Minnesota Press
Minneapolis   Oxford

"Criticism as National Culture" first appeared as "The Importance of
Being Minor," *Journal of Modern Greek Studies* 8 (1990): 5–33. By
permission.

Published by the University of Minnesota Press
2037 University Avenue Southeast, Minneapolis, MN 55414
Printed in the United States of America on acid-free paper

Library of Congress Cataloging-in-Publication Data

Jusdanis, Gregory, 1955–
    Belated modernity and aesthetic culture : inventing national
literature / Gregory Jusdanis.
        p. cm. — (Theory and history of literature : v. 81)
    Includes bibliographical references and index.
    ISBN 0-8166-1980-8
    ISBN 0-8166-1981-6 (pbk.)
    1. Literature—History and criticism—Theory, etc. 2. Literature,
Comparative—History and criticism. 3. Canon (Literature)
4. Aesthetics. I. Title. II. Series.
PN81.J85   1992
809—dc20   91-11964
                                                                CIP

A CIP catalog record for this book is available from the British Library.

The University of Minnesota
is an equal-opportunity
educator and employer.

For Julian

Contents

Acknowledgments

In the following pages I state often that my study must be regarded as part of a collective inquiry into the historical emergence of literatures. This is true on a personal level as well. I am greatly indebted to many friends, colleagues, and institutions. The bulk of the research was financed by a generous two-year postdoctoral fellowship from the Social Sciences and Humanities Research Council of Canada. The College of Humanities at the Ohio State University kindly provided me with grant-in-aid to conduct further research in Greece as well as two academic quarters free from teaching and administrative duties. Portions of the manuscript were presented at the University of Birmingham (England), the University of Bonn, Indiana University, the colloquium "The Canonization of Greece in the Human Sciences" at Harvard University, Queens College, and the Middle East Literary Seminar at Princeton. I am grateful to all participants for their valuable insights and comments. The Johns Hopkins University Press has offered permission to reprint a revised version of the first chapter originally published in the *Journal of Modern Greek Studies.*

I would like to thank Kui Qiu as well as Evangelos Gegas for assisting me in my work with efficiency, energy, and meticulous care. I am indebted to Ann Klefstad for her careful copyediting. Dimitris Dimiroulis, Wlad Godzich, Michael Herzfeld, and Dimitris Tziovas read the entire manuscript in its early stages and made many helpful suggestions. I cannot overemphasize my gratitude to the students of three graduate seminars at the Ohio State University with whom I discussed many of the issues covered here and whose comradely advice helped sharpen my arguments. Carl Anderson read the manuscript twice over with patience and painstaking attention, tactfully suggesting improvements. Jochen Schulte-Sasse devoted many hours to the project, discussing it with me extensively and helping to bring it to fruition. Vassilis Lambropoulos has been involved with this project from the beginning. I am beholden to him for our ongoing dialogue which has left its trace in the text. My greatest debt is to my wife, Julian Anderson, for her tranquillity and generous criticism in the writing of this book. In more ways than one, it is written for her.

Introduction

This is a study of national culture and belated modernization. It traces the emergence of an autonomous cultural identity, a sphere of shared sentiments and experiences, in response to the social, political, and economic transformations taking place in European societies during the seventeenth and eighteenth centuries. By examining the function of this imaginary realm in the construction of the state, the dominant mode of sociopolitical organization in modernity, it reflects on the factors that made the invention of national culture so inevitable. At its inception national culture is really literary in nature, for literature, in the extended sense of stories and specific meaning as fiction, is thought to mirror the nation as well as encourage the acquisition by the population of socially important values and norms. My project therefore investigates literature's role in the building of nations, its establishment as an institution, and then its aestheticization as a compensatory form. I wish to show how narratives, once essential in the creation of collective identities, eventually become a means for orchestrating an ideological consensus.

My examples are taken from western Europe and primarily from Greece. While I look at developments in Germany, England, and France, I am interested particularly in the formation of culture on the periphery of Europe. The approach is comparative. I look at the emergence of art and literature in western European countries, then follow their introduction into a stratified, agrarian, and noncapitalist society often hostile to rationalism, Enlightenment, and secularism. My aim is to discover the implications of purposeful modernization in the cultural realm and the fate of the modernizing project in a society unprepared for it. The work thus seeks to reveal an-other modernity, an experiment on the margins, which, having internalized the tensions between dominant and minor, periphery and center, prototype and copy, imitates and also creates, follows but resists. Implicitly I examine how and why a society defines itself as modern and western.

The Greek enterprise to attain ethnic, linguistic, economic, and territorial integration constitutes one of the earliest attempts at modernization outside western Europe. In an unprecedented geopolitical calculation, Greek-speaking Orthodox subjects of the Ottoman Empire aspired in the eighteenth century to orient their community to the West. Believing that the power center was no longer the Ottoman Empire, nor even the Russian Empire, they sought access instead to the expanding capitalist states of Europe. Having become aware in the seventeenth and eighteenth centuries of different social, economic, and political structures in the West, and believing that their interests lay with them, they proposed a fundamental reordering of their community. The changes ranged from the founding of an independent state to devising new protocols of social behavior. National culture proved necessary as both binding agent for the state and means of instilling the new patterned order.

One of the most prominent successes of this project was the insertion of the story of Greece into the master narrative of the then-powerful nations. Greek intellectuals, scattered throughout Europe, learned how to deal with the dominant cultures and how to present their own society to their hosts. But this came at a price: they ended up replacing Ottoman domination for cultural, economic, and also political dependency on the West. The Greek state, once integrated into the capitalist system, actually became a peripheral area in relation to those regions, a pattern later repeated by former colonies of the Third World after independence. To be sure, Greece has been characterized by some observers as the earliest Third World country (Kaklamanis 1989: 15).

The first modern feature the Greek elites sought was national unification. This, of course, is not the only characteristic of modernization. Modernity in this context usually signifies those structural attributes of western European society that began taking shape around the sixteenth century and that distinguished it from previous periods and other contemporaneous societies. These attributes include industrial expansion; constitutional restrictions on the exercise of political power; the rise of civil bureaucracies; the growth of urban centers; the spread of literacy and mass education; secularism; the appearance of the interior, psychological self; and functional differentiation. The last category, which incorporates some of the previous features, occurs when the institutional spheres of politics, economy, science, law, education, and religion are dissociated from one another and become autonomous systems. The emergence of an autonomous aesthetic and a separate institution of art, two concerns of my study, forms part of this process.

By the modernization of Greek society I mean the enterprise launched by the intellectual and mercantile elites in the late eighteenth century to designate the Greek-speaking Orthodox a national community, free the Greek territories from Ottoman control, and define the Greeks as western. They took a gamble by trying to create a new territorial, social, and administrative entity. A national culture, replacing the ethnoreligious identities in the Ottoman Empire, acted as a source of legitimation for the new state by harmonizing local loyalties and linguistic variations in an imaginary realm. This domain of symbols and meanings was conceived, as in many though not all nationalist projects, prior to actual independence. In short, national unity was experienced discursively before it was attained politically.

The modernization of Greece, however, did not follow the blueprints of the elite, any more than it does elsewhere. The contingencies of local context, social and cultural variations, and structural dependence on the West do not permit this. The bulk of the Greek population did not consider itself European. Political and cultural institutions were imported into a decentralized and feudal society incapable of integrating them and suspicious of western life and thought. The modernization of Greece was therefore "imperfect." Belated modernization, especially in nonwestern societies, necessarily remains "incomplete" not because it deviates from the supposedly correct path but because it cannot culminate in a faithful duplication of western prototypes. The imported models do not function like their European counterparts. Often they are resisted. The project of becoming modern thus differs from place to place. This is why it is possible to speak of many modernities. Peripheral societies, however, internalize the incongruity between western originals and local realities as a structural deficiency. The lack of modernity is seen as a flaw. Hence, "incomplete" attempts to catch up with the West are followed by calls for a new phase of modernization. Ironically, however, the flaw lies not in modernity's absence but in its purposeful introduction, ignoring autochthonous exigencies.

My study begins with a critique of the Eurocentrism and chronocentrism in modernization theories, namely, the way they project the traits of western culture to other times and other societies. In the post-World War II political order this thinking resulted in developmental policies that proposed modernization as an inexorable process of change ending in the complete reproduction of western paradigms (Tipps 1973: 207). When social scientists, for instance, turned their attention to the Third World, which they understood as underdeveloped, they expected it to reap the "benefits" of technology by following the same path toward modernity as western nations. Their Darwinist theories saw social evolution as a predictable progression toward increasing complexity, culminating in the abandonment of all traditional features and the creation of "advanced" social systems (Hoogvelt 1978: 14; Roxborough 1979: 13). They foresaw the establishment in these countries of western social, economic, and political institutions. Having defined tradition and modernity as diametric opposites, they regarded the transformation from the former to the latter state as unilinear. The European experience was extrapolated to nonwestern societies in the belief that the history of the West could be repeated and that any country would pass through comparable stages of development (de Souza and Porter 1974: 9).

All proponents of modernization adopt this deterministic approach. The Greek intellectual and mercantile elites expected Greeks to become western. For them modernity and the West were synonymous. They too generalized from the European situation in their hopes to achieve economic, social, and political union according to European paradigms. The Greek case indicates that the dichotomous thinking underlying the whole argument for Third World modernization has been present right from the beginning. The initial encounter with modernity launched Greek society on a cataract of ideological oppositions (East-West, traditional-modern, purist-demotic, classical-contemporary, ethnicity-state) which led to instability and sometimes violence. To resolve these tensions, if only in an imaginary way, another modern construct was imported, the autonomous aesthetic.

The relatively early experience of the Greeks with modernization is instructive because, in a sense, all such projects after the Netherlands, England, and France are belated. In their deviation from these prototypes, they share some common features. German modernity, for example, was less a product of internal conditions than a response to French domination. It was a purposeful act, imposed from the top as a theory of the Enlightenment. Delayed modernization necessitates centralized planning, since it entails the anxious attempt to acquire the characteristics of a model. Canada offers another good example of this. A British colony until 1867, it became culturally and economically dependent on the United States in the twentieth century. In order to affirm its own national integrity against the influence of these two giants, Canada invested in cultural institutions promoting unity: the Canadian Broadcasting Corporation, the National Film Board of Canada, the National Research Councils. To this day the federal government funds culture heavily as a means of resisting American hegemony. Culture plays an indispensable role in modernization because it promotes national cohesion. Often, however, as in the case of Germany and Greece, it permits an imaginary perception of unity before it is achieved politically and administratively. Germany as a national idea had its beginnings in German *Bildung*, which created a national literature allowing individuals of the various states to participate in a common narrative.

Modernity can be experienced late by both western and nonwestern societies. When discussing the latter, however, western writers encounter some problems regarding their position, most significantly the very presentness of their own language, the hermeneutics of their modernity. We live in an age which, as Foucault observes, has designated itself modern. As inheritors of the *Aufklärung*, we problematize our own "discursive present-ness" (1986: 89). Our discourse "takes into account its own presentness, in order to find its own place, to pronounce its own meaning, and to specify the mode of action which it is capable of exercising within this present" (90). Even when we undertake excursions into other epochs and cultures we still may be looking for ourselves, posing the questions: "What is my present? What is the meaning of this present? And what am I doing when I speak of this present?" (90). These questions often lead to critique. (Alas, we still write within the horizons of critique!) If we cannot escape the modern, we can at least reflect on its effects.

Throughout this study I refer to the building of national culture as fabrication, invention, and construction in order to emphasize the contextual, historical, and interpretive nature of this project. It goes without saying that my own narrative is also a "fiction," not because it tells conscious lies but because it is a provisional attempt, based on the assumptions I outline here, to grasp the topic at hand. Like all tales it makes use of rhetorical tropes and, though I hope to discuss representative factors in the production of national literature, is determined by principles of exclusion. My account claims no universal validity but intervenes in contemporary discussions of critical theory, cultural studies, and comparative literature in two ways: first, as a critique to counter current perceptions of peripheral or nonwestern traditions, and second, as a constructive assertion of differences to enable these traditions to represent themselves.

Aware that discussions of modernity in nonwestern cultures have ideological consequences, I would like to add some qualifications: I do not pose modernity as an ideal nor do I impose it as a model. Furthermore, though I must refer to terms such as modernity and tradition, I do not imply that they are antithetical. My intention is not to reinforce these antitheses, therefore my use of them should be understood as being "under erasure." The split between tradition and modernity has been, as I argue earlier, a function of the modernization project, which assumes that modern societies have completely eradicated traditional elements and, conversely, that traditional societies have no modern features. I would like to see these concepts as continuous rather than separate, dialectically related rather than diametrically opposed (see Rudolph and Rudolph 1967). For instance, although some Enlightenment thinkers such as Voltaire and Korais thought that religion and modernity were incompatible, religion has often functioned as a vehicle for modernization (Werblowsky 1976: 31). Traditional structures do not simply yield to modernization but coexist with new institutions. "Belated" societies, however, exhibit an uneasy fit between traditional and modern constructs. The history of Germany in the twentieth century, for example, indicates the coexistence of hyperindustrialization and "premodern" forces. Modernity fails because it rarely leads to the creation of western clones and the complete annihilation of indigenous practices. The local quite often defends itself against the alien.

The ultimate aim of studies like mine is the formulation of alternate theories within the boundaries of a reclaimed symbolic space. These theories would be based on the problematic of minor or peripheral paradigms, though not universalized. If students of marginal disciplines do not wish to be confined to the borders of the humanities and social sciences, vainly communicating only with each other, if they do not wish to speak the language of others, limited by those others' questions and answers, they must study their own practices, and discuss their own theoretical crisis. As Cary Nelson puts it, only a theorized discipline, engaged in self-criticism, "can be an effective site for a general social critique" (1987: 48). Writers could invent such theories by reflecting on their own situation, be it of belated modernization, colonialism, racism, or whatever.

Ashcroft, Griffiths, and Tiffin, for instance, suggest that the Canadian experience of cultural mosaic could generate discourses of literary hybridity and spatial plurality to replace the linear models of nationalism (1989: 36). The phenomenon of purposeful modernization may also lead to its theorization involving questions about the tension between Europe and the local culture; the latter's internalization of feelings of inferiority; the use of European thought to resist the importation of western ideologies; the implications of belatedness. Such discourses will develop their own concepts of text, representation, interpretation, author, value, meaning, reading, and canon, as well as other concepts impossible to conceive in the western critical framework. These theories, having emerged from their own specific historical situations as well as being responses to western hegemony, would be better positioned to explain the developments of their own paradigms.

My own study, not an attempt to draft an "alternate" theory, simply maps out the cultural differences in order to prepare the ground for such a theory's eventual configuration. Its institutional home is the new field of modern Greek studies in the Anglo-Saxon world. Modern Greek culture has occupied an ambivalent position in western scholarship, on the one hand attracting the attention of classicists who sought in Greek culture material for the elucidation of ancient Greek society, and on the other, regarded by them as less than fully European, let alone modern. This prejudice is encountered by the field itself, situated in the epistemological ghetto of ethnic studies, a soft option for those interested in "exotic" cultures but also, by its own "exoticism," evidence of the university's pluralism. My project is partly a response to and a reflection on this situation. It is related to attempts of some modern Greek specialists (for instance, Herzfeld 1987 and Lambropoulos 1988) to question the status of modern Greek as another curious example of ethnic studies and to transform it into a theorized field able to participate in interdisciplinary discussions.

My general goal is rather straightforward—to show that things have not always been so and can therefore be changed. In choosing to write about the construction of a national literature in a peripheral country as an example of belated modernization, I wish to demonstrate that current practices in western culture constitute not reality but a field of contingencies to which neither our present nor future should be held hostage. Only current ideologies terrorize us into believing that there are no alternatives. What Johannes Fabian observes in cultural anthropology is certainly valid for criticism: "The methods, channels, and means of presenting knowledge are anything but secondary to its contents" (1983: 116). By focusing on what was practiced prior to literature, by examining how literature was institutionalized in another culture, we can come to understand that the "methods, channels, and means" of present literary knowledge are not timeless and shared by all humanity but are the products of western European culture of the last two hundred years. If we restore to the institutions of literature and criticism their history and otherness, we can realize that our apparently individual reactions to universally recognized literary works are more than innocent responses to self-evident truths.

What follows is a summary of the book's five chapters. As I explain in chapter 1, the study contributes to the reevaluation of the totalizing strategies of western thought, which, in projecting its values as universal, seeks their reproduction in other societies. I argue, for instance, that both critical practice and critical theory operate like a national culture insofar as they seek to fabricate an ideological consensus on an international scale. They aspire (aesthetically) to a conflation of cultural differences by projecting the idea of common interest and collective heritage. In chapter 2 I outline the project of the Greek elites to define their community as modern and western by generating a collective identity to serve as a basis for national solidarity. Chapter 3 concerns the role of the literary canon in the formation of the national narrative. After examining the theoretical concept of canon, I trace the emergence of a national literature by investigating anthologies of poetry and prose. I relate this venture to attempts to modernize the social, political, and economic infrastructure. In chapter 4 I explore the rise of an autonomous aesthetic in western Europe in order to compare it with developments in Greece. This leads to a discussion of opposition to western models and the failures of modernization. Chapter 5 examines the social spaces of literary discourse and the composition of a public sphere where literature emerged and national consensus was contrived.

A note on transliteration from the Greek: I have tried to use the system of transliteration suggested by the *Journal of Modern Greek Studies,* though I have retained the familiar spelling of well-known names (i.e., Cavafy, not Kavafis). Of course I follow standard practice in cases of classical Greek (*techne* as opposed to *tehni*). All translations, unless otherwise identified, are my own.

Chapter 1
Criticism as National Culture

The topic of this book, the relationship between literature and national culture, is frustrated by dominant critical practice that either dismisses nonwestern literatures as parochial or, more important, incorporates them into its cosmopolitan category of the literary. For more than a century critics have worked to show the interdependence of the world's literatures and have argued that local variations are really part of a celestial unity. They searched for continuities, origins, and grand narratives. But criticism's celebration of common interest and its projection of a few dominant literatures as universal paradigms have come at the expense of most other traditions in the world.

The production of shared characteristics is, of course, the hallmark of nationalist discourse, which attempts to enforce a linguistic and ethnic uniformity in the state through culture. The totalizing strategies of literary criticism function much like the attempts of national cultures to homogenize differences within their territorial and symbolic spaces. Criticism's nationalist operations are not surprising given its initial participation in the nation-building process. Philology evolved into modern criticism during the eighteenth and nineteenth centuries when this new discipline committed itself to the construction of civil and national imaginaries in western Europe. It continues to function as a national discipline, though at the end of the nineteenth century it extended its aspirations outside the boundaries of western Europe. Its aim in the era of multinational concerns is the preservation of western identity from external threats. By posing western developments as global models it implicitly affirms their superiority over other literatures.

The Ecumenicity of Comparative Literature

Even comparative literature does not escape the integrative procedures of nationalist thought. Although it takes as its aim the comparison of two or more literatures, it has to date concerned itself primarily with the traditions of northern Europe and has promulgated the ideas of European or world literature. In an influential text, "La littérature européenne," Ferdinand Brunetière articulated his notion of "European literature" (a province of the greater category of comparative literature), which subsumed various national literatures within one totality (1904: 1–5, 49–51). He subordinated national literature to European writing, which itself belonged to the genus of general literature. Frédéric Loliée similarly promoted the universal vision of comparative literature. Referring to the literatures of western Europe, he affirmed that they, "more or less distinct in origin and character or more or less interwoven finally, are united in an all-embracing unity" (1904: 358). Comparative literature was becoming the discipline concerned with the literary traditions of the "nation" of Europe.

The comparative approach appeared partly as a response to literature's active involvement in the building of nations. In reaction to literature's production of cultural identities, critics wished to activate its potential to criticize and transcend these identities. The cosmopolitanism of comparative literature sought "to reduce the murderous competition among nationalities by subsuming all nations in one higher unity" (Chaitin forthcoming). The importance of linguistic barriers, Wellek and Warren state, was "unduly magnified" during the nineteenth century when nationalism was closely allied with literary history (1963: 51). After decades of narrow-minded nationalism the perspective afforded by literary world citizenship is welcomed (Weisstein 1973: 19) because it looks "beyond the narrow boundaries of national frontiers" to discern movements and trends in various national cultures (Aldridge 1969: 1). The advantage of comparative literature, S. S. Prawer argues, over traditional disciplines is that it studies literature without regard to national borders (1973: 4). Comparative literature, according to Henry Remak, teaches scholars a more comprehensive understanding of literature "as a whole" rather than of departmental fragments. Indeed, he implores students of single national traditions to widen their perspectives by undertaking excursions into other literatures (1961: 10, 17).

Few would disagree with Remak. The project of comparative literature is as valuable now as during its inception. Indeed, nothing is more deplorable than Anglocentric critics who know no other languages save the current lingua franca and who presume their experience of the literary to be universal. Comparative literature, with its broader vision of genres, periods, styles, movements, and interdisciplinarity exercises, as Jonathan Culler asserts, "a critical demystificatory force on the cultural pieties of a nation" (1986: 30). Yet no matter how commendable the theory, its practice reveals a deep chasm between ideals and scholarly realities. For the Weltanschauung of comparative literature in terms of both departmental policy and epistemic investigations has tended to limit itself to the dominant linguistic traditions. Mary Louise Pratt argues that comparative literature is "primarily oriented toward creating a [western] European Continentalism" to the exclusion of most of the world's literature, including that of the United States. When comparatists broadened their glance to the classical literatures in Chinese, Japanese, Sanskrit, and Hebrew, they did so with the intention of studying not contemporary Third World writing but the literature of "Europe's fellow high civilizations—refined, ancient, and classical, though in modern times equals no longer" (1986: 33).[1] Furthermore, the differences critics seek to compare between national units turn out to be dimensions of a vaster union. Comparative literature aspires to demonstrate both the interdependence of various literatures and their participation in a grander process. All literatures are seen as species of a higher class defined by their linked traits. The basis for this uniformity is a common inheritance. "Only within a single civilization," Ulrich Weisstein claims, "can one find those common elements of a consciously or unconsciously upheld tradition in thought, feeling, and imagination which . . . beyond the confines of time and space often constitute an astounding bond of unity" (1973: 7–8). Weisstein's plea for a shared imaginary is a classic example of statist thought. Critical discourse imposes this unity on an international scale rather than within the territorial space of the nation.

The general concept of literature determines the way comparatists view individual national paradigms. Wellek and Warren regard literature as a "totality" and exhort their readers to trace its development "without regard to linguistic distinctions" (49). The great strategy of comparative literature, they believe, is to falsify the notion of a self-enclosed national literature. "Western literature, at least, forms a unity, a whole" (49). They applaud developments in criticism that demonstrate the unity of western civilization and ask for "a widening of perspectives, a suppression of local and provincial sentiments" (50). Wellek demands that we transcend all provincialisms, however respectable and hallowed. Literature is one, he concludes, as humanity and art are one; "and in this conception lies the future of literary studies" (1953: 5).

This transcendence, of course, sacrifices the individual to the general. Although comparatists claim not to neglect national paradigms, their sweeping project casts aside "provincial" and local elements and those traditions unable to compete according to western terms of greatness. Ironically this cosmopolitanism, far from escaping nationalism, becomes a means of asserting nationalism on a supranational scale. In an attempt to transcend the reactionary forces of nationalism, comparative literature has in fact embraced its integrative and exclusionary maneuvers.

For instance, one of the most distinguished projects of comparative literature, Curtius's *European Literature and the Latin Middle Ages,* is based on the notion that European literature forms a unified structure: "The starting point of our inquiry was the historical fact that the Mediterranean-Nordic West was culturally one. Our goal was to demonstrate the same unity in its literature. We had, therefore, to make manifest certain continuities which had hitherto been overlooked" (1973: 228). Curtius no doubt includes classical Greece in his Procrustean scheme but not the literature of the modern nation. Though located on the Mediterranean, modern Greek literature does not conform to this plan. Comparatists have presumed from the beginning the existence of a universal literature, the founding paradigm of all literary production. Yet an examination of contemporary literatures from the Mediterranean would have demonstrated that this notion hardly corresponds to the reality of Europe, let alone the rest of the world.

Critics need not spend much time reading to arrive at this conclusion; they could also simply set foot in a country outside western Europe. Charles R. Larson discovered that, when he began teaching English literature to Nigerian high school students in 1962, they asked questions he did not anticipate about the English novels and brought concerns to the class unrelated to his literary tradition. His pedagogical experiences and subsequent study of African fiction led him to abandon his cherished belief in the "idea of universality" (1972–73: 463). The patriarch of comparative literature in the United States, however, has defended this discipline as the study of "all literature from an international perspective, with a consciousness of the unity of all literary creation and experience" (Wellek 1970: 19).

This ideology demands that others be like us. Western audiences, Ivan Sanders writes, are attracted to those authors from Hungarian literature who "violate norms and rattle establishments" (1987: 279). In other words, they prefer writers engaging in the modernist ethic of code and rule breaking; they are interested in that aspect of the foreign most similar to their own experience. It is this parallel of experience that even critics of marginal literature invoke to win international recognition of works. Read Cavafy and Seferis, Greek scholars tell their western readers, since these poets are much like yourselves: they are not Greek but universal. African scholars often argue implicitly that African literature is worthy of study because it is European. In this way they ask audiences to understand Africa by embedding it in European culture (Appiah 1984: 146).[2] Such an attempt to prove the relevance of nonwestern texts ends up denying local specificity in the understandable pursuit of global recognition.

We Are the World

The idea that literature constitutes a unity not only rejects the possibility of separate development of the Others but also demands their conformity to the designs of western Europe. General literature cannot accommodate all traditions, as it is modeled very much on the literatures that comparatists know well: English, French, German, Italian, and Spanish. Since the discipline is organized in European terms, critics of other traditions are guilty of parochialism and their writings amount "to no more than the expression of pious hopes, local pride, and resentment of centralizing powers" (Wellek and Warren 1963: 52). The minor or the peripheral is by definition "provincial," since its concerns have not been universalized. Furthermore, as the rules governing general literature are based on western European prototypes, works from marginalized traditions receive scant attention. Given that African literature, as Robert Clements argues, has contributed fewer literary works fulfilling criteria of "international acclaim and enduring values," African authors will play a "minor" role in the new universal literature curricula (1978: 32). They are ignored for not being western enough or condemned for being themselves. "From Homer to the nineteenth century," William F. Buckley asserts, "no great book has emerged from any non-European source" (in Adhikari 1988). "Who is," Saul Bellow contemptuously asks, "the Tolstoy of the Zulus? The Proust of the Papuans?" (in Atlas 1987). Bellow's denunciation of the Zulus and Papuans for not having created (European) novelists justifies, in a circular manner, the necessity of studying western classics. Bellow's objective is to maintain the only *literature*. But if—as Cornelius Castoriadis says of Marxist conceptions of universal history—in order to have a literature, it were necessary to exclude from it "almost everything, except what has occurred over a few centuries on a narrow strip of land bordering the North Atlantic, the price to pay is really too high" (1987: 28).

Bellow is willing to pay the price. Even poststructuralists blur differences between literatures and affirm paradigmatically the primacy of the "great" literatures. They often implicitly or explicitly demand European concerns from their nonwestern texts. Rey Chow, for instance, accuses Fredric Jameson of conducting this type of criticism in his discussion of Chinese texts. She argues that Jameson's introduction of the term *postmodernism* into Chinese writing is not only misleading but also ethnocentric (1986–87: 84,

93). Postmodernism is a culture-specific periodizing concept that cannot gratuitously be transplanted into a foreign situation.[3] This argument cautions against the search for references to language and textuality, a concern of western European postsymbolist literary and critical practice, in non-western texts. The current preoccupation with meaning is not everybody's problem.

Feminism has had to face such criticism for its exclusion of issues of race and class in its critique of patriarchy. As Hazel Carby insists, most contemporary feminist theory, concentrating on patriarchy alone, does not adequately account for the experience of the black woman, who must confront racism as well as sexism (1982: 213). White feminists, she argues, become ethnocentric when, in referring to "women," their ostensible subject turns out to be "white women" and when they seek the liberation of African and Asian women in terms of "progressive" customs of the metropolitan West (216–17). In their emphasis on gender-specific problems, white women are reluctant to see that in an environment of racism they too can be oppressors—insofar as they reap the benefits of economic exploitation—instead of being only the oppressed (221). While many white feminists are sensitive to problems of race and class, black feminists argue, their almost exclusive preoccupation with gender prevents them from seriously considering these additional factors affecting the lives of other women.[4]

Quite often, disregard for the validity of the Other is shown by the imperialist way in which dominant discourses claim concepts and categories as their own. Terms such as *criticism* and *literature,* for instance, are bandied about as if they were ecumenical forms and not simply national entities. The title of Terry Eagleton's *The Function of Criticism* (1984) assumes the existence of a homogeneous criticism and deems it unnecessary to mention that its real subject is English criticism. This is also true of an article, "Literature's Romantic Era: Historicists Re-Interpret it and Generate Controversy among their Colleagues," in the *Chronicle of Higher Education* (April 13, 1988). The word *literature* in the title promises an exploration of literature in general or a comparison of the romantic periods of several countries. But the discussion never departs from the boundaries of England, thereby equating once more the textual tradition of that nation with a general category of literature. Despite its unrestricted title, Gerald Graff's *Professing Literature: An Institutional History* deals solely with American material. Graff himself acknowledges that a more suitable subtitle would have been "A History of English Studies," but decided that "essential traits had been similar enough to warrant the broader label" (1987: 2). Similarly, the title of Terry Lovell's *Consuming Fiction* (1987) presumes a global identity in literary studies. Such a designation would be understandable only in an interpretive community concerned exclusively with English writing.[5]

Radical Otherness

These all-embracing claims to knowledge have the effect of dispossessing any literature not preceded by the epithets "great" and "universal," and they divide writing into, on the one hand, the prototype and major, and on the other, the imitation and minor. While critics of major paradigms appropriate for their traditions the general appellations *literature, criticism, institutions,* and *fiction* (thereby guaranteeing maximum attention for their work) the burden falls on the shoulders of critics of the other literary traditions to differentiate their disciplines by supplying the names to their Otherness. Increasingly, however, critics are challenging the universalist perspective that proposes the western European literatures as models and seeks to territorialize dissenting identities. Third World scholars, feminists, and minority critics propose that attention be given to divergent traditions not as ethnographic aberrations but as instances of separate development.

They contend further that western discourse is either irrelevant to or cannot be imposed upon nonwestern cultural artifacts. As Chinweizu bluntly states, African literature represents a separate tradition; "its historical and cultural imperatives impose upon it concerns and constraints quite different, sometimes altogether antithetical to the European" (1980: 4). The Kenyan intellectual Ngugi Wa Thiong'o similarly argues that the "European imperialist bourgeois" experience of history as reflected in its art and literature is not a universal experience of history (1981: 38). The teaching of European and mostly British literature in schools means that Kenyan students are exposed solely to the European perspective and to the European reflection of itself,[6] whereas the African conceptions of "art" and "literature" have little in common with western models. In Africa, Ngugi observes, the writer and the politician are in many cases the same person. Writers often participate in political struggles; for them the gun, pen, and platform serve the same ends—the liberation of their countries (1981: 73). Art for art's sake has no meaning in Africa. The African situation necessitates not an aesthetic, but a political understanding of writing. In literature, he argues, there are two opposing aesthetics: one of exploitation and oppression and one of struggle for total liberation (38).[7] For African writers to cease writing about colonialism, race, color, and exploitation and to address issues such as the "human condition" is, according to Ngugi, tantamount to rejecting African realities and embracing the

"European mania" for timelessness, universality, and a man without history.

Parallel colonial experiences have prompted the Peruvian writer José Carlos Mariátegui to abandon western theories of literary development and to propose those relevant to the situation of Peru. Because of the special character of Peruvian literature, he concludes, it cannot be studied within the framework of classicism, romanticism, and modernism. Peruvian literature did not proceed from an ancient through a medieval to a modern era; nor is the Marxist evolutionary process of the feudal, aristocratic, bourgeois, and proletarian periods applicable (1971: 190). In the Peruvian context the only valid theory is one organizing literature into the following categories: colonial, when the literature is still dependent on the metropolis; cosmopolitan, when literature assimilates elements from various foreign traditions; national, when literature shapes and expresses the identity of the national character (191).

Caliban does not continue to speak Prospero's language, as Retamar has eloquently argued (1989). Alternate experiences demand alternate theories and methodologies. At the very least this means that aesthetic autonomy, the determining feature of western literature, does not necessarily characterize all cultures. Resistance literature, a writing that has emerged in the organized national liberation struggles of Africa, Latin America, and the Middle East, does not seek to distinguish art from ideology, theory from practice. Such texts, Barbara Harlow insists, differ from other types of writing by their involvement in the struggle against oppression. A poem or a novel constitutes simultaneously part of the struggle and an arena in which the struggle is waged (Harlow 1987: 39). These texts are predicated on their social functionality: they not only express opinions but also teach moral lessons, history, and geography. "The theory of resistance literature is in its politics" (30). This mode of writing, Harlow argues, presents serious challenges to western critical discourse because it cannot easily be assimilated into traditional departments organized according to national criteria, and it does not lend itself to formal aesthetic exegesis.

Such texts may challenge our understanding of the aesthetic but it is doubtful that "they remain unavailable to the literary institutions of the west" (35). History has shown that any text can be made the object of (aesthetic) interpretation. To think otherwise is to believe in the "closedness" of a text and in its innate power to inhibit certain methodologies. Texts of resistance literature differ from other writing not in an essential or absolute way, as Harlow assumes, but in their use. Hence the challenge they pose has nothing to do with inherent features. It is a community's refusal to detach language from political reality and its integration of literature into social struggles that challenge the alleged universality of aesthetic autonomy. These differing cultural contexts, in which literary writing consciously intervenes in the historical process, cast doubt upon the western injunction against the association of literature and politics. Such cases of cultural difference deconstruct the dominant notion of nationalist discourse that *a* representation of reality is *the* representation. This monistic view of history equates a particular world with the world at large, imagining that world to be an extension of itself.

Alternate Theories, Alternate Practices

A theory emanating from western Europe or North America is inapplicable in other cultural situations not as an exegetical methodology, since any text is interpretable, but as a mode of explanation seeking to understand cultural settings with foreign conceptual tools. Both approaches may be reductive and inappropriate but only the latter can be resisted on political grounds. While one cannot prevent someone from interpreting a revolutionary poem with ahistorical structuralist techniques, it is possible to argue that the search for a system of aesthetics, a literature, a concept of a canon in contemporary Kenya, Peru, or fifth- or nineteenth-century Greece is futile because such notions had not or have not developed in these contexts. All analysis is culturally centered and flows from ideological assumptions and worldviews.

Current critical theories, therefore, informed by theoretical practices in the West, fail to come to terms with cultural differences and thus, according to Molefi Asante, cannot be applied intact to African texts (1987: 159). Asante finds a "hostile silence" toward other realities in the works of Frye, Saussure, de Man, and Derrida (160). Houston A. Baker criticizes his African-American colleagues for suggesting that criticism is transcultural and for co-opting the language and assumptions of white critics (1984: 89). Joyce A. Joyce argues that a poststructuralist methodology imposes a strategy upon black literature from the outside, whereas a direct relationship exists between Euro-American literature and theory (1987b: 382). She thus strongly resists the translation into the black idiom of white literary theory and its attendant preoccupation with linguistic matters rather than the economic, social, and political reality imposed on black people by "white America" (1987a: 338). "The poststructuralist sensibility," she argues, does not aptly apply to black American literary works (341).

These critics propose alternative frames of reference which would make African and African-American culture the subject and not the object of study. Joyce espouses a polemical African-American criticism, directly involved in the liberation of black people, and exhorts the black critic to affect, guide, and "arouse the minds and emotions of Black people" (345).[8]

Baker proposes "holistic, cultural-anthropological" investigations of African-American literature and culture instead of close textual readings (109).[9] In his *The Afrocentric Idea* (1987) Asante calls for Afrocentric theories that would draw on African experiences and posit Africa as the reference in the approach to problem solving. An African criticism will situate works in the traditions of its African audience and illuminate the social and philosophical conditions that the works address. The only alternative is for Africans to develop discourses that are as embedded in their own "plot of history and mythology" as European theories are defined by European perspectives.

All methods are valid in their own contexts. The fallacy lies in masquerading a particular ideology as universal. As a European-oriented discipline, literary criticism cannot evade its Eurocentric character. Western theories do not automatically have validity outside the traditions that produced them. Critics cannot presume that the development of the novel in Middle Eastern societies followed western paradigms, or that prose existed before the advent of modernity.[10] In their attempt to draw parallels between both Europe and its past and Europe and its Other, researchers inevitably discover modern European concepts in epochs and settings that could not have produced them. Such Eurocentric and chronocentric practices have the effect of imposing upon the object of study a modern European orientation. Eurocentrism demands European motifs, strategies, and concerns from non-European societies; chronocentrism searches for modern concepts in earlier cultures. When scholars examine the artifacts of past societies, Jean Baudrillard argues, they quite often perceive them as aesthetic objects and, as a result, deposit them in the museum. "But these objects," he stresses, "are not art at all. And precisely their nonaesthetic character could at last have been the starting point for a *radical perspective* on (and not an *internal critical* perspective leading only to a broadened reproduction of) Western culture" (1975: 89).[11]

The discourse on the Other can undertake such a "radical perspective" by deterritorializing the landscape of dominant criticism that leads ultimately to the reproduction of western models. The discourse of minor or marginal cultures insists on the possibility of separate development, which cannot be integrated within the national paradigm of criticism. This notion of ethnographic specificity may appear (particularly to cultural anthropologists) like an unoriginal and unexceptional plea, but the theory and practice of contemporary literary criticism prove otherwise. From job descriptions to actual methodologies, criticism betrays an expectation, charged with hubris, for others to be like itself.

My work, written in opposition to such thinking, disputes the assumption that all literatures are alike or that they share the same attributes. I borrow my strategies from the project of cultural critique I outlined here—the defamiliarization of dominant notions and the demonstration of differences. One of the initial tasks of cultural critique lies in questioning the transparency of the values of criticism. The juxtaposition of marginal and dominant perspectives will draw attention to the fallacious notion of literature as natural, immutable, and universal. The goal of such a study would be to replace the "shifting monologues of self and other (which, however disordered or decentred, remain the orderly discourses of the bourgeois subject) with a genuinely dialogic and dialectical history that can account for the formation of different selves and the construction of different epistemologies" (Sangari 1987: 186).

The Greek as Minor?

Disciplines like modern Greek, though marginalized at the university, need not be irrelevant. On the contrary, they can transform their very peripheral status into an advantage. Instead of bewailing their banishment to the fringe they can benefit from their ostracism by conducting a critique of the center. Critics of these cultures are strategically positioned to reevaluate the nationalist operations of criticism. They can scrutinize concepts such as aesthetics, canon, literature, and art, which have been used to efface differences between social and ethnic groups and to privilege the values of a few dominant communities. In this task, Abdul JanMohamed and David Lloyd insist, marginality can be a supreme asset (1987: 10). It can disrupt the totalizing strategies of criticism by perpetuating suspicion of all attempts (actual or aesthetic) at the reconciliation of political differences.

As such, modern Greek can play the role of minor in the supranational territory of criticism, even though it is not minor in the sense defined by Deleuze and Guattari, as a "literature a minority constructs within a major language" (1986: 16). Deleuze and Guattari cite the case of the Jews in Prague writing in German, that is, within the perimeters of a "great" literature and in a language not their own. Situated within a major literary tradition, a minor literature assumes an oppositional posture with regard to its established host. It evades the homogenizing and reconciling tendencies of major writing by "deterritorializing" its language and by implacably affirming the perspective of the minority. A minor literature chooses to be minor in the culture it inhabits.

Modern Greek literature is not minor in this sense, since it was used for constructing a national identity. It does not deterritorialize within its cultural space but actually dominates the writings of other minorities. Nor do Greeks of the diaspora constitute minorities like blacks, Chicanos, or the native peoples in North America, oppressed communities that for historical reasons have maintained a distinct identity, often in opposition to the dominant white European culture.[12] But it can function as minor in the kingdom reigned over by western criticism, which seeks the transcendence of cultural differences. From the margins of Europe it can activate the critical potential of culture to deterritorialize the integrative tendencies of criticism, deny its authority to represent others, and question its universalist strategies.

The radical potential of marginal literatures to undo cultural identities is counterbalanced by their capacity to produce and maintain them. The contradictory nature of these cultures, that on the one hand possess authority nationally but on the other are disenfranchised internationally, should caution critics against celebrating endlessly their radical otherness. Herein lies the hubris of the position taken by Deleuze and Guattari. They demonstrate the unique ethos of the minor, but they resort to the artifices of the major when they generalize its operations and seek for it political privileges. In proposing the situation of Czech Jews as the "problem of us all," they grant this literature representative status (19). At the end they triumph in the ability of minor literature to violate: "Nothing is revolutionary except the minor" (26). Deleuze and Guattari exult in diversity for its own sake and hence universalize the distinctiveness of this concept beyond usefulness.[13] After deconstructing the global strategies of dominating literatures they make the individual stand for the whole once again, a maneuver that elevates it to the status of the major.

The aim of critics, however, should not be to proclaim the greatness of the minor but to learn from its problematic. Only by reflecting on the specificity of these traditions and developing theories about them can they prevent the major from setting the agenda and presiding over the discussion. Indeed, the ambivalence toward the West and the center brought on by belatedness can be transformed by peripheral cultures into a productive impulse. The internalized tensions can lead to both a reflection on identity from the margins and a critique of identity and literature's role in its creation.

Chapter 2
From Empire to Nation-State:
Greek Expectations

Greece as a Special Case

Europeans have long been fascinated by Greece. Around the sixteenth century they began to celebrate Hellas as the mainspring of western civilization. Greece came to be regarded as the birthplace of the West, the source of its cultural institutions. It became a privileged topos in the European imaginary, a shimmering fantasy on the far horizon. But Europe's geography contained a physical reminder of this utopia, a rocky peninsula where Greek was still spoken by a population nearly forgotten by Europeans after the Ottoman capture of Constantinople in 1453. In the ideological transformations of European identity and the nationalist struggle for a Greek nation the boundaries between imagination and geography dissolved. The intellectual elite of the Greek community discovered and began to exploit the fusion of the classical and modern in their attempt to modernize the Greek community—to liberate the territory from Ottoman control, found an independent state, and orient it culturally, politically, and economically toward capitalist western Europe. They sought to draft the story of modern Greece in a spirit of European Hellenism and to incorporate it into the master narrative of the West.

Their enterprise was successful to the extent that modern Greece came to be and is still regarded as a special case in comparison with other countries on the margins of Europe. The declaration of the War of Independence of 1821, for instance, initiated the most fashionable international cause of the century, a pan-European phenomenon rivaling that of the Spanish Civil War of the following century. The passion with which Europeans, dedicated to liberal causes, supported the struggles of the Greeks may be compared with the indifference they showed to the revolts by the Serbians, Bulgarians, and Armenians. None of those ethnic groups could elicit the same concern, let alone the logistical aid of the Europeans; unlike the Greeks they could not relate their own nationalist imaginings to the core of European identity. European Hellenism provided Greeks with access to Europe unavailable to other nations. The only other people to make a similar appeal to the West would be the Zionists. Whereas Greeks laid claim to the cultural and secular roots of western civilization, the Zionists would exploit the foundational role of the Hebrew Bible in the Judeo-Christian tradition.[1]

Greece is still a special case, now as then. In the first meeting of the Council of Europe following the coup d'état of the colonels in 1967 a socialist deputy from Austria voiced the philhellenism of the previous century when he declared that "the members owed it to the Greek people, who gave the world the organization of the democratic state which was today banished from their country, to do everything to help them" (cited by Holden 1972: 53). The ideological connection between ancient and modern Greece made the Greek tragedy European. The deputies thus ignored the arguments of an Italian delegate who reminded them that a few years earlier Turkey, a member nation, experienced a far bloodier coup that the council had hardly noticed. Even the British foreign secretary in the House of Commons in 1970 expressed his "sense of distress that it should be Greece of all countries, with her dazzling history, who is estranged from the democratic countries of Europe. (Cheers.) It gives to many of us a sense of deep distress that Greece should be estranged from European countries who owe so much to her heritage" (in Holden 1972: 54). It is no accident that Greek democracy, Pericles' funeral oration, and the Acropolis were freely adduced in European discussions of the dictatorship. They point to the historical continuity drawn during the two previous centuries between ancient and modern Greece. But these images had as much to do with Europe's self-imagining as they did with the events in Greece.

The Greek case illustrates how a peripheral nation can gain recognition in the international arena by embedding itself in the identity formations of superpowers. The prime minister of Greece, Konstantinos Mitsotakis, gave a speech to the National Press Club of Washington in June 1990 in which he argued for the relevance of his nation to his American audience:

"Democracy" is one Greek word that every American knows. It is
a Greek concept that is now transforming Eastern Europe and
shaking the foundations of the Soviet Union and China. I am

proud that today "Democracy" is not only your form of
government but also the name of the party ruling Greece, my
party, New Democracy. Coming from the birthplace of Democracy
to find so much of my country reflected in the ideals and
aspirations of your country has been a wonderful experience. It has
shown me how significant our small country is to your great one,
and has taught me how important it is that we strengthen the ties
that join us and work together for our mutual good. (*Greece: The
Week in Review,* June 11, 1990, Embassy of Greece, Press and
Information Office)

Basing his argument on the connection between ancient and modern Greece,
Mitsotakis is able to take credit on behalf of Greece for both the political
transformations in Europe and the form of government in the United States.
Greece's claim to be the birthplace of democracy as well as its bid for the
1996 Olympic Games (in celebration of the centenary of the first modern
Olympics held in Athens in 1896) was made possible by the links established
in the eighteenth century between modern and classical Greece and between
Greece's new story and Europe's own history.

Greece has not always elicited this enthusiasm from Europeans. During
the four centuries after the fall of the Byzantine Empire the inhabitants of
that territory were largely ignored by westerners. If scholars took any notice
of the modern Greeks they often regarded them as degenerate descendants
of their glorious ancestors. William Martin Leake, for instance, in his widely
read book on Greece, observed that the "modern dialect of the Greeks
bears the same comparison with its parent language, as the poverty and
debasement of the present generation to the refinement and opulence of
their ancestors" (1814: 11). Jakob Philipp Fallmerayer, who shocked Greeks
with his arguments about their descent not from classical Greeks but from
Slavs, also chastized them for not having an infinitive. "A language without
an infinitive," he stated dismissively, "is not better than a human body
without a hand" (1845: 2. 451–52).

European travelers began to arrive in the Greek-speaking provinces of
the Ottoman Empire after the 1750s (Jenkyns 1980: 5) but they were concerned more with the ancient monuments than with the modern Greeks
themselves. Winkelman's *Gedanken über die Nachahmung der griechischer
Werke in der Malerei und Bildhauerkunst* (1755) and *Geschichte der Kunst
des Altertums* (1764) helped to transform taste from Hellenistic art (which
could be obtained in Italy) to classical art, and thereby made a visit to
Greece essential for Greek revival architects, artists, and scholars (Tsigakou
1981: 21). These travelers could not ignore the Greeks they encountered on
their visits and often made comparisons between them and the ancient
Greeks. Some even began taking an interest in the life and manners of

Greeks themselves, although many still considered the Greeks despicable, vicious, and deceitful (Angelomatis-Tsougarakis 1990: 9).[2] Byron, perhaps the most influential of such travelers, visited the area in 1809 and 1810 and later incorporated in the first two cantos of *Childe Harold's Pilgrimage* thematic material on Greece. The immediate translation of this work into many European languages contributed to the rise in Europe and the United States of a vigorous literary philhellenism.

Byron forced the condition of Greece on Europe's attention. But the Greeks themselves turned literary philhellenism into a political program for the benefit of the Greek cause (William St. Clair 1972: 19). Enthusiasm for Greece swept through Europe, capturing the European imagination. Committees were formed to support the Greek revolution, money was collected, men arrived in Greece ready to fight. A British aristocrat, Lord Guilford, devoted his entire fortune to the establishment of a Greek university in Corfu. Hölderlin, for whom "seliges Griechenland" was a "Haus der Himmlischen alle," composed *Hyperion oder der Eremit in Griechenland* (1797–99) as a plea for Greek national revival. Delacroix painted canvases with Greek themes, the most famous being *Scenes from the Massacre at Chios* and *Greece Expiring on the Ruins of Missolongi.* Victor Hugo wrote "The Heads of the Seraglio," a poem about the decapitated heads of the Greek soldiers exhibited in Istanbul. Beethoven composed *Ruins of Athens,* operas were performed that dealt with Greece, exhibitions organized, benefit concerts staged, books on Greece published. On the whole the Europeans were inspired by the ideal image of classical Hellas, hence the disappointment of the volunteers when upon their arrival on the Greek mainland, they discovered the eastern habits of the Greeks and their virtual indifference to the ancient tradition. For them Greece possessed an identity only in relationship to its past. The philhellenes expected to fight alongside the descendents of Leonidas's warriors, not peasants with oriental manners and dress. Thus even on the battlefield the Greeks were judged not on their own terms but according to the criteria of their classical predecessors. Philhellenism would certainly not have mobilized European public opinion had Hellas not been posited at the center of European identity.

The War of Independence was portrayed not only as a fight for democracy and freedom from oppression but also as a struggle between Europe and Asia, like the wars between the Greek city-states and the Persians two thousand years earlier. For the Europeans the Christian Greeks were fighting against Muslim despots; they saw the War of Independence from the perspective of orientalism. The Greek intellectuals understood this very well and thus tried to portray Greeks as European. Adamantios Korais (1748–1833), the famous scholar and promoter of French culture, believed that if

Greeks did not accept the values of the Enlightenment, Europeans would adopt a pro-Ottoman policy. "Enlightened" Greeks, on the other hand, could steer Europe toward a position favorable to the Greek cause. Enlightenment for Korais was synonymous with hostility to the East (Kondilis 1988: 205). The task facing westernizers such as Korais was the transformation of the ethnoreligious identities defining Greeks in the Ottoman Empire and the erection of a new political structure for social organization— the state. They appropriated the discourse of the Enlightenment and exploited the spirit of philhellenism to enable the Greek-speaking subjects of the Ottoman Empire to imagine themselves as fellow nationals and members of Europe.

The Greeks and the Ottoman Empire

With the gradual disintegration of the Byzantine Empire a successively greater size of its territory came under Ottoman control. When the Ottomans finally seized Constantinople, known then as simply the City, in May 1453, most Greek-speaking Orthodox Christians had already become subjects of the Ottoman Empire. The seizure of the City gave an apocalyptic shock to the people of Byzantium. For the Greeks, the dominant ethnic group in the Byzantine Empire, it induced a collective trauma that gave rise to a series of messianic prophecies foretelling the recapture of the City. The most famous of these, the popular song "Ayia Sofia," which lamented the sack of Constantinople, ended with these sentiments: "The Holy Virgin was seized with trembling, and the icons wept tears. / 'Be silent, Lady and Mistress, do not weep so much: / once more in years and times to come, all will be yours once more.'"[3] The wide circulation of such songs and prophecies after 1453 seems to indicate that Greeks regarded their religious community as conquered and that they hoped one day with the aid of divine intervention to seize the City and reestablish Byzantine rule.

On the whole, however, despite the capture of Constantinople and the forced relocations of portions of the population, the Greeks accepted their lot under the new authority and eventually became the most prosperous of the Balkan people under the security guaranteed by the Ottomans. The Ottoman Empire allowed conquered Christians and Jews, as people of the Book, but not polytheists and idolaters, religious autonomy under their own ecclesiastical authority. There was no equivalent to the Inquisition under Ottoman rule. Nevertheless, non-Muslims had an inferior legal status and were subjected to certain discriminations: they paid higher taxes, they were not allowed to bear arms, their evidence was not valid in court against Muslims. The most controversial of such practices was the periodic levy of unmarried male children to be raised and then trained to become part of the elite military corps, which was imposed on the non-Muslim peasants of the empire from the fourteenth to the sixteenth centuries. Although oppressive, the Ottoman Empire did not perpetrate the contemporaneous excesses, for example, of the Spaniards in South America.

The Christians, Jews, and Muslims were separated into ethnoreligious communities known as millets. The largest of the Christian millets, the Orthodox or Rum[4] millet, established in 1454 by Sultan Mehmet II (1451–81) was administered by the patriarch of Constantinople. Ironically the patriarchate acquired more authority after 1453 than during Byzantine times because, in addition to its religious duties, it was responsible for the civil governance of the millet (education and legal matters pertaining to non-Muslims such as marriage, divorce, and inheritance). Though the Ottomans initiated a new social and economic order they permitted the captured populations religious and cultural autonomy. Greek society at the time was agrarian, precapitalist, and stratified. The community was the basic organizational unit of the millet with the priest acting as an intermediary between village and both the upper ecclesiastical and Ottoman authorities. The family, as the foundational unit of the community, became the repository and transmitter of culture (Karpat 1983: 142). Cultural practices were of course influenced by the Ottoman occupation but they were free from direct state control.

The Ottomans, however, introduced a new social structure cutting across ethnic and religious affiliations. They organized people horizontally into millets and vertically into social estates according to vocation (Karpat 1973: 113). The four major estates were: a) military men and dignitaries; b) religious leaders, scholars, cultural figures, and scribes; c) merchants and craftsmen; d) peasants. The majority of subjects were peasants who were assured hereditary rights to till lots in the *timars* (fiefs) as long as they paid a tax to the local notable (Stavrianos 1963: 16–17). The *timar* system of land tenure and the social estates provided the economic and social foundation of the empire during the fifteenth and sixteenth centuries, which were characterized by relative order and security. In the seventeenth century, however, a series of internal and external changes led to the dissolution of the social estates and millets and eventually to the emergence of the nation. By the end of the nineteenth century the multiethnic, multireligious, and multilingual empire broke up into autonomous states.

Externally the empire faced its greatest threat from the increasingly powerful capitalist centers of western Europe (Wallerstein 1974), which, with extensive world trade networks, began to penetrate its economy, destroying the traditional Ottoman craft industries (Shaw 1976: 173). The capitalist countries purchased raw materials from the empire and shipped to its territories manufactured goods, causing trade imbalances. The growing populations of the western states also necessitated the importation of food from the Balkan provinces. Corn, introduced into the Balkans in the seventeenth century and widely cultivated for export, made the estates increasingly dependent on western markets (Stavrianos 1974: 190). The landlords of these export-oriented estates began to accumulate wealth, land, and power. Exploiting the weakness of the central government, they increased levies arbitrarily, evicted peasants who refused to pay taxes, and kept the land for themselves, an act impossible under the *timar* system, which assured the notables authority to collect taxes but not ownership of the fief. This new *chiflik* order of land tenure led to the large-scale dislocation of peasants who, no longer possessing rights to their lots, were reduced to serfdom, overtaxed and exploited by the notables.

The oppression of the peasants was one of the reasons they supported uprisings that under the leadership of intellectual and economic elites increasingly assumed a nationalist direction. Many of the landless peasants resorted to banditry as early as the 1680s. At this time their brigandage was generally a response to arbitrary taxation and impoverishment rather than an expression of ethnic identity (Sugar 1972: 243). But during the War of Independence the Greek bandits, or *klefts,* as they were called, consolidated forces with the revolutionaries against Ottoman rule. Other peasants simply remained serfs on the estates of notables such as the Ali Pasha of Ioannina (1788–1822), who defied central authority by forging a quasi state within the empire.

The economic, social, and technological changes undermined the social estates by intensifying social mobility and creating demands for new criteria in assigning status and position. In the seventeenth century, as a consequence of enhanced occupational differentiation, a new social order emerged comprising three main groups: a) an upper class of government officials, Phanariots (Greek aristocracy), dragomans (interpreters and undersecretaries of ministries), rich merchants, landowners, and heads of millets; b) a middle class of merchants, tradesmen, and manufacturers; and c) peasants (Karpat 1973: 37). By far the most important development was the rise of the merchant class, whose members, particularly the Greeks in the Orthodox millet, acquired wealth and later political appointments in the Ottoman bureaucracy and influence over the patriarchate. The merchants were based in the expanding market towns of Anatolia and the Balkans, such as Adrianople, Thessaloniki, Smyrna, Sofia, and Serres, which became centers for the exportation of agricultural commodities and distribution of foreign goods. They received trading privileges from western powers as a result of treaties with the empire and gained increasingly greater contact with Europeans: the Serbians in southern Hungary, Bulgarians in southern Russia, and the Greeks scattered widely throughout Europe.

With their acquired wealth they sent their sons to study at European universities, but they also set up schools within the empire and endowed them with books and scholarships. (A notable example is the Society of Friends of the Muses, founded in Vienna in 1815 to distribute funds for education in Greece, propagate learning about classical civilization, and preserve antiquities.) Economic expansion created a class of intellectuals who provided their respective ethnic communities with a historical past and interpreted their future according to the precepts of the Enlightenment. They were also instrumental in endowing the ethnoreligious identity of the Orthodox millet with a political consciousness. These merchants and intellectuals shared an attitude to the West substantially different from the xenophobic and antiwestern position of the patriarchate, the Ottoman authorities, and the masses. Unlike the church, they were not suspicious of the West as a Catholic menace nor, like the Porte (the Ottoman government), as an economic and political threat. They viewed it as a model to be imitated. Many merchants came to regard the nation-state as a legitimate area in which to exercise their interests—to enhance commercial contacts with the expanding economies of the West free from clerical control (Karpat 1983: 151; Stavrianos 1963:17; Yerasimos 1988: 37). In a nation-state authority would rest with indigenous civilians and not, as in the millet, with the church and the Ottoman bureaucracy. The aim of the intellectuals was first to undermine the church's jurisdiction over cultural production and then to devise a secular culture that would act as the binding agent in the state. They strove to create a new realm of shared values to attain and preserve national unity. Eventually they introduced literature as a realm where people could experience their imagined solidarity. The leading role played by the intelligentsia and westernized merchants before and after the revolution "explains to a great extent why from the very start there was a persistent attempt to organize national life along liberal-bourgeois lines, despite the weak capitalist development and the non-existence of a strong Western-type autochthonous bourgeoisie" (Mouzelis 1978: 14).

The English traveler Henry Holland, in his visit to the city of Ioannina during the years 1812 and 1813, commented that the Greeks had extensive commercial connections with foreign countries that resulted in both economic gain and the acquisition of European cultural practices: "The active spirit of the Greeks, deprived in great measure of political or national objects, has taken a general direction towards commerce. But, fettered in this respect also, by their condition on the continent of Greece, they emigrate in great numbers to the adjacent countries, where their activities can have more scope in the nature of the government" (1815: 148). The inhabitants of Ioannina had relatives scattered in cities of western and central

Europe from whom they learned about western culture. Holland pointed to the Zosimadis brothers, who contributed annually to Ioannina books and large sums for education. They also supported the publication of Korais's Hellenic Library, an influential collection of classical texts. Holland characterized such benefactions as "a splendid instance of genuine and well directed *patriotism*" (151; my emphasis). The merchants Holland met had traveled much in Europe, were "well instructed in European habits," and spoke several European languages.

Holland also commented on the "literary habits" of these merchants and their families: "The wealth acquired by many of the inhabitants gives them the means of adopting such [literary] pursuits themselves or encouraging it in others. The connections in Germany and Italy, and frequently residence in these countries, tend further to create habits of this kind, and at the same time furnish those materials for literary progress, which would be wanting in their own country" (151). He referred to Ioannina as a "mart for books," particularly of translations that the Greeks used in "forwarding the literature of their country." It was in urban centers like Ioannina, in these spaces of commerce and writing, that a new narrative came to be woven, a story telling the Greek subjects of the empire that they constituted a people in their own right.

Not all members of the new class of merchants and traders may have been enthusiastic supporters of a literary culture, but their wealth contributed to an intellectual revival and sustained an intelligentsia interested in literary pursuits. The merchants, as Holland describes them, were Europeanized and clearly eager to reproduce European culture at home. They achieved this, as I shall discuss in the last chapter, primarily through the endowment of cultural institutions. William Martin Leake commented in 1809 that Ioannina, for instance, had two "colleges for education and libraries belonging to them," both founded by wealthy merchant families (1835: 206). The library holdings, Leake noted, were of a general nature befitting the schools while the books of the church concerned the "Fathers and Byzantine history." These and other institutions were no longer under the jurisdiction of the church and their curriculum was thus not theologically based. In 1818 the English traveler William Jowett, during a visit to the academy of Ayvalik (Kydonies) in Asia Minor remarked that lectures were given on classical Greek literature and the natural sciences as well (in Clogg 1972: 647). The bitter reaction of the patriarchate to the introduction of secular humanist education and the condemnation by the educated elite of the church's position demonstrate the struggle between these two interests for the appropriation of Greek culture.

The Tilt toward Europe

The Greeks of the Orthodox millet, on account of their unequaled commercial and cultural ties with Europe, were the first ethnic group to approach the West. This was a daring political speculation for it was not always certain that western Europe would become the new economic, political, and cultural center and that nationhood in an expanding capitalist world economy, rather than the empire, would become the mode of political organization and economic distribution. As Immanuel Wallerstein argues, before the thirteenth century the Mediterranean was the focus of trade carried out by Byzantines, Italians (from the city-states), and North Africans. Northwestern Europe with its feudal system was marginal in economic terms (1974: 17). Only a series of historical, ecological, and geographic accidents made it better situated in the sixteenth century to diversify its agriculture, develop industries (textiles and shipbuilding), and thereby become the core area of world economy (1979: 18). The states of western Europe reached an economic equilibrium in the sixteenth century with the two other world systems: the Russian and Ottoman empires. But it was not at all clear that these states and their untested world economy would surpass the Russian Empire.

Indeed, many Greeks looked favorably at alliances with Moscow, the self-appointed Third Rome of Orthodoxy. Such designs were reinforced by Catherine the Great's "Greek project." She intended to break up the Ottoman Empire, divide the territories between Austria and Russia, and organize the Greek, Bulgarian, and Serbian regions into a revived Byzantine Empire with Constantinople as capital but under Russian protection (Barbara Jelavich 1983: 70). Many Greeks lived in Russia. The large number of Phanariots serving in the Russian bureaucracy and administration regarded that empire as a restored realm of the Byzantines (Holden 1972: 81). They, however, favored the revival of a Byzantine Empire controlled by ethnic Greeks. Ultimately the Russian option fell out of favor with the Greek elites. They were convinced that prosperity was to be found in neither the Russian nor Ottoman empires, indeed not in an empire at all, but in a strong centralized state connected to the capitalist world economy. The fight against the idea of empire did not end definitively, of course, until 1922, when Greek troops, pursuing the glories of the *Megali Idea* to establish Greek jurisdiction over the former Byzantine territories, were defeated by Attaturk's forces. (I shall discuss alternative models of Greek identity and forms of resistance to the western paradigm in chapter 4.)

A dominant group to become disaffected with the Ottoman Empire was the westernized class of merchants, which found the instability and uncertainty of the seventeenth and eighteenth centuries increasingly intolerable for their interests (Stavrianos 1963: 25). Trade, of course, flourished in urban centers like Ioannina, as the testimony by Holland and Leake indicates, but it had become more difficult to conduct. That the arbitrariness and rapacity of the officials and the inefficiency of the system impeded the maximization of profits is shown by the view of a typical merchant, Ioannis Pringos, established in Amsterdam between 1755 and 1774. Pringos valued the order and commercial independence possible in Holland; characterizing Amsterdam as a "great place to trade," he spoke with admiration of its social and economic institutions:

> All these cannot be organized under the Turk... for he knows no order and justice, and when the capital equals one thousand, he designates it ten times as much, so as to seize it, to impoverish others, not understanding that the wealth of his subjects is the wealth of his empire. They [the Dutch] organize their affairs with justice but he [the Turk] is totally unjust and cannot achieve anything but can only ruin. May the Almighty destroy him, and may Christianity flourish, may *governments be established like the above, like those in Europe,* where every one has his own without fear of injustice, where justice prevails. (Pringos 1931: 851; my emphasis)

Pringos's chronicle attests to the circulation among diaspora Greeks of new stories recounting the "liberation of the Christians from the tyranny of the Turks" (852) and the emergence of a new society. They told that corruption, injustice, and the absence of central political authority made life intolerable and undermined commercial activity. Increasingly Greeks of the diaspora came to believe they could pursue their fortunes under modes of "government like those in Europe" which, after the decline of the feudal system, restored internal order and enabled social prosperity. As the first Greeks to be integrated into western capitalism, they favored a structure of economic distribution and a form of political organization to facilitate their trade activity. The economic system desired by Pringos required a stable and neutral authority to secure financial transactions. The differentiation of the economic sphere necessitated sociopolitical unification with a strong central state. Such a territorial unit, administered by a bureaucracy and defended by a standing army, was to be linked to the capitalist economy of western Europe. I should emphasize, however, that Pringos's narrative differed from that of Enlightenment scholars because it advocated Christian rule rather than a secular state. Although these stories represented diverse interests and had not been incorporated into a unified nationalist cause, they shared one common purpose—the liberation of the Orthodox Christians from the "evil" Turks.

The scholars Daniil Filippidis (1755–1832) and Grigorios Konstantas (1758–1844) in their influential volume, *Yeografia Neoteriki* (1791) also addressed the political chaos and economic decay of the empire struggling to maintain authority over a huge territory and multiethnic population. They blamed the discontent of the Greeks on the absence of law and reliable structures for commercial interchange. Many Greeks, particularly the wealthy, they argued, fearing for their lives and property, flee to neighboring countries where "laws are sovereign and rights of life and property are sovereign" (1988: 116). Conditions in the empire are not conducive to trade: "What heights of commerce do you expect in a place where the sea teems with pirates, and the land is full of *klefts* and thieves. The roads are all threatening and unsafe, which is why the merchants gather in caravans. . . . Those of the modern Greeks . . . who are given to commerce are subject to harassment by the Turks who have the custom houses. . . . Therefore many rich merchants who know other states and who have decided to live by commerce exile themselves and establish themselves in other countries" (118).

Filippidis and Konstantas held the "despotic government" of the Ottomans responsible for the lawlessness of the land. These Europeanized authors were of course aware of states in which "good government" contributes to the well-being of its citizens. They advocated such structures for the empire, as the interests of commerce and prosperity lay in them. For them good law was the soul of society, the protector of "life, property, honor, and life" (116). The belated modernization of the Greeks would be promoted by the codification of law, a step to be followed later by the codification of the entire culture. This normative framework would then guide individual action and bring society under the authority of the state. The first stage of this process would be the invention of tales that would allow Greek Orthodox Christians to imagine themselves as a united people rather than as subjects of an unjust empire. The discourse of these stories was to varying degrees orientalist.

The situation under the Ottomans was, according to Adamantios Korais, one of tyranny, ignorance, and enslavement ([1803] 1970: 172). This was not inherent in the Greeks, he argued, but imposed by Ottoman occupation. He pointed to the islanders of Chios, who by seeking the "protection of some magnate in the empire" have solved their most pressing problem: "how to lead a life most devoid of oppression under an arbitrary government" (172–73). Their elected municipal assembly, unlike the Ottoman administration, "never abuses its power" and has set up an "educational establishment on the European model" that could serve as an example for other Greeks. Korais pointed to the other features of Chiote society—"an industrious population, silk factories and various other lucrative trades"—

as demonstrable proof of the capabilities of the Greeks when freed from Ottoman rule. The success of the Chiotes proved, according to Korais, that the backwardness of the Greeks reflected the corruption of the empire rather than the state of Greek society.

The story narrated by westernizers like Filippidis, Konstantas, and Korais was that with the capture of Constantinople a darkness befell the Greeks, educational institutions vanished, and teachers fled to the West. This was an effective strategy both in soliciting western aid and in establishing a history and collective identity. The story enabled them to think of themselves as a nation aligned with the West and blessed with a unique tradition. Greece had to turn to the West, believed the influential thinker Iosipos Misiodax (1730–1800), for Europe "overflows" with the "lights of learning" while Greece is denied them (in Valetas 1947: 316). Europe pities Greece not so much for its bondage as for its state of ignorance; but in coming to the aid of Greece, Misiodax asserts, Europe is only repaying a debt for originally having taken the flame from the Greeks (318). The notion of Europe's obligation to Greece became a common topos in the discourse of Greek nationalism, a feature noticed by foreigners such as Henry Holland (1815: 161). Misiodax, Katartzis, and Korais, the major figures of the Enlightenment, repeatedly exhorted youths to educate themselves, become teachers, and enlighten their fellow Greeks. Enlightenment of course presupposed the acquisition of European culture. "The enlightenment of the nation [yenos]," argues the old man in a story by Ioannis Vilaras, "is the holy and necessary duty of all learned men" (1935: 298). For Vilaras there was a direct relationship between political autonomy and cultural production. Subjugation to the Ottomans, according to him, resulted in the disappearance of the arts and sciences. They would reemerge only with the return of independence—the "fountainhead of the arts and sciences" (351). A national culture in his eyes was possible only within the borders of an autonomous state and on the basis of a shared vernacular, not the classical language some scholars wished to resurrect in order to "acquire independence, sciences, and arts" (352).

The intellectuals of the eighteenth century, who had knowledge of western culture and systems of government, conceived the idea of a national community distinguished by language. By transferring to the Greek context the ideas held in Europe on nation and language, they made it possible for Greeks to imagine themselves as a collective group bound by language and a unique heritage as well as by the Orthodox faith. The European states, wrote Dimitrios Katartzis (1730–1807), a court official in Wallachia, rejected Latin in favor of their own vernaculars, creating thereby their own unique cultures (1970: 21). He supported similar reforms of Greek, since the cultivation of the spoken idiom, according to him, would create a nation (*ethnos*) rivaling the ancient Greeks (10, 24). Education was central to his project: "The complete education of the nation and the common happiness follow necessarily from the good education of the youth" (41).

The idea of a national culture, the invention of a new identity, was made possible by cultural engineering. Katartzis's work testifies to this. A Greek (Romios) Christian should love his nation more than his family, he argues, and be ready to die for the sacred soil that has given birth to his illustrious ancestors. That someone should die for an abstract concept like the nation instead of his family, kin group, or religion was, as Benedict Anderson observes, a radical idea and one that had to be instilled. A Greek, Katartzis insists, should learn those cultural traits that differentiate his society from the Turkish, French, and Italian polities (46). "When I refer to a Greek Christian I mean a citizen of a nation . . . a member of a civil society from which he takes his name. This [civil society] has its own familiar laws and explicit ecclesiastical rules which make him different from other [citizens] and members of other societies and religions" (44). Katartzis had to acknowledge, however, that in the 1780s the Greeks had not constituted a true nation but one "subordinate to a greater power." In order to attain national independence scholars like Katartzis fashioned for Greek Orthodox Christians a new consciousness. They were motivated strictly speaking not by economic reasons but by emotional ones. Caught up in the nationalist fervor of Europe, they sought the benefits of nationhood for Greeks.

In order to achieve this goal they had to remind their western audiences of Greece's significance. This was the thesis of a lecture delivered by Korais in January 1803 in Paris to the Société des observateurs de l'homme. Korais understood that the French perceived Greeks through orientalist eyes, as uncouth vassals ruled by eastern despots. He undertook to revise this image by demonstrating that Greece had not turned its head from the rays of enlightenment (183). Instead of ignorant orientals, he tellingly referred to his compatriots, particularly his fellow Chiotes, as the "Frenchmen of the Levant." Greece was interesting, he told his French listeners, because it resembled their own country. Korais's arguments and those conceived by other Enlightenment figures remain central to the self-imagining of Greece; they contend that since Europeans constructed their culture upon the foundations of classical Greece, modern Greeks have a legitimate claim to European citizenship. These thinkers masterfully appended the story of modern Greece to the larger narrative of European civilization.

In pleading the relevance of his own society, Korais resorted to blurring its differences from the great powers and highlighting their similarities, as people of marginal cultures still do (see chapter 1). The Other has to adopt the values and ideology of the dominant in order to demonstrate its own efficacy. This strategy, however, paradoxically results in the loss of autonomy, and in the repression of indigenous values that are exotic to Europeans. The Greeks, for their part, exchanged political domination by an empire for political, cultural, and economic dependency on the West. Furthermore, the pursuit of purposeful modernization lodged Greek culture between a series of ideological antinomies.

As we have seen, Korais buttressed his appeal to Europe by invoking the past, a classic strategy in nationalist documents. A distinguished history is an essential attribute of any new state, since a past justifies the right to a future. The intellectual elite must confer upon the new nation the prestige of a renowned genealogy and relate this tradition to the community as a national myth. In this, Greeks had a much easier task than other ethnic groups—for instance, the Armenians—because they could boast a history more illustrious than any claimed by Europeans themselves. Since, according to Korais, Greeks were the direct descendants of Miltiades and Themistocles, they had never "considered the Europeans as other than debtors who were repaying with substantial interest the capital they had received from their own ancestors" (158–59). The link between ancient and modern was crucial.[5] The glow of their ancestors' splendor inspired the Greeks, for they implicitly told themselves: "We are the descendants of Greeks . . . we must either try to become worthy of this name, or we must not bear it" (184). But the vast gap between contemporaneous realities and past glories, paralleled by the difference between European modernity and Greek belatedness, was internalized by the Greeks as a deficiency in their society. For them Hellas and modern Europe constituted two poles of anxiety of influence.

Korais read to his Paris audience a passage from a circular letter sent to Greek merchants of the diaspora soliciting funds for a school in Greece. The nationalist rhetoric of the school's administration was directed at both the merchants' "patriotism" and their sense of European cosmopolitanism. "Established in the midst of enlightened cities," the letter stated, "you witness with your own eyes the advantages that arts and sciences bring; able to frequent European theaters, where you may see representations of [classical] Greek plays and Greek actions, who is better able than you to appreciate your ancestors' values, virtues, and learning? . . . In founding this establishment [the school] we have done nothing but obey the voice of the fatherland, nothing but realize the wishes of all Greeks, and especially yours, because you in your position are best able to judge how far enlightenment might help to gain once more for our nation the *esteem of the foreigners* which it ought never to have lost" (171; emphasis mine). The need of the Greeks to win the "esteem of the foreigners" was based on a sense of inferiority to them. In order to gain their favor they had to emphasize Greek qualities most familiar to them, the classical heritage, while suppressing the oriental elements altogether. In effect they promoted a picture of Greece already developed by European Hellenism.

Korais's text indicates how early the ideology of nationalism had begun to spread beyond the countries of its origin and how quickly the concept of the nation began to reproduce itself in nonwestern societies. His lecture is an early statement of themes to recur later in nationalist doctrines of Asia and Africa (Kedourie 1970: 42). The Greek nationalist project was successful because diaspora intellectuals identified their cause with western political, economic, and cultural interests. Though on the margins of geopolitical concerns, the Greeks related their mission of national integration to the concerns of the great powers of the time. The Greek modernizers based their nation upon the originary myth of the West. More than any other ethnic community (apart from the Jews) Greeks could demonstrate that they were European and conversely that the Europeans were really Greek.

The ultimate mission of nationalism is the establishment and reinforcement of an autonomous state. The state, however, requires a network of linked values and sentiments to hold it together. Nation building entails the invention of collective narratives, the homogenization of ethnic differences, and the induction of citizens into the ideology of the imagined community. Greek intellectuals understood from their experience in Europe that culture was indispensable to the process of national integration. In order to create such an entity for Greeks they had to wrest education away from the jurisdiction of the church. The goal of the struggle over education was control of cultural production, which had been in the hands of the church in the stratified millet. The struggle ended with the transformation of the church into a national institution. Although Greeks still considered themselves Orthodox, their identity was determined not by their faith alone, as in the millet, but by their nationality. Their new community was made imaginable by a profane discourse as opposed to a sacred script. The church of Greece, having been converted to the secular values of Greek nationalism, became "an official arm of the Greek state" (Kitromilides 1989: 166) and contributed to the legitimation of that state.

The anticlericalism of Enlightenment intellectuals was vehement. Korais, for instance, directed much of his rhetoric against the "superstitious and ignorant clergy" whom he held responsible for the wretched state of learning among Greeks ([1803] 1970: 156). His first political tract was a fiercely anticlerical text and defense of republican values, the *Adelfiki Didaskalia* (Brotherly teaching), published in 1798 in Rome. The document, addressed to all the "Greeks of the Ottoman dominions," was a response to the *Patriki Didaskalia* (Paternal teaching) published in Istanbul earlier the same year and attributed to Patriarch Anthimos of Jerusalem (though the author-

ship has been disputed even by Korais himself). Korais accused the author
of following a pro-Turkish policy and of trying to prevent Greeks "from
copying current movements for freedom of many European nations" (1949:
44). Korais very cleverly cited passages from the New Testament to justify
opposition to the "illegal Turkish administration" (50). All "oppressed"
people, he declared, have the right to break away from the "yoke of tyranny" (59). The real object of Korais's animosity, however, was the notion
that Ottoman occupation was a blessing from God to protect Orthodoxy
from a worse menace: Catholicism and secularism.

The *Patriki Didaskalia* not only condemned Enlightenment teaching as
blasphemous but also praised Ottoman rule for saving Orthodoxy from
inner and outer corruption: "Our Lord . . . has undertaken to guard once
more the unsullied Holy and Orthodox faith. . . . He raised up the empire
of the Ottomans . . . to assure all the faithful that in this way He deigned
to bring about a great mystery, namely the salvation of this chosen people. . . . For this reason he puts into the heart of the Sultan of these Ottomans
an inclination to keep free the religious beliefs of the Orthodox faith and . . .
protect them" (Clogg 1969: 104). Korais attacked the notion that acqui-
escence to the Ottomans was necessary for the preservation of the Orthodox
faith. He also called attention to the compatibility of views between the
upper ecclesiastical authorities and the Porte. Both feared the establishment
of a Greek nation, the former because it threatened the ecumenicity of
Orthodoxy, and the latter because it undermined the integrity of the empire.
To be sure, even today neo-Orthodox thinkers denounce Korais for sabo-
taging the mystical and Eastern traditions of Orthodoxy with the "cor-
rosive" values of the rational, Catholic, and Protestant West. They hold
him responsible for inaugurating the gradual destruction of the indigenous
structures enabling Orthodox society to survive Ottoman occupation (Iliu
1989: 74).

The *Patriki Didaskalia* was the target of other liberal thinkers, particularly the anonymous author of *Elliniki Nomarhia* [Greek Constitution];
or, A Speech about Liberty published in 1806. The two factors keeping
Greeks in tyranny, he claimed, were the "ignorant clergy" and the absence
from Greece of its best citizens, the merchants and students of the diaspora
(Anonymous 1957: 151). Greece, he maintained in a text brimming with
republican rhetoric, could be liberated sooner from the "Ottoman yoke"
if the clergy would teach about freedom and harmony and all the other
"means of human happiness" (178). This happiness could be realized only
with a constitution (*nomarhia*) (64), free from the tyrannical Ottoman
administration, its incomplete laws, barbarous customs, and ignorance
(127). Although the *Elliniki Nomarhia* was more nationalistic and xenophobic than Korais's texts, it used European liberal ideology to promote a

revolution, and it proposed a western mode of government as a model. When in fact a bourgeois form of government was instituted in 1828, it had a tenuous relationship with previous political practices. Modernization from the top was frustrated by this incongruity between local and imported structures.

The tilt toward Europe necessitated the cleansing of all oriental "blemishes" accumulated over four hundred years. It also put the Greeks at the vanguard of the struggle between Orient and Occident, between "barbarism" and "civilization." The Greek War of Independence, having been regarded by Europeans as a specific struggle in the general conflict between Europe and Asia, democracy against authoritarian empires, contributed, according to Martin Bernal, to the decline of the "ancient model," which had acknowledged the Egyptian and Phoenician heritage in Greek culture (1987). It was replaced by the "Aryan model," a product of German *Altertumswissenschaft,* which denied Afroasiatic roots in favor of Indoeuropean sources.

As Greece became more European it grew increasingly dependent on the West.[6] The newly independent nation also became an instrument of western policy in the Balkans and Near East. But to the extent that certain groups promoted both the unification of Hellenism throughout the Near East and the expansion of comprador activity into Egypt, Sudan, and Anatolia, western interests coincided with the irredentist and capitalist aims of those communities (Yerasimos 1988: 38).

The War of Independence

The movement toward independence was not a unilinear process. It was marked by conflicts among groups representing differing political, economic, and cultural interests, each competing to determine the identity of the Greek Orthodox subjects of the empire. The War of Independence itself was characterized by particularization and sectionalism. I have referred to the clash between the patriarchate and Enlightenment scholars over the modernization of Greek culture. Other interests were also opposed to, or at least ambivalent about, an autonomous Greek nation. The identity formation of the millet system, insofar as it encompassed many ethnic groups, was not national but religious. The empire itself, a multiethnic entity, contradicted the concept of an independent state. Indeed, only at the end of the nineteenth century did the Ottoman Empire come increasingly to be associated with the dominant ethnic group, the Turks. The state, defined by a single ethnicity at the expense of the minorities, undermined and eventually destroyed both the millet system and the empire.

The principal social group that contributed to the dissolution of the millet was the Phanariot aristocracy. These Greeks from the district of Phanar in Istanbul began to be appointed toward the end of the seventeenth century to ranks of the central government without, as had been previously necessary, their conversion to Islam. Their education, knowledge of European languages, and contacts with European countries made them indispensable in the administration and diplomatic corps as intermediaries between the empire and Europe. They served from 1709 to 1821 as governors of the grain-producing Danubian principalities (Moldavia and Wallachia) and monopolized the offices of the dragoman of foreign affairs and that of the navy. (Although *dragoman* means interpreter, the position was the equivalent of permanent secretary.) Having developed into an oligarchy, they acquired formidable power and prestige. With their wealth they were also influential in the nomination of the patriarch, since each candidate was required to pay a huge sum of money to the Ottoman authorities before assuming office.

The Phanariots were tied to both the empire and the patriarchate. Though their policies favored Greek merchants, they were reluctant to support the nationalist drive for fear of losing their positions. They opposed the formation of an autonomous state until the revolution itself made this cause inevitable. Inspired by visions of Byzantinism, they supported the reconstitution of the Byzantine Empire—whose heirs they considered themselves to be—governed by an Orthodox/Phanariot regime. Their hold on the patriarchate facilitated their project of Hellenization by making Greek the language of liturgy even in non-Greek areas[7] (see Runciman 1968).

The patriarchate, which from Byzantine times was an ecumenical institution representing all of Orthodoxy, became under their influence increasingly identified with one linguistic and ethnic group. Its ecclesiastical and civil jurisdiction over all Orthodox Christians was threatened, and in fact diminished, especially after the establishment of autocephalous churches in the new states, beginning with the Greek church in 1833. The Phanariot policy of Hellenization similarly broke the unity of the millet, as it emphasized language over faith, making language rather than religion the distinguishing mark of the Orthodox millet. The dominance of the Phanariots and their Hellenizing mission introduced to the Greek-speaking Orthodox (indirectly—that is, not in response to western nationalism) a new self-image as a distinctive linguistic group. Thus the task of the westernized intelligentsia to instill in Greeks a national consciousness was facilitated by the disintegration, initiated by the Phanariots, of the former religious identities. Since the unraveling of the millet's ethnoreligious fabric had already begun, the creation of a new identity to unify all Greek speakers made itself more pressing. Thus the formation of a Greek state was not just the product of western nationalism but also a response to the dissolution of previous cultural identities.

The other dominant group ambivalent about independence, the landlords *(kocabasis),* feared the probable demands of peasants for land reform after the departure of the Turks (Mouzelis 1978: 13). Since they also collected taxes, they did not want to lose this source of revenue or their privileges in the administration. As intermediaries between the Ottoman authorities and the peasants, they were welded to the status quo, forming a powerful propertied class. During the eighteenth century they actually profited from the absence of central authority by paying fewer taxes and gaining power to increase taxation of the peasants. Like the lords of the manor in feudal Europe, they thrived when the state structures were weakest. It is not surprising that they favored the current system while many merchants, frustrated by political instability, advocated a centralized state.

The various bands of brigands, the *klefts,* were already engaged in acts of insurrection against Ottoman power and thus formed the bulk of the fighting force. One of the most important military men, Theodoros Kolokotronis, was a *kleft* before the outbreak of the revolts. Many, however, believed they were fighting for Orthodoxy and not necessarily for a national state. They did not have a sense of a common homeland beyond their own regional identification nor did they have a basis for a shared national identity. Fierce family rivalries were common (see Petropulos 1968). Their captains had intense factional loyalties: they fought for the overthrow of the Turks in order to replace them on the local level rather than that of the nation. Though moved to action by nationalistic Greeks, the captains and brigands did not support the liberal ideas of egalitarian democracy and parliamentary government.

This oligarchy of landlords and military men infiltrated the new state apparatus by means of clientelistic relationships. These networks, which extended kinship patterns into the state mechanism, blurred the bourgeois distinction between private and public and disabled the expected neutral functioning of western institutions. This is one example of how modernity "failed," thwarted by indigenous forces. Since the administration in the millet system was decentralized, there was no precedent for a strong core authority, hence the incompatibility of new and old institutions. The church resisted the central government's appropriation of education, social welfare, and ideology. Furthermore, the notables and captains feared the diminution of their authority. The rivalry among the groups led to the assassination in 1831 of Ioannis Kapodistrias, the first governor of Greece and proponent of a conservative centralized state, who tried to enforce state authority upon sectional interests.

The introduction of political and cultural institutions, the products of a functionally differentiated society, into a stratified order created a "tense and sterile symbiotic relationship between state and society" which reinforced the distrust, always present under Ottoman rule, of the state apparatus (Diamandouros 1983: 47). Indeed, the experience of domination at the hands of non-Orthodox rulers, the increasing lawlessness from the seventeenth century on, and the imposition of a Bavarian monarch after independence engendered in Greeks lasting attitudes toward the state, power, and official culture that manifested themselves in the form of distrust and manipulation of state institutions. The pattern of state-society relations in Greece was one of antagonism: "to the state's attempt to rationalise society from above, the latter responded by eroding and particularizing the state from below" (Diamandouros 48).

The western-type state had to be imposed because conditions were absent for the emergence of a powerful autochthonous bourgeoisie. It is important to emphasize that the uprisings in 1821 did not constitute a bourgeois revolution for the simple reason that a powerful bourgeoisie, eager to establish a new civil society, had not yet formed (Filias 1974; Kaklamanis 1989). The diaspora on the whole functioned as the Greek middle class. Notions of individual rights, private property, and a free market therefore did not figure prominently in the struggle for independence (Pollis 1987: 149). The oligarchs sought not the overthrow of feudal bonds but their continuation. The scattered bourgeois elements could not unify the rival sectional forces. Unlike the French Revolution, the Greek War of Independence was not a class struggle against a monarchy and aristocracy but a fight against foreign rule. Subsequent attempts to limit the power of the monarchy were also not class oriented. Even by the end of the nineteenth century political parties did not represent class interests but those of individuals, professions, and geographic regions (Dertilis 1977: 135; Pollis 1987: 151).

The major participants in the uprisings were the largely uneducated[8] and politically fragmented peasants. They joined the revolution to ameliorate their deteriorating economic lot rather than establish an independent nation, a concept largely foreign to them. To be sure, while they were aware of their community as Orthodox and non-Muslim, they did not define themselves as a distinct ethnolinguistic group. Nationalism taught them to think of themselves in this way. This is the whole idea, as Anderson insists, behind the invention of the imagined community. It brings individuals together in a common social experience which becomes the space for the acquisition of their shared identity. It enables people to relate to one another on the basis of a linguistic unity and a canon of stories. Members of this union recite to each other the tales they have learned about themselves, their nation, and its history. The secret society Filiki Eteria, for instance, was organized in Odessa in 1814 by merchants to inculcate in peasants a national consciousness by spreading revolutionary pamphlets and establishing secret cells in the Balkans. (The Holy Synod, in a move underscoring the irreconcilable differences between it and the westernizers, anathematized its members in March 1821 for their seditious activities [see Frangos 1973]).

Though the peasants were inspired by prophetic beliefs in the liberation of Constantinople, their greater concerns were material: land, security, and a check on the rapaciousness of the landlords. Their resistance to Ottoman authority increased because of the prevalent chaos and, significantly, because Turks owned the majority of the land. At the beginning of the nineteenth century, for instance, the 40,000 Turks in Peloponnisos owned three million stremmata (one stremma is about one quarter of an acre) while the 360,000 Greeks controlled only one and one-half million stremmata (Karpat 1973: 75; Stavrianos 1963: 24). On the average the Turks had eighteen times more land. Furthermore, a third of the Greek land was in the hands of a local Greek oligarchy whose lots the peasants worked as either laborers or serfs.

The Turks and the Greek landowners were not the only targets of peasant resentment. The higher clergy also incurred their wrath. A saying that circulated at the time claimed that the people were plagued by "three curses: the priests, the *kocabasis,* and Turks" (in Clogg 1973: 18). Peasant anticlericalism, however, did not have sources in Enlightenment philosophy but in the suspicion that widespread corruption in the church was fleecing them. As a result of the payment demanded by the Ottoman authorities upon his confirmation, the patriarch sought money not only from the Phanariots but also from the archbishops, who in turn demanded more from the bishops, who then tapped the priests, who finally extracted the requisite amount from the peasants. The anonymous author of the *Elliniki Nomarhia,* albeit he is biased, described the transactions in the following way:

> The Synod buys the patriarchal throne from the Ottoman grand
> vizir for a large sum of money. Afterwards it sells the throne to
> whoever gives it the greatest profit and designates the purchaser
> patriarch. He, then, to get back whatever he borrowed for the
> purchase of the throne, sells the dioceses, that is, the archbish-
> oprics, to whoever gives him the largest sum, and thereby appoints
> the archbishops who themselves sell their bishoprics to others. The
> bishops then sell these to the Christians, that is, they skin the
> people to get back what they spent. This is the way that the
> positions of the different ranks are chosen, that is, with gold.
> (Anonymous 1957: 164)

The financial burdens imposed by the church, a manifestation of the general corruption resulting from the diminution of central authority in the eighteenth century, fanned peasant resentment, particularly toward the upper ecclesiastical authorities. Their anticlericalism, however, had no effect on their Orthodox identity; indeed, many considered their struggle to be religious. But the westernized elites, who wanted to redefine that identity, tried to limit the powers of the church in secular affairs. When the Autocephalous Church of Greece was proclaimed in 1833, its previous overwhelming authority in civil matters was curtailed.[9] Greek nationalism, observes Kitromilides, transformed the "whole tradition of eastern Orthodoxy by drawing the nation and the Church together as integral parts of the same symbolic universe" (1989: 166).

Given the ideological differences among the revolutionaries and the absence of central leadership in the movement, it is remarkable that the Greeks won the war. Crucial to their success was the involvement of the superpowers of the time: England, France, and Russia. Because of Greece's strategic location in the eastern Mediterranean and the cultural factors discussed earlier, the Greek revolution became a major diplomatic conflict. Sensing the imminent disintegration of the Ottoman Empire, the great powers strived to gain as much advantage as possible while keeping each other in check. Every state had specific concerns. The Hapsburg government feared Russian expansion into the Balkans. The Russian policy aimed for a stronghold in the Mediterranean and control of the Dardanelles. The English wanted to protect their routes to the East. The French hoped for Ottoman territory, particularly after they acquired the Ionian Islands in 1797, from which they spread revolutionary propaganda into Greece (Clogg 1969: 89–91).

The great powers finally intervened in 1827 and sank the Ottoman fleet, thereby guaranteeing victory for the Greek side. The Greeks, however, were not simply pawns to the powers, for they coaxed them to join the conflict. They secured foreign loans in European banks to guarantee the interest of the powers in order to protect their investments; they dangled the possibility of a throne to sons of royal families;[10] and they also petitioned England in 1824 to assume protection of the Greek cause to instigate action from France and Russia, countries suspicious of British dominance in the area (Couloumbis, Petropulos, Psomiades 1976: 18). These strategies were, of course, part of the project to cement Greece to Europe. But they also initiated a pattern of direct foreign involvement in Greek political and economic affairs that has continued to the present day.[11] Greece was going to be a part of the West; indeed, it is the only Balkan nation to be a member of NATO and the EEC. While Greece gained independence from the Ottoman Empire, it became an appendage to western Europe. The British minister to Athens put it imperialistically in 1841: "A Greece truly independent is an absurdity. Greece is Russian or she is English; and since she must not be Russian, it is necessary that she be English" (in Stavrianos 1974: 198).[12]

Other States

The Greeks were the first people in the Ottoman Empire to form an autonomous nation and Greece continued to be the only independent country in the Balkans until the 1860s. The Serbians had arisen against the Ottomans in 1804 but the revolt was suppressed in 1809; its implications were limited, although it provided a model to the Greeks (see *Elliniki Nomarhia*). Coming as early as it did, Greek nationhood had enormous implications beyond the borders of the new state. It sent a message of nationalism to the other communities of the empire, which was incompatible with the idea of empire. Above all, the Greeks became one of the first peoples outside western Europe to participate in the experiment of modernity.

At the beginning of this chapter I examined some factors accounting for the invention of a Greek culture and establishment of an independent nation. It is helpful to examine briefly why other important communities of the empire did not form independent states. After their expulsion from Spain in 1492 large numbers of Iberian Jews emigrated to the Ottoman Empire, which, with an expanding economy, welcomed skilled urban labor. Since Turks shunned international trade (Mantran 1983: 135), the Jews became intermediaries, particularly in commerce between the empire and their coreligionists in Italy and other regions of the Mediterranean. The Jews were the prominent merchants during the sixteenth century. But as trading patterns shifted toward central Europe, the Sephardic Jews were replaced as traders and intermediaries by the Greeks and Armenians, who had stronger ethnic and religious networks there. In the seventeenth and eighteenth centuries the Greek Orthodox became the most prosperous non-Muslim subjects of the empire and played a dominant role in its international trade. Faced with increasing competition from the Christian communities, the position of the Jews declined, but they continued to see their future within the empire. Of the non-Muslim communities, they were Ottoman subjects by choice, not conquest, and hence regarded the empire as a haven from persecution. Nationalism, therefore, never found a receptive audience among the Jews (Braude and Lewis 1983: 24). In the struggle between modernizers and traditionalists, the former lost among the Jews whereas they won among the Greeks. They did not question the notion of empire as a form of political organization. Even after the introduction of reforms the Jews cast their lot with the conservative Ottoman forces; their situation deteriorated along with that of the empire (26).

The Armenians, on the other hand, struggled for independence at the end of the nineteenth century, and in their case the reformers won. Following the Greeks, Serbians, and Bulgarians and convinced that the future lay in a nation-state, they launched a campaign for autonomy. A national consciousness emerged much later among Armenians than in the other communities, about the last quarter of the nineteenth century (Walker 1980: 96). It was the result of a cultural revival when schools were established, Armenia's classical past was discovered, and a literary discourse was developed to bridge the gap between the vernacular and the archaistic liturgical language. Armenian cultural life flourished among the educated elite of Istanbul, and particularly in Russia. The Russian Armenian nationalists, however, directed their efforts toward building a nation in Ottoman Armenia, which they regarded as their true homeland. The Armenians began to organize themselves politically in the 1870s, and the first revolt erupted in 1890 in Erzerum.

But the Armenians could not make their cause meaningful to Europe, since Europeans had not posited Armenian history as the source of civilization. The Greeks, having at their disposal the discourse of Hellenism, were able to trace a descent from classical Hellas and claim an Ur-European identity. The Armenians, like many ethnic groups of the eastern Mediterranean and Near East, could similarly boast a distinguished genealogy, but European philologists gave primacy to the Greeks as inventors of culture. Given the centrality of classical Greece in the European imaginary it was rather simple for the Greeks and their philhellene supporters to translate this into sympathy for the Greek cause. The triumph of the Greeks lay in their ability to graft their national text upon the narratives of the states powerful at that time. They cast their attempts at nation formation as central to the Eastern Question and entangled the superpowers in their fate. In contrast, the Armenians could not identify their struggle with the policies of the great powers. The British, for instance, toward the end of the nineteenth century had been supporting the Ottoman Empire as a bulwark against Russian expansion. They also wanted to protect their sizable investments there. In the negotiations of the Treaties of San Stefano and Berlin after the Ottoman loss to the Russians in 1878 the Armenian demands for local autonomy were disregarded. The Armenian delegation to Berlin protested the unfavorable treatment they received in comparison to the Bulgarians:

> The Armenian delegation expresses its regret that its legitimate demands . . . have not been agreed upon by the congress. We had not believed that a nation like ours, composed of several million souls, which has not so far been the instrument of any foreign power, which, although much more oppressed than the other

Christian populations has caused no trouble to the Ottoman government (and, although our nation had no tie of religion or origin to any of the great powers, yet, being a Christian nation it had hoped to find in our century the same protection afforded to the other Christian nations)—we had not believed that such a nation, devoid of all political ambition, would have to acquire the right of living its life and of being governed on its ancestral land by Armenian officials. The Armenian delegation is going to return to the East, taking this lesson with it. It declares nevertheless that the Armenian people will never cease from crying out until Europe gives its legitimate demands satisfaction. (in Walker 1980)

This document makes here the classic attempt of claiming compatibility with the great powers to win their support. But as the delegates themselves recognized, Armenia had not become an instrument of foreign powers nor could it trace ties of religion or national origin to them. Hence Europe did not heed its pleas for autonomy. Furthermore, Armenian hopes for national independence met with increased resistance from the Ottoman Turks, who were developing their own sense of nationhood. While the Turks could ultimately forfeit Greece, Serbia, and Bulgaria, the loss of a major territory in Anatolia represented a severe threat to their emerging nationalism. When the Greeks launched their revolt the Ottoman Empire was still intact if weak. The emergence of Armenian nationalism coincided with the transformation of the empire into the modern Turkish state. Armenian aspirations for nationhood ended with the widespread massacres and forced dislocations of 1915–16. Russian Armenia declared its independence in May 1918 but was annexed by Stalin as a Soviet Republic in 1920.

The Jews of the empire chose not to modernize, the Armenians tried and failed. The Egyptians launched a program of modernization in 1808 but without success. Egypt's encounter with Bonaparte's troops in 1798 was shattering to traditional society. Subsequent rulers, particularly Mohammad Ali (1805–48) and Ismail (1863–79), attempted to bring Egypt, an autonomous province of the Ottoman Empire, into a more favorable military and technological balance with the West. Mohammad Ali, an Ottoman installed by the Porte, attempted a rapid modernization of education, agriculture, industry, and the military. He established academies, language centers, and professional schools. Graduates of these institutions formed a new class of educated Egyptians who advocated further introduction of western culture. Ali also encouraged the settlement of vast numbers of foreigners in Egypt. Ismail in turn opened Egypt to foreign capital and indebted the province heavily to European banks before the British invasion in 1882. He tried to integrate the rural segment of the economy with the urban and to differentiate society into autonomous parts: the bureaucracy, educational network, military, and political institutions (Tignor1966: 42–44). This project met with limited success because of its forced nature, its scant effect on the peasantry, and the relatively small size of the westernized class.

Modernization failed in Egypt because of the discrepancies between imported prototypes and local practices. It was left to the foreign merchants and professionals stationed in Egypt, along with the British, to promote further change. But, like a true comprador bourgeoisie, this class functioned as an intermediary for the implementation of foreign capital; its activities assumed a speculative nature and were concentrated in finance, banking, and commerce.[13] Their capital was invested not in industry but in irrigation, agriculture, and public works (Tignor 1966: 358). The Greeks, forming the largest foreign community, penetrated all sectors of the society except the bureaucracy and thereby were instrumental in determining the country's development. For instance, in the 1860s one third of the Chamber of Commerce consisted of Greek firms and organizations (Issawi 1983: 271). By 1927 the community had a population of 100,000 (Kitroeff 1989: 2). The fortunes amassed by the Greeks in Egypt and the diaspora allowed them to intervene in the politics, economy, and culture of Greece.

The Greek program for modernization provides an interesting case when compared with that of the Jews, Armenians, and Egyptians. Many Latin American countries predated Greece and most other European nation-states in their independence. Argentina proclaimed its autonomy in 1816, Chile in 1818, Mexico in 1821, and Brazil in 1822. All these cases differ from that of Greece. Though they rebeled against empires, on the whole they shared the language and culture of the polities they rejected. Language and national culture thus did not constitute major issues in these struggles; a European-style middle class had not emerged at the end of the nineteenth century; and an intelligentsia had not yet developed (Anderson 1983: 50). The republics existed from the sixteenth century to the eighteenth as separate administrative and economic units which assumed over time a self-contained character. Only after independence did they develop a sense of nationhood. Unlike Greece, where a culture was being shaped by intellectuals decades before the revolution, Brazil declared its statehood in 1822 without a specific Brazilian identity. This was so because prior to 1808 the Portuguese crown had prohibited printing and access to higher education (Barman 1988: 4). A national consciousness formed in the period between independence and the 1850s. The establishment of the nation-state was promoted by educated elites whose familiarity with print gave them mastery over communication, and by mercantile groups striving to promote their interests in the new political and administrative configuration. The nation-state afforded these groups an opportunity to strengthen their dominance, but the bulk of the population did not perceive the consolidation of the state as serving their needs until after the 1850s (Barman 1988: 5). The Brazilian case demonstrates that political independence is not necessarily coterminous with the construction of a nation, an imagined realm of shared identity.

In Greece, by contrast, the two projects coincided, for the Greeks conjoined the idea of an autonomous state and a fund of common sentiments and beliefs. This process, however, took a long time. This is one of the reasons philhellenes were dismayed to discover that the Greeks did not share a common purpose; that is, they did not exhibit the traits of national subjects. At the onset of the uprisings the bulk of the population, as I have argued earlier, did not see itself collectively as a people. It was the task of culture to induct Greeks into the imaginary space of national values and experiences. Identity, as a repertory of conventions and beliefs, has to be acquired.

But this was the case in western Europe as well during the revolutionary upheavals. "In 1789 not many people were nationally conscious, and fewer, certainly, were national patriots" (Shafer 1972: 87). Only half the population of France in 1789 could speak standard French. Similarly, when Italy was unified in 1861 less than 10 percent of the people communicated in Italian; the rest used various dialects. A "national" tongue was gradually introduced through urbanization, education, conscription, and the mass media (Forgacs 1990: 17). Since individuals have to be made into citizens, the cultural apparatus of a nation assumes great significance. Nations, Stathis Gourgouris writes, "exist as dreams before they become politically and geographically signified as nations" (1989: 109); the purpose of culture is to preserve and reinvoke this original dream state. At the initial stage of nation building, therefore, the carriers of nationalism are eager to set up those institutions that designate and codify a national consciousness. Literature is one such institution. Of all the arts, as I argue in the next chapter, it participates most forcefully in the formation of nations. The novel, for instance, joins the newspaper as the major vehicles of the national print media, helping to standardize language and encourage literacy (Brennan 1990: 58). Literature serves as a mirror of the collective identity and also recites its story.

The spread of nationalism from western Europe to neighboring lands went hand in hand with the diffusion of European ideas and values. Since the founding of a state was posited as desirable, those drafting the blueprints for a nation naturally sought the very institutions Europeans developed to cement their own national unity: language, literature, art. The ideology of nationalism and its symbols reinforced each other. The Greek experience is thus not entirely exceptional. What is unique is that Greek nationalism appeared first outside western Christendom, in a society ruled by non-

Christians and hostile to western influences (Kedourie 1970: 42). Greek nationalism manifests the quick dissemination of this discourse beyond the borders of western Europe.

The Language Conflict

The most important instrument for the creation of a national consciousness is the vernacular. The intelligentsia has to call on the masses to fight for a revolution in the language they understand. Nations emerged in Europe after the vernaculars gained equal footing with the classical languages, particularly Latin. The codification of the vernaculars, facilitated in part through print, created unified fields of exchange and communication that enabled people to think about themselves in new ways: as cohesive groups bound not necessarily by their loyalty to a king or duty to the church but by a "deep horizontal comradeship" and a sense of linguistic community (Anderson 1983: 47, 15). By promoting the accumulation of shared experiences the vernaculars helped to differentiate groups from one another. Each national community consisted of individuals who spoke, read, and wrote in a standard language and worked in a realm of (contrived) cultural consensus.

The question of language was profoundly important to Greek identity and continued to have repercussions for the state until the 1980s. The Greeks of the diaspora understood from the European experience the centrality of language in the formation of nations. They, however, were faced with a number of registers (the vernacular, the archaistic language of the patriarchate and scholarship, and classical Greek) competing for the authority due to the national language. Although Greeks imported the discourse of nationalism, their specific situation altered its character. The question of diglossia, the contemporaneous presence of two registers of the same language, meant that the nationalist project had to depart from the program set in western European countries.

Greek, along with Chinese constituting one of the two longest unbroken linguistic traditions in the world, has almost always experienced some sort of diglossia. Although Greek has been transformed in its long evolution, no radical discontinuity has occurred comparable to that between Latin and the Romance languages (Alexiou 1982; Browning 1983; Mackridge 1985). Ancient Greek is not as strange to contemporary Greeks as Anglo-Saxon is to English speakers, and Homeric Greek is probably closer to modern Greek than Middle English to modern English (Alexiou: 161). The average Greek can at least recognize much of the vocabulary in a classical text, and the frequent churchgoer has a passive knowledge of the language in the New Testament. A person with minimal education can read vernacular texts from the thirteenth and fourteenth centuries. All this is possible partly because, alongside the popular language, there has always existed a scholarly linguistic paradigm in which many of the older forms have been preserved and which has enforced a certain conservatism on the language.

A diglossia emerged as early as the first century B.C. with the phenomenon of Atticism, an archaistic revival of classical Attic, spoken in the region of Attica and considered the language of literary prose. With the dissolution of the city-states and their amalgamation by Alexander the Great, Attic and the other Greek dialects began to disappear, being absorbed into a new common language, the *koine,* which spread throughout the eastern Mediterranean and became the language of the New Testament. The *koine* developed as a common language in the Hellenistic world among peoples whose native tongues were not Greek. The changes in Greek culture and language, made inevitable by the spread of Greek culture and its contact with other societies, distressed those committed to the preservation of tradition. In order to prevent the eventual disappearance of Attic, teachers of grammar and rhetoric began to advocate its adoption as the written language. They exhorted their students to employ esoteric literary words instead of their "vulgar" equivalents. Their aim was to thwart linguistic change, regarded by them as decadent, and a betrayal of the classical heritage. While this movement consolidated itself in pedagogic practice during the next two centuries, the spoken idiom lost its authority as the language of teaching and writing. Scholars, teachers, students, and orators wrote in an imitation of classical writers while the person in the street continued to use the *koine.* This separation of the spoken language from the written persisted in one form or another from late antiquity, the Byzantine era, up until modern times.

Diglossia developed into a political problem during the eighteenth century as a result of modernization. The question of a national language arose only when the nation was posited as a desirable mode of political organization. This new entity required a standardized linguistic medium of its own. Since then language has continued to be a contentious issue involving politics of every order: in writing, on the street, in Parliament. As early as 1852 the scholar Spiridon Zambelios remarked that the question of language was not simply "philological" but broadly political, since it directly concerned Greece's "destiny" and relationship to both East and West (1852: 368). The clash over the national idiom was about national education, and more important, the relationship of Greeks to their classical and Byzantine past, and their self-definition as a western society. Because of its centrality to national identity, the language question mobilized forces struggling over culture, history, and the community's relationship to Europe. The establishment of the state in no way resolved these conflicts. Political autonomy entailed the importation or creation of cultural constructs, such as national language, for which there was no need or precedent in the millet system. The introduction of the European models in an undifferentiated, precapitalist society led to ideological turmoil that polarized Greek culture along a series of antinomies: tradition-modernity, East-West, nation-empire, classical-Byzantine.

The archaistic contingent, which held ancient Greece as its referent, imposed a puristic language on the nation. The modernizers strove to fashion Greece along western prototypes by importing European models even though there was no context for their implementation. The demotic populist current, often with pro-Orthodox or Hellenocentric tendencies, attempted, as a reaction to mechanical imitation of the West, to isolate Greece from Europe, even though its ideology had western sources. Nikos Svoronos believes neither the socialist nor the demoticist movements of the late nineteenth and early twentieth centuries escaped these contradictions (1976: 24).[14]

The language question was implicated in these oppositions and was understood as a conflict between them. Liberal thinkers supported the vernacular. The education of Greek children, argued the author of *Elliniki Nomarhia,* would be much easier in "our simple idiom" (Valetas 1957: 200). He decried the years pupils spent acquiring scholarly Greek. Institutions such as the church, under whose purview education fell during Ottoman rule, defended the classicizing language as the tongue of the church fathers. For the church, it also served as a bulwark against the Enlightenment. In an encyclical of 1819 Patriarch Gregory V (1745–1821) condemned the neglect of this language in the schools and attacked secular learning (sciences, mathematics) as a corruption of religion.[15]

This view was shared by the Phanariots and by conservative scholars like Evyenios Vulgaris (1716–1806), Dimitrios Darvaris (1716–1823), and Neofitos Dukas (1760–1845), who regarded ancient Greek as a path to classical Greece and to a rebirth of its civilization. By returning to an uncorrupted form of the ancient language, they believed the Greek people would once again assume their rightful place in Europe, a position worthy of their illustrious ancestors. The cultural renaissance, based on the resurrected language, was to provide "the linguistic proof of the continuity of Hellenism and of the 'Greekness' of the Greeks" (Babiniotis 1979: 3). The guiding principle of this linguistic revivalism and of much Greek ideology was mimesis—the reproduction of the original (Dimaras 1975: 161). In the same spirit, building in Athens took on a neoclassical appearance and parents chose classical names for their children—Themistocles and Alexandra rather than Peter and Maria.

Their opponents, although criticizing the classicists as outmoded, themselves often made references to classical Greek in support of demotic. Filippidis and Konstantas, for instance, asserted that the vernacular evolved from the "great Greek language" as its fifth dialect (1988: 114). A nation that neglects its "natural language," they insisted, actually rejects itself and is not worthy of its ancestors. The authors buttressed their arguments with allusions to classical culture but they also pointed to the example of European nationalism. Many European nations experienced problems with their script language, Latin, but they resolved them by developing their "spoken idioms" (148). They exhorted Greeks to follow suit by reforming their own vernacular; otherwise, as descendants of "demigods," they appeared inferior to the "Celts and Teutons." When, they asked (citing Condillac), will the Greeks begin to "copy the English and the other nations of Europe, for a nation perfects its soul when it begins to cultivate its language" (86). Enlightenment thinkers understood from the European experience that a standardized vernacular enabled the creation of a homogeneous culture by facilitating communication among members of the linguistic community. They realized that a shared vernacular rather than a scholarly idiom would enable Greeks of the empire to think of themselves as a corporate group. Their task was to endow demotic with the prestige of classical Greek and to demonstrate its capacity to grow into a national language.

Katartzis, the leader of the demotic camp, argued that only the demotic could serve as the "national" tongue and engender a unified culture (1970: 14). The standard language would enable the emergence of arts and sciences and the evolution of a "civilized nation" (7). Vilaras similarly fought for a common language, used by both learned and uneducated people, to reconcile the tension between orality and literacy (1935: 315). A language, he asserted, should be written as it is spoken; only in a shared idiom can members of a society communicate with each other (325, 332). European nations "do not have two languages, one for the masses and another for scholars" (372); their national unity depends on a communal language. For these intellectuals codification of demotic was connected to the very possibility of a modern Greece.

The language problem was initially resolved by moderate demoticists and classicists. Chief amongst them was Korais, who proposed his *via media*, the *katharevusa*. Korais's compromise was a language based on popular speech, "purified" of Turkish loan words and foreign dialect features and "embellished" on the model of the ancient language. *Katharevusa*, although an archaistic language, was not the traditional atticizing form encountered in previous centuries. It was a hybrid of the demotic and learned registers. After the War of Independence in 1821 it was installed as the official language of the state, education, and "serious" writing. Government, cultural, and religious institutions became bulwarks of *katharevusa*. But these institutions were dominated by individuals who favored a classicizing interpretation of the linguistic compromise. The use of archaizing form and syntax was considered a sign of distinction. Thus *katharevusa* became increasingly distant from the vernacular under the pressure of conservative scholars and poets such as Panayiotis Sutsos (1806–1868), Alexandros Rangavis (1809–1892) and K. Kontos (1834–1909).

By the last two decades of the nineteenth century, however, its dominance in the state apparatus provoked a reaction from supporters of demotic. The years between 1880 and 1917 saw the rise of a militant demoticism; proponents of the vernacular struggled to establish it as the language of poetry and prose, education, and the state. The first battle was won in the early part of the twentieth century but not without the use of both discursive and physical violence. Riots broke out in the streets of Athens in 1901 when Alexandros Pallis published a demotic translation of the New Testament and again in 1903 when the National Theater performed the *Oresteia* in modern Greek. Two people died and many were wounded in these demonstrations. In 1911 a clause in the constitution officially secured *katharevusa* as the national idiom; it remained the language of the state, church, army, press, and most scholarly discourse until the 1970s. In the meantime, Greeks faced a peculiar and dispossessing situation most of their lives, being compelled to switch continually between the two linguistic modes.[16]

During most of the nineteenth century the only area for demotic literary production was the Ionian Islands, where a school of poetry connected to the Cretan tradition flourished. But poets like Solomos (1798–1857), Tipaldos (1814–1883), and Valaoritis (1824–1879), who were hailed by demoticists as the founders of Greek poetry, remained on the margins. The situation changed when the Generation of the 80s launched the demoticist movement and a new project of modernization. The demoticists, unable to have demotic recognized as the language of either the state or education, withdrew into the realm of culture, which since the 1880s had become a demotic domain. Blocked from official institutions, they used literature and criticism to promote the vernacular. For much of the twentieth century neither the language nor the culture of the intelligentsia corresponded with that of the schools.

In the twentieth century demotic gained ground after the publication of an influential modern Greek grammar by Manolis Triantafillidis in 1941. Its prestige grew in the favorable climate fostered by the reforms of the Center Union Party in the mid-1960s and was increasingly incorporated into the educational system. These policies, however, were immediately abandoned by the junta coming to power in 1967, which confined the use of demotic to primary schools. Dictatorships always supported the purist language. Then, after the downfall of the junta in 1974, the Konstantinos Karamanlis government passed a law in 1976 declaring demotic the language of education and state. Finally the administration of Andreas Papandreou introduced the monotonic system in 1981, in which pupils were no longer required to learn the complex use of accents introduced during the Hellenistic era. Only in these recent years has the linguistic controversy largely been resolved, the ghost of diglossia put to rest, and a standard language established for all uses, official and unofficial.[17]

The acceptance of demotic as the language of schooling and government indicates a possible integration of state institutions and national culture. The disjunction between these two realms has frustrated the formation of a unified field of communication and a cultural homogeneity. The incongruity between symbolic and political structures created extraordinary tensions in a society considering itself belated and marginal. Yet, despite the lack of a cultural consensus, Greeks experienced a shared sense of community, first in literature and later in an aesthetic realm. The problems created by the exposure of Greek society to modernity were resolved by that most modern feature, the autonomous aesthetic.

Literature and Nation

"A nation in order to become a nation needs two things: to extend its boundaries and to create its own literature [*filoloyia*]. . . . It has to extend not only its physical but also its mental boundaries." So wrote Yiannis Psiharis (1935: 25), one of the most implacable supporters of demotic, in his autobiographical treatise on the language controversy, *To Taxidi Mu* (My journey, 1888). In these two sentences he posits the formation of literature on the same level as the territorial construction of a nation. Earlier he equates language with the nation: "Language and nation are one. The struggle is the same, whether one fights for one's country or for its national language" (25). Demoticists and purists alike understood that literature and language were key components of a national culture. Language produced the extended fields of communication essential for the genesis of national culture while literature generated stories about its identity. Since the value of literature was already acknowledged by the intellectual elite, one of the demoticists' tasks was to gain recognition for demotic by showing that it could produce a national literature.

The association of language, literature, and nation was one of the hallmarks of European nationalist thought. As early as 1767 Johann Gottfried Herder observed that "der Genius der Sprache ist also auch der Genius von der Literatur einer Nation [the spirit of a language is also the spirit of a nation's literature]" (1877: 148). Language was considered the deepest expression of a nation's individuality. Literature was the imaginary mirror in which the nation reflected itself, where people experienced themselves as members of such a union. It was both a manifestation of the nation as well as part of the nation-forming process. As a collection of narratives, the literary canon contains the tales by means of which members of a community understand their common links. Literature in a sense is the nation's diary, telling the story of its past, present, and future. Literary culture has been indispensable to ethnic communities wishing to cement their integrity as nations and to demonstrate (belatedly) their modern credentials.

The Russian critic Vissarion Belinsky, for instance, observed that foreigners disregarded Russian literature as too young, capable only of copying European models (Belinsky 1976: 11). "The national spirit of European nations," he concluded, "is so sharply and originally expressed in their literatures that any work, however great in artistic merit, which does not bear the sharp imprint of nationality, loses its chief merit in the eyes of Europeans" (12). Many times a literature is ignored because it does not conform to the standard of its neighbors. Until the 1960s, for example, Canadian literature was neglected by the rest of the world and, significantly, by Canadians themselves. The indifference of Anglo-Canadians to their own literature prompted Margaret Atwood to write *Survival,* a study of "what is Canadian about Canadian literature" (1972). In response to the overwhelming presence of the British and American literary traditions in Canadian critical discourse the intelligentsia demanded a Canadian literature. Canadian literary texts had, of course, been composed but they were not recognized as literary by the cultural institutions, which promoted largely foreign work. African-American literature, Henry Louis Gates insists, arose in part as a reaction to charges that its authors could not create literature. Gates sees the effort vindicated, arguing that in a few years "we shall at last have our very own Norton Anthology, a sure sign that the teaching of Afro-American literature has been institutionalized and will continue to be so" (1987b: 26–27). The existence of such a literary tradition provides African-Americans with one of the most potent symbols of ethnic unity. Although this nationalism is not territorially based, African-American intellectuals nevertheless consider it indispensable in the nation-building process. All national groups, it seems, must have a literature. In African-American society, however, as in diasporas generally, literature faces a major challenge in shaping a culture that, not rooted in its own soil, is imagined on a much more abstract level.

Literature serves as a positive agent in the production of cultural identities. The three examples above indicate a conscious effort on the part of intellectuals to produce a national literature. But in putting literature in the service of nationalism they destroy its potential to reflect critically on the nation and the identity it helped shape. At the initial stage of nationalism literature can assist a people in constituting an autonomous state free from external domination. But since literature, like modern art in general, aspires to a negative function as well—to criticize all totalities, including the national one—it occupies a paradoxical position in simultaneously mediating identity and reflecting on it from a distance.

By positing a transcendent realm of essential identity nationalist doctrines often tend to enforce a uniformity of belief. This is true in multi-ethnic states such as Spain, or in many African countries whose borders, drawn arbitrarily by colonialism, contain warring communities. The liberal ideal of diversity within the whole often regresses into a negation of differences. It also leads into the forceful imposition of linguistic conformity upon a heterogeneous political map. Indeed, the creation of a standardized language and a homogeneous culture usually involves the valorization of one dialect and the identity of one community. The purists in Greece designated an artificial code as the official language of the nation. But even the demoticists, in the name of the spoken idiom, elevated the dialect of Peloponnisos as the new national tongue at the expense of the vast number of local dialects and even other languages. The writings of groups excluded from the consensus of dominant culture can defamiliarize the representations of nationalist discourse operating both within the boundaries of a state and, as I argued in the previous chapter, on a supranational level. These counter-narratives resist the homogeneous space and time of national culture and interrupt the continuous narrative of its history.

Chapter 3
The Making of a Canon:
A Literature of Their Own

Modernization entails the formation of a national culture to replace the ethnoreligious identities of the stratified system. In contrast to the absolute laws of the empire and the coercive customs of the church, national culture federates individuals through communal habits, experiences, stories, and, of course, language. Members of the state, linked to one another by this engineered unity, experience their common heritage, humanity, and destiny. The literary canon, as a collection of texts recounting the story of the nation, facilitates the experience of solidarity by allowing people to see themselves as citizens of a unified nation. The canon, however, not only represents national identity but also participates in its producton by instilling in people the values of nationalism. The canon records—in the vernacular— the history of the nation, articulating a chronological continuity that helps members of the community overcome the shortcomings of an uncertain present. In the temporalized order of modernity the canon, a utopian projection into the past, longs for a time rather than a place. In a period of disintegrating identities and differentiating social relationships, the canon looks back to a previous plenitude, offering hopes of cultural revival. Like the contemporaneously emerging disciplines of philology, archaeology, and mythology, it seeks to recapture the past.

The Ins and Outs of Canonicity

Canons and their formation have received attention in contemporary literary study as part of a broader inquiry into the institutions of criticism, artistic

49

production, evaluation, taste, interpretation, and nationalism. Interest in the constitution of literary canons is related to work investigating the emergence of art and literature and their roles in the construction of cultural homogeneity. An analysis of the canon is necessarily historical; it goes beyond the borders of autonomous texts, with their "inherent" devices and properties, and examines how those texts were and are processed and to what uses they are put at specific institutional sites, such as the university, publishing house, journal, newspaper, lecture, and library.

Such an examination asks not what a text means but rather how and why it is made to mean what it means at different stages and spaces in a community. Not an exegetical enterprise salvaging the hidden truths of individual works, an inquiry into canon formation concerns the position a text has occupied in a hierarchy and the movement of texts within this rank. All canons, be they religious, aesthetic, or philosophical, contain examples of texts that were exiled permanently, others that jumped suddenly into prominence, and others still that slid into temporary oblivion. In the formation of the New Testament, for instance, the Gnostic gospels were suppressed in favor of texts which the church fathers considered holy and authentic. Another notorious case is the fate of Plato and the Sophists within Greek philosophy: while almost all of Plato's works have survived, little but fragments remains of his adversaries' texts. The history of art and literature can furnish countless other such examples. Francis Haskell points to the "discovery" of Vermeer in 1792 by Le Brun, "one of the first art lovers who consciously tried to 'discover' neglected artists" (1976: 18). The rediscovery of El Greco in the late nineteenth century, Eliot's successful revaluation of Donne and the metaphysical poets, and the reversal of the reputations of Mozart and Salieri in the musical repertoire all provide similar examples. Those who were once celebrated are often forgotten.

Hölderlin lived his last thirty-seven years in a turret in Tübingen, his work virtually ignored. After a century of neglect interest began to focus on him; he is hailed now as one of the foremost poets of European romanticism. Today, Flaubert's *Madame Bovary* is unequivocally regarded as a classic of European literature, but in 1857, the year of its publication, it was overshadowed by the success of Ernest Aimé Feydeau's *Fanny,* which went through thirteen editions in one year. While Flaubert's novel caused a sensation by offending public mores, most people, it seems, were reading *Fanny.* Now the reverse is true and Feydeau's novel is remembered only by specialists (Jauss 1982: 27). There is the parallel case of Bouguereau and Cézanne. While in his time Bouguereau achieved sensational success, was awarded prizes, and had his paintings displayed in the Salons, Cézanne struggled in vain for recognition. In the current value system of art history Cézanne rates as the foremost master of the modernist tradition whereas

Bouguereau is known only to art historians (Alsop 1982: 411). In the areas adjacent to literary criticism one can think of Giambattista Vico, Charles S. Peirce, and Mikhail Bakhtin, who were "unjustly" neglected. Vico is now celebrated as a major thinker in the philosophy of history, Peirce as the founder of American semiotics, and Bakhtin's work is esteemed as a precursor to current work in popular culture and literary sociology. Then there are the myriad works that seem to have been mercilessly passed over by history. Of the 5,000 operas and 14,000 symphonies composed in the eighteenth century, only a modest sum form part of the current repertoire. The rest were performed once or twice and then forgotten (Velimirovic 1986: 373).

An investigation of canon formation seeks the reasons behind the survival of certain texts and the suppression of others.[1] Barring the accidental destruction of works (particularly those from the ancient world), in most cases texts are read or not read—they survive or they disappear—for specific reasons. It is clear, as the cases of the Gnostic gospels and the writings of the Sophists demonstrate, that only those supporting a particular system or the idea of system-building can found a tradition or be accepted by one already in existence. This hypothesis does not presume a conspiracy theory. Texts are either interesting or useful to a specific end or they are not; some lend themselves more easily than others to the founding of a church, the consolidation of a philosophical paradigm, or the weaving of a national narrative. They exist in a context. If this context is modified, the position of the text also changes in relationship to others. It does not suffice, therefore, to examine solely the entry of, say, Joyce or Cavafy into the canons of English or Greek literature; of more importance is to analyze the conditions enabling the canonization of modernism in a national culture, since the consolidation of this literary movement clearly facilitated the admission of individual authors. An exploration of canonicity should concern itself with the evaluational criteria, the principles of taste, the epistemological assumptions, and the institutions of literature and criticism in which individual authors or entire literary movements become significant or disappear. A study of canonicity seeks out the production of literary truths not in mysterious depths, but on what Foucault has called surface practices. It examines the uses to which texts have been put in a national tradition and then compiles these uses. The word *use* is preferable here to *meaning* because it foregrounds the exercise of power, the role of interests, and the dynamics of struggle, all forces unexamined in the pursuit of veiled signification and hermeneutical meaning.

The canon, a product of the differentiating process of modernity, is the sum of literary uses at a particular time. As a collection of texts belonging to the national institution of high literature, it contains texts that, because they narrate a community's own tale, are deemed worthy of being saved and transmitted to other generations. These texts serve as objects of criticism, enter school curricula, are included in histories of literature, and are annotated in anthologies. The literary canon is composed of those texts from the past that are made relevant to the present. It is the history of literature made monumental. In the segmented bourgeois society that perceives a break between past and present, the canon facilitates the experience of an idealized tradition. It expresses a melancholia for a time that can no longer be.

Because of literature's instrumental role in the invention of national cultures, canonicity confers special privileges on texts; it posits them as objects of serious interpretation and protects them from neglect and loss. Books belonging to the canon, as Frank Kermode remarks, are not only granted a high value; almost a "rabbinical minuteness of comment and speculation" is exerted on their behalf. They are also credited with myriad internal relations and secrets (1985: 89). "Licensed for exegesis: such is the seal we place upon our canonical works," Kermode contends (83). Since the canon guarantees that after every reading something is necessarily omitted that demands another reading (as in biblical exegesis), canonical works remain always new, inexhaustibly open to fresh interpretations. In this way their immediacy and range of meaning are maintained.

Classical Canons

The reference I made to religion is not fortuitous, since many striking parallels exist between the modern literary canon and the Christian and Hebrew Bibles. They are structured and seem to function similarly. The canon is as indispensable to the formation of religious traditions as it is to that of national cultures. If the literary canon does not have the Bible as its origin, it is certainly patterned on it, for the theological canon served as a model for the creation of hierarchies in literary studies. Rudolph Pfeiffer believes the modern notion of canon was first introduced in 1768 by the philologist David Ruhnken in his *Historia Critica Oratorum Graecorum,* where he wrote: "Itaque ex magna *Oratorum* copia tanquam in canonem decem duntaxat retulerunt" (Ruhnken 1823: 386). From the vast number of orators, Ruhnken noted, only ten were kept in the canon, and he listed them. He referred to this list of orators as the canon and proceeded to call all such selective lists by this same term. Ruhnken borrowed this usage from the biblical tradition, where the word signified a series of books. His adaptation of the term to literary studies met with success and is current in all modern European languages (Pfeiffer 1968: 207).[2]

The modern word *canon* stems from the Greek *kanon,* which in turn is derived from a Semitic word meaning reed or rod. *Kanon* was an important concept in discussions of sculpture, music, philosophy, rhetoric, and grammar during the classical and Hellenistic periods and proved indispensable in the unification of the various Christian scriptures into the Bible. It had specific uses for the Athenian sculptor, Hellenistic grammarian, and church father. An investigation of these uses provides an interesting comparison to the modern concept of canon. In making this comparison I do not wish to suggest a continuity between the Greco-Roman period and modernity, but rather to explore some revealing similarities between the Alexandrian lists of the best Attic authors, the selection of the texts serving as the Bible, and national canons.

In the classical period *kanon,* as H. Oppel's study (1937) points out, meant a straight object, or a measure (such as a carpenter's rule) used for sculpture, carpentry, and architecture. It was a way of expressing and measuring exactitude (*akribeia*) and eventually acquired metaphorical meaning: as the right measure or proportion. Thus the sculptor Polyclitus created a statue according to his tenets of symmetry and perfection of form and called this a *kanon.*[3] The statue rendered the proportions of the human body at their most symmetrical. He is said to have also written a treatise entitled *Kanon,* on the beauty of the human body as expressed in the perfect execution of its proportions. In both cases *kanon* meant a rule or a standard of excellence. Metaphorical connotations of the word made their way into ethics, in discussions concerning the *kanon* of human conduct, the righteous man, and the ideal (von Fritz 1939: 113–14). The term became closely related to the notion of example and model, a meaning that grew increasingly significant in the Hellenistic age, after the emergence of the concept of the classic and the tendency toward imitation of earlier monuments.

The Hellenistic period, following the celebrated achievements of the fifth and fourth centuries, was perhaps one of the first to experience so intensely the feeling of cultural belatedness. The Alexandrians placed themselves in a position of unavoidable comparison with their classical forebears, a comparison from which they emerged as inferior. Scholars of the time were convinced that a great period, whose deeds could never again be matched, had come to an end. The Alexandrians were burdened with the belief that they were incapable of equaling, let alone surpassing, their predecessors. They saw themselves as epigones whose only conceivable action was the copying of their classical forefathers (*mimesis ton archaion*). In this context of belatedness the word *kanon* was used in relation to *mimesis* (Oppel 1937: 45). Hellenistic grammarians became obsessed with Attic, the dialect spoken by the Athenians, and sought authors whose language best exemplified what they considered to be standard Greek. Dionysus of Halicarnassus, a rhetor and historian who lived and taught in Augustan Rome, used the word in just this way. In his discussion of Greek orators he chose Lysias as the representative of the pure Attic prose, characterizing him as "the best *kanon* of the Attic language" ("Lysias" II, 1, 5). *Kanon* in this sense suggested the best, the supreme example of a kind, and referred to the work of one individual.

The phenomenon of Atticism, which I mentioned in the previous chapter, had its beginnings here. Although there is no monolithic continuity between the ancient and modern Greeks, the anxious response of subsequent ages to their perceived ancestors has some similarities. During the Hellenistic age grammarians and rhetoricians began devising lists of classical orators and poets whom they considered representatives of a particular style or language. These philologists classified the authors they chose as "the received [into the selection]," the *enkrithentes,* from the verb *enkrino,* meaning to admit and approve. The *enkrithentes* authors were the *prattomenoi,* those who were treated—that is, commented upon—by future grammarians (Pfeiffer 1968: 208). They were read in schools, copied by scribes, and thus saved, while those not registered in these selective lists perished. Aristophanes of Byzantium (257-180 B.C.), the librarian in Alexandria, was one of the first to draw up lists of ancient poets who in his opinion were foremost in various forms of poetry. This is inferred from a passage in the *Institutio Oratoria* (X, 1, 54)[4] of Quintilian, a rhetorician and teacher (A.D. 30–100), where he states that "Apollonius [of Rhodes, author of the *Argonautica*] is not admitted to the lists drawn up by the professors of literature, because the critics, Aristarchus and Aristophanes [of Byzantium], did not include contemporary poets."[5]

The term *kanon* acquired particular weight at that time of Greek history when people came to believe that they were living in an age of cultural exhaustion, when the only option available was the copying of masterpieces of the past. Whereas in the fifth century B.C. it was seen as a measure, rule, or standard, in the Hellenistic age it was conceived as the best, the representative of a style. Although the word *kanon* itself was not used at this time to refer to the catalogues of authors, these lists did exist and were seen as models. They were called, as we have seen, the *enkrithentes* (a term translated into Latin as the *classici,* the writers of the first class).[6] These lists of orators and poets were used in instructing students to write in the manner of their forefathers—that is, in Attic Greek. On the one hand this promoted a stylistic and linguistic archaism of Atticism, which lasted until the eighteenth century. On the other, it encouraged the copying of chosen texts, which in turn ensured their survival. What we know as classical literature is, on the whole, the result of the choices made by Hellenistic grammarians and rhetoricians. What they found interesting for study was preserved in the classical canon as the best works created by the Greeks and Romans; what escaped their attention has disappeared.[7] The idea of canon, by permitting the past to shape the present, provided a certain degree of linguistic and stylistic stability. It was used to bestow on Alexandrians and Byzantines (and later modern Greeks) a sense of cultural continuity with the classical age.

The Bible as Canon

A text belonging to a canon wields power over those accepting its jurisdiction. This holds true for the most influential and certainly most durable canon, the Hebrew Torah, one of the earliest examples of a text to exert authority over a people. The whole point behind canonization is to underwrite this authority of a text over its community (Bruns 1984: 464). The significance of such writing lies not only in what it contains but also, and perhaps above all, in the effect it has. The Hebrew Bible narrated to the Jewish people the story of Israel. Although the nation dispersed, J. A. Sanders writes, it preserved its identity by virtue of its Bible/canon, which was indestructible, commonly available, and portable (1972: 534). Although its ultimate authority was beyond question, hermeneutics enabled it to remain adaptable, diversely meaningful, and hence powerful. To those who remembered and repeated it, the canon legitimated their relationship to the community. The canon as a divinely ordained collection of texts was essential for ritual worship and the establishment of legal norms; it also allowed an exiled people to trace its institutions back to divine inception.

The Christian Bible was composed according to this model, or it may be more correct to say that it was written against it. It combined the notion of *kanon* current in the Hellenistic and imperial ages with Jewish philosophy (Oppel 1937: 59). The original meaning of *kanon*—a norm, standard, or rule seeking to determine and measure other entities—acquired a legal connotation. Whereas the grammarians spoke of linguistic rules (*kanones*), for the church fathers *kanon* assumed moral significance. In the church this concept was used as an ethical law, a standard of judgment by which to unify myriad doctrines and opinions. As Edgar Honnecke shows, *kanon* designated what was ecclesiastically obligatory (1963: 23). It was understood in three ways: *kanon tes aletheias* (the rule of truth), *kanon tes pisteos* (rule of faith), *kanon tes ekklesias* (rule of the Church). Paul proclaimed *pistis* (faith) as the new *kanon;* for him *kanon* meant the rule of faith, the norm of revealed truth in the teachings of Christ. *Kanon* then was the law to which everything in the church had to accommodate itself, the standard according to which all things were measured. Eventually this original meaning was modified as *kanon* began to signify not only the thing contained but also the container: the scriptures incorporating the rule of faith, that is, the canon (as revealed truth and law), came eventually themselves to be referred to as the canon. Thus it was possible for Clemens of Alexandria to speak in the *Stromata* of the scriptures as canon of faith, *ton kanona tes pisteos* (IV, XIII, 98).

Since the scriptures were composed of a series of texts, *kanon* increasingly came to mean a list or paradigm. Thus *kanon* referred not only to the truth in the text but also to the list of texts embodying this truth. It began to signify the boundary of the permissible, revealed, and holy, within which one had to remain. To canonize a text meant to place it within this framework, to recognize it as part of the norm. By the fourth century A.D. *kanon* suggested a collection of recognized documents containing the revelation of God. Eusebius in his *Ecclesiastical History* (c. 325) may be the earliest source for the use of the word *kanon* as scripture. While discussing Origen's review of the collective scriptures, Eusebius observes that "in the first book of his [Origen's] commentaries on the Gospel of St. Matthew, following the Ecclesiastical Canon, he attests that he only knows of four Gospels" (VI, 25, 290). About a quarter of a century later Athanasius, the Bishop of Alexandria, also used this term to mean a list of authoritative writings, noting that Hermas "is not part of the canon [*me on ek tou kanonos*]" (cited in Oppel 1937: 70). At this time it was possible to differentiate between *kanonika biblia* and *akanonista biblia,* between canonical and noncanonical texts, those whose authority was acknowledged and those that were considered spurious. In not conforming to the norm, in expressing unorthodox opinions, the latter were suppressed as *hairetika* (heretical) or *apokrypha* (apocryphal), the hidden writings that remained uncanonized. This process of course was political, involving the exercise of deliberate choices disguised as the uncovering of ecclesiastical truth.

The Christian canon was delineated and the church established only after the writings of the Gnostics were effectively suppressed.[8] In its early stages Christianity existed as a multiplicity of doctrines. But by the end of the second century one orthodox view had asserted itself as dominant. The Gnostics constituted the most powerful group vying with orthodox Christians for ecclesiastical authority. They challenged the orthodox conception of God, Christ, and the Church. Gnostics, for instance, believed that Jesus was a spiritual being who adapted himself to human perception rather than an actual person. Hence they interpreted the Resurrection metaphorically, in contrast to the orthodox, who saw it as a real event. This difference in interpretation had institutional consequences, as the Resurrection, the dominant event in Christianity, enabled those who had witnessed it to claim a privileged place in the organization of the church (Pagels 1979: 6). The orthodox version asserts that first Peter and then the other apostles saw the resurrected Christ. As direct witnesses to this miracle they had incontestable authorization to spread the word of Christ, become leaders of the Christian community, and choose their own heirs. The apostolic succession of bishops and in fact papal authority (insofar as the pope traces his authority back to Peter) depend on the interpretation of the Resurrection as an actual occurrence (1979: 10). In order to consolidate its institutional power, orthodox Christianity had to deny the authenticity of those texts that, first, insisted that the Resurrection symbolized Christ's presence, and second, proclaimed that this presence could be experienced by everyone, and not just by the apostles. It had to ensure that its narration of events was the only one heard and read.

Gnostics differed from the orthodox in other ways: they questioned the concept of monotheism, described God as a dyad embracing both masculine and feminine forms, and appointed women as priests and bishops (and hence attracted many women to their teachings). In short, they threatened the organizational and theological structure of the increasingly powerful orthodox believers and incurred their wrath. Their story of Christ had to be silenced. Indeed, their texts were burned, branded as heretical, and in time disappeared. Those able to choose a different way—the verb *haireo* means to choose and also to seize, to get into one's power—were denounced as *hairetikoi* and expelled from the chosen lists. By the end of the second century orthodoxy had codified its particular narrative as the Christian canon and consolidated itself as "one holy, catholic, and apostolic church." (Ironically, its catholicity was dependent on the suppression of all creeds incompatible with it. As in the case of national integration, the individual was sacrificed to the general.) Winners, Pagels writes pithily, write history and they do it their way. The Christian canon recites the story of the victors. The unity of the Christian faith depends on its account of the events.

The destruction of the Gnostic gospels, like the disappearance of the Sophists' philosophical works, represents one of the most notorious attempts in western history of a dominant tradition suppressing a rival narrative. In both cases these texts survived for a long time as fragments enmeshed in the invective of their opponents. The Gnostic gospels have fared better, in that a few extant examples became known in modern times and thirteen complete texts were uncovered by chance in the Egyptian desert in 1936. Clearly, Christianity would have been substantially different if these antagonistic texts had been allowed to exist even in the fringes of the canon. But, as Pagels hypothesizes, if the Christian church remained multiform, it would probably have vanished like many other cults of the time. It survived because of its Procrustean ideology—an inexorableness significantly absent from the Gnostic practice—which necessitated the elimination of all other creeds (142). The process of establishing orthodoxy ruled out every other option. The literary and philosophical canons similarly cannot tolerate pluralism. The texts allowed to survive reflect the interests of those doing the choosing; they also determine the nature of the canon they comprise. The case of the Gnostic gospels, like that of the Sophists' writings, leads us to wonder whether a tradition can ever be built on a theology or a philosophy that is open-ended, antiauthoritarian, and sceptical.

The expansion of the church required that a body of "attested" writings be isolated from the multiplicity of doctrines and texts claiming to be holy. The life of Jesus Christ was the chief principle used in the division between canonical and noncanonical scriptures. Only those documents purporting to tell the story of Christ were canonized; they were advanced to the rank of holy texts because they were witness and testament to God (Honnecke 1963: 32). Christ, Hans von Campenhausen writes, is present in the Gospel and is its "guarantor" (1972: 115). Albert Sundberg (1975: 369), James Turro, and Raymond Brown (1968: 17) point to the idea of inspiration as another factor in the delineation of canonicity. Whatever the reason, canonical status was defined not by the internal worth of the texts themselves but by external factors representing the values of the dominant community. The collection of writings, which all members of the Christian community would consider authoritative and binding, was determined only after many struggles.

Three stages were involved (Sundberg 1971: 1217-23). Originally there existed an oral tradition lacking formal authentication. But the expanding church required the codification of these stories and parables (as would nation-states many centuries afterwards). The Gospels originated in the first century after Christ as a written alternative to these oral accounts, though based upon them. Other gospels were composed that cited earlier ones. In this nascent stage—when the spoken stories acquired the status of scripture—canonization was secondary to the conferment upon the texts of authority rivaling the Hebrew Bible. The second step was characterized by a conscious grouping of writings into closed collections, such as the fourfold Gospel, the Pauline collection, and the Catholic letters. From a wide variety of texts certain writings were retained while others were excluded. The Gospels of Mark, Matthew, Luke, and John were considered authoritative because in them the apostles delivered what was enjoined on them by Jesus. They were witnesses to Christ Himself. In the final stage canonization proper occurred—lists were formulated and boundaries drawn between canonical and noncanonical. Around 325, Eusebius, as noted earlier, acknowledged this unity of scriptures when he referred to the books considered canonical in his work on the church. Some years later Athanasius wrote that Hermas did not belong to the canon.

By that time the Christian canon had been established as an authoritative collection of holy texts to which nothing could be added and from which nothing could be subtracted (*mete prosthenai mete aphelein*). It consisted of a group of documents given a special normative position with respect to the Christian community and the Hebrew Torah. The Christian Bible, a public possession and permanent collection of writing, a self-authenticating "literature" endowed with inner cohesion, served as the ultimate authority for the Christian community, attesting to its special relationship with God.

The Function of the Literary Canon

A religious document such as the Bible exercises infinitely more power over its readers than a secular one such as the *Odyssey*, as Erich Auerbach writes in his comparison of these two texts in the first chapter of *Mimesis:* "The Bible's claim to truth is not only far more urgent than Homer's, it is tyrannical—it excludes all other claims. The world of the Scripture stories is not satisfied with claiming to be a historically true reality—it insists that it is the only real world, is destined for autocracy. . . . The Scripture stories do not, like Homer, court our favor, they do not flatter us that they may please us and enchant us—they seek to subject us, and if we refuse to be subjected we are rebels" (14–15). A literary work nevertheless performs important functions for a community accepting the necessity of literature, and its place in the canon may be guarded with religious fervor.

Literary canons underwrite the authority of certain texts, demarcating the acceptable from the unacceptable, the literary from the nonliterary; they preserve a tradition and connect the present with its past achievements; they help establish and maintain the identity of an entire nation; they organize a community's stories in neat hierarchies. The canon serves as a utopian site of continuous textuality in which a nation, a class, or an individual may find an undifferentiated identity. Central to its operation is the notion of founding geniuses (i.e., Homer, Shakespeare, Dante, and Goethe) who seem to produce and validate it with their language and authority. These founders express the spirit of the entire nation and, in so doing, paradoxically transcend their national borders to become universal figures. Their double role as local and global authors, however, does not undermine the canon's national status but actually gives it international prestige.

Canons seem to form within those discourses that value tradition and possess a strong consciousness of the past. Be they philosophical, religious, juridical, or literary, such discourses put a premium on the preservation of the documents of their respective histories.[9] The notion of literature depends for its validity on the existence of a corpus of classics that by definition are superior to the products of the day. Past monuments remain vital parts of current aesthetic taste and artistic production. The canon renders the products of the past relevant to a contemporary audience. Canons have arisen as a means of keeping the past alive and enforcing its authority on the present. The survival of societies and traditions depends not only on memory to retain the past but above all on the formation of a hierarchy of prized texts transmitted through time.

Unlike the Bible, literary canons can be revised, though not without a struggle. It would be almost inconceivable, for instance, for such classics as Homer, Shakespeare, Dante, and Goethe to be displaced from their positions in their respective national literatures or from the hierarchy of "world literature," as such changes would involve fundamental transformations in contemporary aesthetic criteria. But revisions do occur. Certain authors and styles do fall out of favor while others are pushed from the periphery to the center. Botticelli's works had been ignored for centuries until he was "discovered" at the turn of this century. Worthy of mention here is Tolstoy's attempt to dislodge Shakespeare from his eminent place in "world literature." The shifts from the margins to the center are continuous, although only the most notorious will be remembered. What is in today may be out tomorrow. The significance of these reversals and fluctuations, as I pointed out earlier, lies not at the level of individual authors but of the discourses in which the writers are posited and, of course, the standards of taste. If the literary criticism of the last twenty years favors "writerly," opaque, difficult writing, then it is not surprising that Mallarmé's work is repeatedly cited and has become so relevant. If the Apollo of Belvedere no longer occupies a prominent place in the canon of Greek art, as was the case from the Renaissance until after the exhibition of the Parthenon marbles in London by Lord Elgin, it is not because critics have now found fault with this statue but because aesthetic tastes have shifted away from fourth- to fifth-century sculpture.[10] While it is interesting to examine the respective fates of artists in the canon, it is more fruitful to explore the fluctuations in the evaluative system controlling those shifts of fortune.

Even these changes, however, are not fundamental. They are modifications of taste within an aesthetic community rather than attempts to alter the course of art and literature or to overthrow them as privileged categories in culture. For instance, supplementations have occurred recently in the canon of American literature with the inclusion of texts by blacks and women and the publication of anthologies of gay and lesbian verse. These previously marginalized texts have been, or are in the process of being recognized as literature. But has the incorporation of these works really altered the direction of American literature? The texts have become literary but the necessity and importance of the canon—or for that matter, of literature—have not seriously been questioned. Thus, while those who disagree with the canon's current composition or who feel that their interests are not represented in its hallowed list may demand alterations, the idea of the canon itself has not been challenged. The literary canon, by its inexhaustible ability to absorb marginal material, ceaselessly proves its "pluralism." It is valuable to the literate bourgeois community and is therefore preserved and transmitted through the schools in order to maintain that community's values. It is the product of this community, though declared binding also on those who do not believe in literature.[11]

When we speak of the literary canon we mean the collection of those written texts and oral poems (given the status of written work) that have been designated high literature. The current literary canon represents a selection of writers and texts out of a vast mass of writing, a reduction in the number of possibilities to a manageable and accessible form. Its formation coincides with the emergence of literature as an institution whose principle of aesthetic autonomy determines the production and consumption of texts. Texts within the canon are classified according to genres, which themselves form their own hierarchy, insofar as some are considered at different times to be more canonical than others (Fowler 1982: 216).[12] For Hegel, tragedy was the supreme literary form; for the symbolists, it was lyric poetry. Epic has been out of fashion for a couple of centuries; if poets choose to compose one today they risk the disappearance of the work in an institution that does not recognize (and hence does not classify) modern epic.[13] Works belonging to a more popular genre have a greater chance of survival.

Though the literary canon functions like the Bible, it actually emerged in western societies when the Bible itself lost its authority as privileged text. In Germany, for instance, the literary canon appeared along with new reading and interpretive practices. As late as 1740, when England and France had flourishing literary cultures, the average German family owned only a Bible and a few other religious books, which were read out loud (Schenda 1976: 17). But around the middle of the century a "reading epidemic" of secular writing began to sweep the country, threatening the elites who feared the effects of this popular "literature." Conservatives, seeing in these texts an assault on established order, advocated state control as a way of restricting them. Liberal writers, on the other hand, though denouncing this literature as escapist and trivial, directed their efforts to contain its proliferation through schooling. Writers such as Johann Adam Bergk and Johann G. Fichte believed they could teach the middle classes to abandon the mass literature of entertainment for a select list of edifying books

(Woodmansee 1988–89: 207–9). Bergk published his *Die Kunst, Bücher zu lesen* (The art of reading books) in 1799 to instruct literary connoisseurship and reform reading practices by encouraging active and analytical reading of texts as opposed to the passive consumption of "light" works. Relying on arguments from the philosophy of aesthetics, he and other writers set out to prove the distinctiveness of "serious" literature.

In modern compartmentalized societies, where institutions perform distinct roles, polite literature, as I shall discuss in the next chapter, was given a specialized function: to cultivate taste and suppress the sentimental feelings evoked by popular works. Of the vast number of texts only a limited number met this requirement and qualified for inclusion in the canon of the new "sacred" writing. The new principles for reading severely curtailed the number of texts entering the secular hierarchy. Unlike the Bible, which was declaimed, the new literature was read silently, in the privacy of the home, the compensatory space of bourgeois society—the chosen texts of middle-class culture belonged to the domestic sphere. At the same time, the task of traditional criticism changed from instructing students to write poems according to the rules of *ars poetica* to teaching them the composition of essays about literary works. Students no longer asked what words did but what the authors meant by them (Kittler 1980: 150–53). Reading became an exercise in the search for deep and veiled meaning. The pedagogical project of teaching people the art of hermeneutics was designed to control reading practice but also to limit the number of books that could *legitimately* be read.

A Question of Value

Canonicity is about status and evaluation, the criteria and standards according to which not only individual works and authors but also entire movements and discourses and even the formations of art and literature themselves come into or fall out of favor. Evaluation occurs at all levels. First of all, literature is a privileged construct in bourgeois society. Although the cultural worth of individual texts may fluctuate, for the last three hundred years literature has been valuable in the construction of a bourgeois public sphere and the formation of national cultures. Canonicity, taking place in this context, is simply a valorization of categories, techniques, or concepts. It is really a process of classification in which texts, styles, and approaches are designated literary and hence become worthy of attention or are pushed to the margins and perhaps allowed to disappear. While canonical texts have been considered important by previous communities, peripheral ones have not been cited, criticized, mentioned in reference books, or annotated in anthologies. Such works, if they happen to go out of print, must await the intervention of major literary figures with immense authority (such as T. S. Eliot) or of specialized presses (such as the British Virago) for their resurrection. In short, survival depends on interest, in every meaning of this word.

A text, to borrow from Michael Thompson's terminology, may be made important or unimportant; it may be transient (value decreasing), rubbish (no value), or durable (value increasing) (1979: 10). Membership in these classes is temporary. But the move from one to another category is a social process which imposes on physical objects or forms of knowledge the properties of lastingness or transience.[14] Evaluation in this sense is a social processing of objects. Value is not a function of essence or personal choice but a matter of social negotiation. A slum tenement, for instance, which is usually expected to have a short life span, receives little maintenance, while a public monument or a residence in a posh area, where life expectancy is high, will be better kept up (37). Of course a decaying neighborhood may be modernized and have its value increase. But this is a matter of public classification, according to which each category forms an integral part of the social system. Slums thus constitute a necessary component of a town in that they serve as negative comparisons, foils for more fashionable quarters, enhancing their value. Like high art, which requires popular craft, respectable addresses need their dialectical opposites to maintain their value.

Durability in society is a prized category.[15] What is canonicity then but a grand cultural enterprise to maintain the durability of prized objects and to prevent a drop in their stock? Of course the danger of neglect always exists, and some works slip into temporary or permanent obscurity. Only a few most celebrated masterpieces, such as the works of Homer, Shakespeare, or Goethe, comprise an almost petrified canon where a shift in status is nearly impossible. These texts would forfeit their privileged positions only if the entire value system supporting them collapsed. But a great deal of time and money is invested by culture to avert such an occurrence. It is commonplace to assume that the best works of art always survive; indeed, their very durability is supposed proof of their aesthetic worth. The project of canonization, by promoting the destiny of certain works, styles, and genres, ensures and makes manifest this process. But the mechanisms of canonicity conceal the classificatory strategies at work to preserve texts by making survival appear natural, self-evident, and deserved. They disguise the struggle waged by social groups over the power to classify.

Certified works will survive. Their very existence will be seen, in a self-fulfilling prophecy, as evidence of their intrinsic worth. Indeed the institution of criticism will provide the tools and references permitting their aesthetic value to be discovered and expressed. In other words, the works will contain the properties expected of them, the qualities for which they were originally canonized. Value, as Barbara Herrnstein Smith points out, is the interactive relation between the classification of an object and the function it is expected to perform (1984: 17). The value of an entity is a product of a subject's needs, desires, interests—the personal economy of the subject, which forms part of the greater economic system (15). There is a constant fluctuation and shifting between individual purposes and the standards of taste accepted by the community. The two systems are interactive and interdependent, with the greater one being formed by the personal economies of producers, distributors, and consumers (17).

On the one hand, there exist the norms and criteria of specialized groups in literary criticism, and those of the broader social community, and on the other the preferences of individuals. The value judgments of individual members may correspond with those of the community or they may conflict with them and thus be considered eccentric. The judgment of an object's value, such as "this is a good piece of music," is the evaluator's observation as to the worth of that object regarding the function it is expected to perform in a particular situation (Herrnstein Smith 25).

If a text is useful in a particular way to a community, the chances for its survival increase. It may, for instance, be regarded as the best of its kind, as exemplifying the characteristics of a particular genre, or lend itself to a certain hermeneutical approach. Critical schools on the whole tend to select texts suitable for their particular interpretive and pedagogical needs. Formalism, for instance, preferred self-reflexive works; structuralism, short poems with complicated and dense structures; deconstruction, opaque, difficult, experimental texts. By bringing attention to a certain kind of text, critical discourses can promote its position in the canon. Works may also be interesting for their antique value. One of the factors responsible for the survival of classical texts was the esteem in which Attic Greek was held by Hellenistic grammarians. Texts written in a favored language can for that very reason be useful in political struggles, such as the endeavor to delineate a national identity.

A text that serves a community may be protected from obscurity through admission into the cultural distribution system. It can then be cited, analyzed, reproduced; in time it will perhaps be canonized. In this respect one of the chief agents of canonicity is commentary. To become part of the cultural stock a work must achieve currency through some form of replication—commonly as a manuscript, typescript, or book (Shils 1981: 145). Works must capture enough attention not to be forgotten. Their existence has to be recorded in many—or at least the most prestigious—places. While not guaranteeing canonization, commentary is a prerequisite for survival.

In the case of nineteenth-century Greece, national value was the criterion most often applied in the evaluation of poetry and prose. Texts were important as symbols at one and the same time of nationhood and Europeanness. Of course anthologists sought "good" works, but their interests went beyond the texts' "literary" worth to their function in the public sphere. Pure aesthetic value was an ideal generally unavailable in the axiomatic system of that society. When contemporary critics, however, discuss aesthetic taste in the context of nineteenth- and early twentieth-century texts they anachronistically privilege aesthetic consumption, positing evaluation as a function of only an autonomous aesthetic system rather than culture in general.

Aesthetic consumption was differentiated in Greece from ordinary consumption only after the aestheticization of literary practice in the 1930s. Of course, texts in the nineteenth century were read for other than political reasons. Individual readers certainly derived pleasure from a poem or the translation of a foreign novel. Moreover, given the low literacy rate in the country, people would have acquired prestige through their ability to read at all. (See chapter 4 on the high priority Greeks placed on education.) Certainly, as I argued earlier, reading is not neutral in modern societies but a category of distinction, useful in maintaining social and cultural exclusion. The legitimation of certain modes of reading and the canonization of privileged texts are related to the manner by which status is assigned, advantages in social selection ascribed, and social stratification preserved. By reading canonical texts individuals separate their taste from popular taste, thereby lending superior value to their own social position.

Pierre Bourdieu (1984) calls this form of knowledge "cultural capital"— the learnable skills (modes of aesthetic appreciation, manners, attitudes, preferences, behaviors) that enable individuals to distinguish themselves and gain access to official high culture. Although distinction occurs at all social levels, cultural capital refers to the exclusivist function of high culture. People gain this prestige by learning privileged cultural symbols from their families, class, and education. But cultural capital is not a form of material consumption; hence intellectuals and artists, the producers of cultural capital, do not necessarily have economic power. Taste, Bourdieu argues, is the acquired disposition to establish and mark differences by the process of distinction (466). Aesthetic objects, like all goods, are carriers of social meaning and direction through which individuals or groups search for their places in the social order. These objects speak to us less of the owners · than of their social pretensions, objectives, and classification (Baudrillard 1981: 38).

The most refined cultural capital is the capacity to perceive form for its own sake.[16] But this cultural practice, which valorizes high taste while delegitimizing pleasures elicited by popular arts, cannot function in societies without an autonomous aesthetic.[17] In nineteenth-century Greece, for instance, official culture was designated for the most part by the ideology of purism. The use of extremely archaic syntactical forms or the appreciation of purist poetry enabled the educated elite to acquire and maintain high status. Through this exclusionary means it protected its privileged position from outsiders. But the consumption of purist texts cannot be understood as a type of cultural capital because the social conditions for its operation were absent. There was no culture industry, no proletariat, and no mass culture from which the refined sensibility could distinguish itself. Purism denounced the vernacular not only because of its low status but also because it offered a competing version of national identity. Though purism designated itself the official discourse of the state, it posited the differences between high (purism) and low (demoticism) in political rather than aesthetic terms. Purism had broader sociopolitical goals than the preservation of prestige and allocation of cultural resources. Its pedagogical mission envisioned *katharevusa* as the national language and purism the national culture. In practice, of course, these plans never materialized, because of popular resistance and opposition from demoticists. But like demoticism, purism strived to indoctrinate the nation into its values, its aim being the production of Greeks.

Anthologies

The canon is a publicly available body of writing, representative of certain national and social interests. Anthologies are a valuable source for an inquiry into the canon because they contain what their compilers deemed worthy of being collected at certain times. An anthology reflects the canonical texts of a particular period, which for various reasons came to the attention of the anthologist. Often anthologists justify their selections in a preface with arguments that reveal their own assumptions as well as the taste of their readers. Their decisions—along with those of authors, teachers, librarians, reviewers—determine what is central and what peripheral, what would be reprinted and what would go out of print. Of course a text's inclusion in an anthology does not guarantee canonicity. Anthologies in their inception, therefore, mirror the canon by incorporating well-known texts. When published they enter literary discourse and become major agents in the (re)formation of the canon.

The earliest Greek anthologies, produced for the Phanariots, appeared toward the end of the eighteenth century, circulating largely in manuscript form and containing anonymous poems. As Margaris (1940: 211), K. Dimaras (1975: 169), and Vitti (1978: 135) observe, such anthologies were distributed for the entertainment of educated Greeks in imitation of the literary habits of cultured Parisians. One of the earliest surviving samples was printed in Vienna by Zisis Dautis (1818). These volumes of anonymous and largely erotic verse represent the first compilations of Greek poetry. With such collections pioneering anthologists hoped to entertain the salons of the aristocrats.

The purposeful codification of "folk" poetry began after the revolution.[18] Before that time anthologists, seeking to establish a national literary tradition, were interested in collecting works of well-known poets rather than the anonymous demotic songs. Folk songs had drawn the attention of some Greek scholars and expatriates, but they did not occupy a central place in contemporary literary concerns and hence did not play an effective role in the formation of the canon.[19] The early anthologies made manifest the problematic notion of tradition in Greek culture. On the one hand, they projected tradition as an idealized continuum while on the other they posited it as a disjunction. Modernization required the rejection of the old; the modern justified itself either by breaking with the past or by proving itself worthy of it. Yet by definition the classical heritage, posited as a temporal utopia, could not be equaled but only longed for.

The relationship of Greeks to the past was laden with anxiety, as can be seen in an anthology published by Andreas Koromilas. In his preface (1835), Koromilas states that he was interested in collecting and saving for posterity poems by popular poets. But he was also motivated by the realization that, while Greek poetry from classical times had been preserved, there was little chance for the survival of contemporary poems. Considering their possible disappearance a "great loss to the nation," he printed the popular verses so as to make them available to a broad readership. Koromilas encouraged others to join his project by sending him poems for inclusion in subsequent volumes. Even though modern Greeks might be less illustrious than their ancestors, he argued, "they have no lesser inclination for poetry."

The notion of unbroken continuity with the past allowed Greeks to represent themselves as the legitimate heirs of European antiquity, hence as true Europeans.[20] The traditionalists among them sought resemblance of past to present, seeing the creation of a national culture as an exercise in similitude, a continuation of time. Modernizers, however, though they accepted classical tradition, believed that the creation of a new culture would serve the needs of a European state. National unity and political autonomy hinged on this contradictory relationship to the authority of Hellas. The peculiar situation of Greek culture is reflected in its very name: modern Greek. The qualifier reinforces the advantages of survivalism yet urges negative comparisons. Modern Greeks feel themselves belated in respect to the European and inferior in respect to the classical.

The introduction of western political and cultural institutions could not be harmonized with the interior realities of Greece. Because westernization was imposed from the top, it was initially limited to political and cultural institutions. After the declaration of independence in 1830, for instance, the westernizers initiated the first official stage of modernization. They established a strong centralized state, a parliamentary government with a liberal system of representation, a bureaucracy, an army, and cultural institutions such as a university, library, and academy. But all these institutions were western only in form, because they were infiltrated and monopolized by indigenous oligarchic elements. (The first check on their power and that of the monarch was the constitution of 1864 guaranteeing universal male suffrage.) In the 1840s the economy was largely based on agriculture; there was little industry and no proletariat; capital was controlled by diaspora Greeks and invested in finance and commerce (Dertilis 1977: 114). Of a population of 850,000 there were 18,296 merchants, 15,343 artisans, 13,679 sailors, and 276 bankers (Kourvetaris and Dobratz 1987: 40). An industrial base, indispensable for the functioning of the western institutions, had not been consolidated. As a result they did not function as expected. Yet the failure of modernization—as is true for Third World countries today—was conceived by both foreigners and Greeks to rest in Greek society exclusively, and not in the lack of fit between imported models and indigenous formations. Greeks internalized this incongruity as an imperfection or a distortion, which cried out for correction through further reforms. Even in the 1980s one of the major positions in the political platforms of the two dominant parties, PASOK and New Democracy, was modernization—catching up with Europe and preparing Greece for the unified European market of 1992.

Paradoxes of Purism

A sense of belatedness imposes upon a community the necessity of overtaking those who initiated modernity. In terms of literary culture this means that Greek scholars had to demonstrate the existence of an indigenous literary practice. The anthology by Konstantinos Hantseris, *Ellinikos Neos Parnassos, i, Apanthisma ton eklektoteron Piiseon tis Anayenithisis Ellados* (Modern Greek Parnassus, or, collection of the choicest poems of reborn Greece, 1845), for instance, was intended to persuade Greeks and Europeans alike that Greece was capable of producing a national literature. Hantseris stated unequivocally that the poems showed to "Europeans that the newly arisen Greek nation possesses a literature [*filoloyia*] and that in a span of a few years has developed a poetic language" (1845: Preface). To his fellow Greeks he wanted to show that poetry formed part of their common culture, which differentiated them from citizens of other nations.

True to his Enlightenment heritage, Hantseris used his anthology as a pedagogical tool, to teach young Greeks about the heroic exploits of their ancestors. This sociopolitical project incorporated mostly purist authors: with the exception of two demotic writers the poets in the anthology wrote in *katharevusa*. The greatest space was devoted to representatives of this purist school: Panayiotis Sutsos, Alexandros Sutsos, and Alexandros Rizos-Rangavis. Dionisios Solomos, chief representative of the demotic tradition in the Heptanesian Islands, was given attention especially scant in view of the illustrious position he would eventually occupy in the canon. This is also true in the case of the Renaissance poet Vitsentsos Kornaros, in which the politics of Hantseris's anthology comes into full view. While acknowledging that Kornaros was worthy of Homer and Aeschylus, Hantseris was appalled by his "loquacity and uncultivated [demotic] language." He therefore emended the chosen passages, removing some of the "vulgar" elements, and adding his own verses "just like a worker building a beautiful altar out of the ruins of a large temple."[21] Hantseris was bent on erecting the foundation of modern Greek poetry upon the ruins of Athens.

This reconstruction necessitated rejection of the vernacular. If literature was to be a reflector of national identity, Hantseris's mirror showed only one dimension. His conception of national culture presupposed the notion of classical revival that resulted in unceasing comparison with the ancients. Regarding only purist texts as poetic, he transformed, ignored, or rejected those not conforming to that paradigm. He determined a poem's worth by its language. To be good the poem had necessarily to be purist. In this anthology we can see the effect of the opposition between demotic and *katharevusa*. The reigning purist ideology excluded poetry in the vernacular, having marginalized the demotic school discursively to the fringes of scholarship and geographically to the outer boundaries of Greece, the Heptanesian Islands (which were under Italian control). Anthologies from this region, such as the selection of lyrics by Athanasios Hristopulos (1847) and the collection of folk poetry from the island of Zakinthos (1850) did not play a major role in the formation of official lists of poetry.[22]

Purist ideology, having consolidated itself in the institutions of the state, attempted to homogenize the sectional interests in culture so as to bring all practices under its control. In language this led to an increasing archaicization of *katharevusa,* and in poetry to the valorization of the Phanariot school in Athens. Ioannis Raptarhis's collection (1868) devoted vastly more space to poets of the Athenian school than to those of the vernacular tradition. This was also true of an anonymous anthology (1873), even though the editor promised a "mirror of Greek lyric poetry from recent years." Official literary discourse had appropriated the category of poetry in its mission to fabricate a repertory of meanings and symbols. But the elevation of extremely formal and ornate writing as the national verse seems to have contradicted purism's pedagogical project.

Although purists aspired toward the invention of shared experiences through the medium of *katharevusa,* the unification of all Greeks in the Near East within common borders, and the resurrection of Hellas, their notion of culture was exclusionary. Not the aestheticized culture of Europe after the dissolution of the bourgeois public sphere, it nevertheless required much formal education and therefore could not be reproduced on a national scale, its declared goal. As the official discourse of the state, education, church, and army, purism gained the authority to designate the high and low institutions of society. It then tried to impose this hierarchy upon what it defined as sites of low discourse—the home, marketplace, village, coffee-house, elementary school—which resisted it. Purist culture then, restricted to the educated elite, had no chance to become a national popular culture. Purism could not harmonize the tension between its Enlightenment vision of a cohesive national order enforced by a code of communal beliefs and its neoclassical predilection for a resurrected civilization.

The contradiction between purism's ideological project and the means for its realization can be seen specifically in Panayiotis Matarangas's *Parnassos, iti, Piitiki Silloyi pros Hrisis ton Pedion* (Parnassus, or, a poetic selection for the use of children, 1880). Children simply could not understand the heavy *katharevusa* of the previous anthologies. Indeed, as demoticists had pointed out, pupils devoted years to mastery of this register, and often never arrived at it. This "national" literature, which should have been a central component of an integrated national culture, excluded, therefore, large segments of the population. To overcome this difficulty, Matarangas chose from the oeuvre of each poet only those poems written in the simplest *katharevusa.* His anthology also contained a comparatively greater number of demotic poems, a fact indicating that the vernacular was gaining increasing recognition in the 1880s.

Demoticism and the Second Modernization Project

The decade of the 1880s inaugurated a militant reaction on the part of the demoticists—comprising writers, linguists, scholars, and pedagogues—to the dominance of the purists in all facets of Greek intellectual and public life. By the turn of the century the demoticists eventually triumphed by exploiting the paradox of the purist project: the construction of a national identity on the basis of a (self-defined) high discourse. Their arguments were on the whole ethnocentric and populist. As Dimitris Tziovas has shown, they aimed to prove the suitability of the vernacular as poetic language. They argued repeatedly, as supporters of the vernacular had done many decades before, that literary discourse did not differ essentially from ordinary discourse but was an imitation of speech (1986: 124). Using the organicist language of nationalism, they connected their concepts of speech, people, and language with the interests of the nation. In other words, they strived for a fusion of the national and popular. Conversely they demonstrated that *katharevusa,* as an artificial and elitist register, was incapable of producing a system of integrated values and experiences. Their most successful strategy was to identify their cause with the major attempt in the late nineteenth century to modernize Greek society. Although their discourse contained notions of autochthonous, popular, and local culture, they promoted their project by embracing modernity while designating purism as a force of reaction. Ultimately, they succeeded in eliminating purism as a cultural alternative.

The modernization of Greece's infrastructure began in the 1880s with the government of Prime Minister Harilaos Trikupis (1875–93). Among his principal aims was the dissolution of the clientelistic system and the reorganization of the army and navy, and of the civil service, which by 1870 measured per capita seven times greater than Great Britain's (Mouzelis 1986: 9). Trikupis also launched a program of public works that continued after his death. By 1893 about 568 miles of railway had been added to the minor network existing in 1882; 4,000 miles of telegraph lines were installed; steamship tonnage under Greek ownership grew from 8,241 in 1875 to 144, 975 in 1885; the Corinth Canal was opened in 1893 (Clogg 1979: 91). His liberal reforms were backed by the nascent industrial bourgeoisie whose size increased at the turn of the century. For instance, industrial production, though still comparatively modest, grew twentyfold between 1867 and 1889. Nicos Mouzelis argues that the period from 1880 to 1922 set the preconditions for development of industrial capitalism (1978: 17). A unified market was created through the expansion of the country's population (28 percent of which was urban by 1879) and territory. The influx of foreign capital, largely in the form of government loans for public projects, was dramatic; interest on the loans, which between 1879 and 1893 totaled 468,358,500 francs, consumed 40 percent of state revenues (Svoronos 1976: 103).

The last two decades of the nineteenth century witnessed a major attempt by the liberal bourgeoisie to create a modern state. But the enterprise seemed to flounder with the defeat of Trikupis in 1893, many of whose social and political reforms were either undone by his successors or undermined by conservative forces ensconced in public institutions. Large budget deficits brought on an economic crisis. In order to distract the masses from internal problems and gain additional territory the conservative government declared war on the Ottoman Empire. But the unprepared Greek army suffered defeat in Thessaly in 1897. The loss of the war dealt a blow to the ideology of irredentism informing the campaign, known as *Megali Idea,* whose objective was the unification of all the Greek-speaking people in the Near East.

The *Megali Idea* attempted to bring about a coincidence between ethnicity and state; at the turn of the century, a very large number of Greek speakers still lived outside the kingdom. The Greek *ethnos* thus extended beyond the borders of the country. This doctrine aimed through war to reconcile the tensions introduced by modernity. But the *Megali Idea* was itself also a product of the disjunction between ethnicity and state. This disjunction, a common feature of nationalism and a result of the attempt to gain sovereignty over a demographically heterogeneous area, manifested itself in another conflict, that between culture and state. In Greece at this time the forces producing culture did not control the state apparatus.

Though demoticists managed to achieve a fusion of the popular with the national, insofar as their culture constituted the national imaginary, they could not integrate culture with the state, from whose operations they were excluded. The culture promoted by the bureaucratic, administrative, and ecclesiastical elites was based on the purist language. In other words, national literary culture was not supported by official institutions. Students did not necessarily learn in school texts that, outside school, formed part of their collective tradition.

The Greek experience differed from that of neighboring Italy. By the 1930s Greeks had developed a shared identity whereas Italians had not. In Italy, according to Gramsci, little integration had been achieved between the national and the popular: "In Italy the term 'national' . . . does not in any case coincide with the 'popular' because in Italy the intellectuals are distant from the people, i.e. from the 'nation.' They are tied instead to a caste tradition that has never been broken by a strong popular or national political movement from below" (1985: 208). Though Italy's modernization was as purposeful as that of Greece—Gramsci's anxious questions about the absence of a national literature in the 1930s are typical of a belated modernity—the fabrication of a national culture from above was limited to the educated elites. This contributed to the emergence of two Italys: a social and cultural space composed of regional traditions and a political and administrative unit (Forgacs 1990: 27).

Though demoticists in Greece failed to secure official institutions, they identified their cultural production as the national one. Indeed, the word *national* (*ethnikos*) figured prominently in demoticist discourse: "national unity," "national progress," "national future," and "national interest" (Frangudaki 1977: 19, 124). The demoticist project for common language and shared ideology was all-encompassing, manifesting itself in the codification of the vernacular, the canonization of its literary tradition, and the invention of folklore. As the poet George Seferis put it, "The movement in favor of demotic was in the first place a group movement for the use of our national means of expression; then, more subtly, for the realization of the true and genuine outlook and idiosyncracy of the Greek race" (1966: 87). Demoticism articulated its grand narrative in the vernacular, the "national means of expression." Its socializing mission to determine the "genuine outlook and idiosyncracy of the Greek race" was a means of attaining national integration.

National progress was going to be achieved by a rationalized pedagogical system responsive to the economic needs of the nation. An inquiry conducted in 1883 revealed the "miserable condition" of the schools and a heavy emphasis on philology. All hopes for the regeneration of the country and the solution to its problems were pinned on schooling, especially after the humiliating defeat by the Turks in 1897. The reforms of 1899 proposed the teaching of chemistry, geology, mathematics, economics, and constitutional history along with humanistic subjects (Frangudaki 1977: 23–25). But the reforms were never passed in Parliament. Indeed, this and the other attempts (in 1933 and 1964) to orient the education system toward the sciences and technology were never realized.

The failure of the liberal reforms points again to the recalcitrance of the prebourgeois forces entrenched in official institutions. These defeats, however, in no way undermined demoticists' faith in pedagogy. To be sure, their evangelism was based on the Enlightenment conviction that attitudes, beliefs, and values can be instilled in people. The creation of a homogeneous culture made itself even more pressing by the territorial expansion of the state into Macedonia and Epirus, which brought to Greece many Orthodox Christians who spoke no Greek and did not consider themselves Greek at all. (The problem was compounded in 1923 after the mandatory exchange of populations with Turkey.) Their sense of nationality had to be cultivated.

In 1907 Ion Dragumis, Kostas Hatsopulos, and other demoticists founded the National Language Society, and in 1910 Alexandros Delmuzos, Pinelopi Delta, and Dimitris Glinos established the Education Society. The scope of their project is encapsulated in an entry from Dragumis's journal, written during his service as Greek consul in Macedonia (1904). "I want to make Greeks into patriots. This is why I try to rouse their national feelings." He would attain his goal through general education: "Greek schools should have two aims: a) to expand the mind and b) to nurture the child with his nationalism [ethnismo]" (1976: 70–71). Dragumis connected education directly to the construction of national identity. He and the other writers, intellectuals, and professionals were going to induct all Greeks into the virtues of neo-Hellenic Bildung.

Nikolaos Politis, the founder of Greek folklore, similarly emphasized the pedagogical mission of popular verse. In the prologue to his authoritative collection of folk songs he wrote that "since demotic poetry is the instrument of national education, all Greeks should learn the principal poems" (1914). Greeks were supposed to know the songs because, as they were told by the intelligentsia, they constituted part of their communal heritage. Also important to this enterprise was Alexandros Pallis's translation of the New Testament from *koine* into demotic, which provoked riots in 1901 after segments of the text were published in newspapers. Pallis hoped to make the reading of the vernacular a daily practice. This translation was intended to enhance the prestige of demotic, and also to prescribe its use in written form as part of ordinary ritual. (The church denounced the translation; to this day the Gospels are read in their original language during the liturgy.)

Since demoticists were prevented from exercising any influence in the schools, they turned to the instruments of culture in their program of national integration. Their control of culture had already begun with the acceptance in the 1880s of demotic as the literary language. Literature, as was explained in the previous chapter, was central to their nationalist strategy. Psiharis's *My Journey* (1888), the manifesto and bible of demoticism, argued that for Greece to be a nation two conditions must be met—the expansion of borders, and the rise of a literature (1935: 25). Irredentism and the invention of a national culture were components of one and the same project. Demoticists promoted both, in the form of an expanded and homogeneous state whose unity could be partly attained and felt through literary texts. When this collective identity came under strain after the collapse of the campaign for a greater Greece in 1922, their successors looked to literature as a means of overcoming the contradictions between ethnicity and state. The antinomies of nationalist discourse, which could not be overcome in reality, could be resolved in the utopian space of literary culture.

Socialists criticized the privileged position of literature in demoticist thought; they felt this came at the expense of social issues. G. Skliros, for instance, argued that liberal demoticists tried "to solve the language problem without addressing the social foundation." They believed, he added, that they could bring about "social change with discussions, poems, and novels" ([1907] 1976: 128). Skliros saw demoticism as a bourgeois movement doomed to failure for disregarding the context of language. Demoticism was indeed a liberal discourse, steering a middle path between a nascent socialism and an entrenched conservative state apparatus. It founded a national culture on the basis of "discussions, poems, and novels." But the priority it gave to literary production as a source of national cohesion led, as I shall show, to the aestheticization of this culture.

Demoticism's successful institutionalization of literature can be seen in the anthologies of the period. In the course of securing the vernacular as

the literary language, demoticists brought into prominence neglected writers. Thus the anthologies from the 1880s onwards began to incorporate
more demotic poets, becoming by the end of the century an eclectic selection
of both traditions. An anthology (1884) edited by Anestis Konstantinidis
contained more than the usual share of demotic authors, with the largest
space devoted to the prerevolutionary demotic poet Athanasios Hristopulos.
The collection (1888) compiled by N. Mihalopulos had a large number of
folk songs and, significantly, the majority of the poems were in demotic.
It even included texts written in demotic by otherwise committed purists
such as Alexandros Rangavis. In 1899 Dimitrios Tagopulos, a demoticist,
published *I Nea Laiki Antholoyia* (The new popular anthology), which
departed from traditional practice. First, although the language of all
included prose was still *katharevusa,* he wrote the prologue in demotic.
Secondly, Tagopulos sought a balance between the two opposed discourses,
treating both linguistic registers evenhandedly; while the established purist
poets occupied their customary place, the editor also incorporated contemporary demotic poets as well as those from earlier generations. As he
explains in the prologue, he wished to select the best and most beautiful
poems from the time of Solomos to the present without regard to linguistic
preferences and literary schools. The title, a "new popular anthology,"
attests to demoticism's attempt to canonize demotic verse by granting it
equal, if not superior, value to that of purist writing.

The initial stages of canonization in poetry formed part of a grander
project to found a literature composed of multiple genres. Until this time
the designation *national literature* really signified national poetry only. The
end of the century marked the emergence of literature consisting of, at the
very least, poetry, the novel, and the short story. The formation of literature
was not a passive phenomenon but was as willed an act of modernization
as the introduction of parliamentary government.

The purposeful nature of literary formation is borne out by one of the
earliest prose anthologies, *Ellinika Diiyimata,* published in 1896 by the
magazine *Estia,* which gave enthusiastic promotion to the short story in its
columns.[23] The editors were troubled by the paucity of prose anthologies
compared to the numerous collections of poetry, and the higher status
granted to verse. Although prose writings had existed before this period,
such as the texts of Rigas, *Papatrehas* (1811-20) by Korais, "The Woman
of Zakinthos" of Solomos (written in 1826 but published posthumously),
and the memoirs of generals and soldiers or the purist novels, there was
no classification in which they could be placed. The publication of the
anthology was motivated by the urgent sense that Greece lacked an indigenous fiction. The main aim of this volume, as the editor Yeoryios Kasdonis
explained, was to introduce the public to "one of the most significant

branches of modern Greek literature" (Preface). The editor extolled the virtues of the collection, asserting that he published it with confidence, and was "not terrified" by the possibility of comparison with European short stories. Here again the anxiety over European literature persisted in tandem with the need to demonstrate the quality of its Greek counterpart. Not only Europeans but also Greeks themselves had to be persuaded of the "choice fruits" of Greek fiction. The Greek public, the editor complained, lacked enthusiasm for this "national enterprise"; the short story, he noted, would develop into an "heirloom of the Greek people" only after readers acknowledged it as a serious form of writing. Patriots were made, not born; and, in the same way, readers had to be taught to appreciate Greek literature. It is no accident that Kasdonis called the promotion of literature a national enterprise.

His anthology aimed to bring attention as well to the authors of the short stories. Although it included purists such as Rangavis and Angelos Vlahos, it anthologized more recent writers, primarily demoticists, such as Kostis Palamas, Yeoryios Drosinis, Grigorios Xenopulos, who were struggling against the purist order. In contrast to the previous century, no one side or group had firm control over literary production. More writers than ever before, through choosing demotic as the medium, were brought to the attention of a large new audience. But at the same time the power of tradition and the authority of purism still entrenched in the country's cultural institutions helped maintain the prestige of many archaistic writers. Anthologies of this period incorporated texts written in both demotic and *katharevusa,* reflecting in this way the era's state of linguistic flux. Emile Legrand points to the dilemma facing many scholars; he explains in his preface to *Morceaux choisis en grec savant du XIX*ᵉ *siècle* (1903) that though a demoticist, he was compelled to recognize the reality of the purist tradition. Therefore his collection of Greek prose, intended as an introduction to Greek literature for French readers, contains numerous short stories by purist authors.[24]

The last two decades of the nineteenth century and the first two of the twentieth embraced the era of militant demoticism. The state of linguistic and literary anarchy fostered an eclecticism unrivaled in Greek history. There was no single national canon, but several, each representing different communities, all striving to be officially crowned. During these decades the terms *Greek poetry* or *Greek literature* were not necessarily identified with the writings of the purists, as was true in the nineteenth century, or with the demoticists, as would happen in the twentieth. No single conception of the literary was naturalized as the national one. Thus Dimitrios Kokkinakis, in his *Panellinios Antholoyia* (Panhellenic anthology, 1902), a collection of poems from the *Erotokritos* to his present, did not confine himself solely to either of the linguistic schools but drew selections from both. The term *panhellenic* in the title refers here to poets from both demotic and *katharevusa*. This comprehensiveness also is found in the collections edited by Konstandinidis (1904) and Saliveros (1911).

This period was short-lived, however, as the demoticists gained increasing authority in cultural institutions. A striking feature of the next series of anthologies was the sense of renewal, revaluation, and reorientation of tradition expressed in the adjective *new* or *modern* in the titles, such as Ioannis Polemis's *Lira: Antholoyia tis Neoteras Ellinikis Piiseos* (Lyre: Anthology of modern Greek poetry, 1910), *Nea Elliniki Antholoyia* (Modern Greek anthology, anon., 1913), and Ioannis Sideris's *Neoelliniki Antholoyia* (Modern Greek anthology, 1921). To varying degrees these anthologies conducted a critique of the past and announced innovative directions. Polemis's collection was almost exclusively devoted to the poetry written in demotic with particular emphasis on recent poets. Though the purist schools were still well represented, demotic authors received the greater exposure both in space and numbers. In most cases they outnumbered their purist counterparts.

In the struggle to win wider acceptance of this revisionary order many collections introduced contemporary poets to the public. A collection edited by the symbolist poet and essayist Tellos Agras (1922) anthologized authors of the period between 1910 and 1920, whose work, Agras believed, could be compared to anything produced in the past. But the tradition to which he assigned them was very selective; it began with Andreas Kalvos, Solomos, and the Heptanesian School, and bypassed what he termed the "sterile" period of "pseudoromanticism and pseudoneoclassicism [the flourishing period of purism]" to reach the second Athenian school of Palamas, Drosinis, and Malakasis. Agras's version of the canon, recounted by proponents of demotic in those decades, consisted of three stages: he denounced or ignored the Phanariot and old Athenian schools, he brought attention to new and recent work, and he reintroduced compatible purist poets like Kalvos.[25] Others followed Agras in devoting entire anthologies to newly published poems: the *Antholoyia ton Neon Piiton mas 1900-1920* (Anthology of our new poets, anon., 1920), *Ekloyi Neoteron Piimaton* (Selection of new poems, 1924), edited by Yeoryios Avlonitis; *Antholoyia ton Neoteron Piiton* (Anthology of new poets, anon., 1925). All aimed to introduce new and young poets to the reading public and forge for them a place in the newly emerging literary canon.

In the late 1920s demotic was firmly established as the idiom of literature, though *katharevusa* maintained its place in official institutions. Thus by the 1930s the struggle to impose the vernacular as the medium of a national literature lost much of its urgency. The new goal was the consolidation of these gains. It was carried out by the Generation of the 30s, a group of writers, poets, artists, intellectuals, critics, and scholars who saw themselves as the inheritors of demoticism. This generation institutionalized literature as a category of diverse genres, giving emphasis for the first time to the novel. As Yiorgos Theotokas stated in *Free Spirit* (1929), the philosophical manifesto of the generation, poetry was not enough; a "new literature" required "discussion of ideas, an authentic theater and an authentic novel" (1979: 54). Increasingly they posited literature as a privileged space of cultural activities and ascribed to it compensatory functions. The socio-political project of the demoticists—to create a repertoire of shared opinions, attitudes, and symbols—became aestheticized in the 1930s. The national traumas and disappointments consequent to modernization, as well as the ideological contradictions inherent in it, propelled Greek culture into an aesthetics of autonomy. The Generation of the 1930s resolved these problems by projecting them into the utopian space of art.

An Aesthetics of Autonomy

Significant to their thinking was the Asia Minor catastrophe in 1922, the Turkish army's defeat of the Greek forces trying to gain control of areas in Asia Minor. Greeks experienced the event as a national trauma of apocalyptic proportions. To be sure, the rout of the Greek army, the destruction of Smyrna, and the ensuing exchange of populations between Greece and Turkey—which Greeks regarded as the end of a 3,000-year-old settlement in Asia Minor—led to the revaluation of national ideology and ultimately eroded the *Megali Idea,* one of the ideological underpinnings of Greek society.

This doctrine, a fusion of Byzantinism and romantic Hellenism, had envisaged the recapture of lost Byzantine territories and the Hellenization of the East, or, at the very least, the unification of all Greeks in one state. While historians and literary critics celebrated the temporal continuity of the Greeks, the *Megali Idea* proclaimed their territorial integrity. The *Megali Idea* served as a populist cause to mobilize the masses. It was politically useful as a guarantee of social cohesion, serving as a panacea for problems of the Greek state and as a medium of communication between people and government (Andreopoulos 1989: 198-200). It also allowed the experience of shared identity, particularly for Greeks outside the state. Its nationalist potential was exploited by the intellectual elite, as was noted by William Miller: "For every Greek from beyond the present frontiers of the kingdom who has studied at Athens goes back to his native town or village imbued with the 'Great Greek Idea,' of which he henceforth becomes a missionary. It is among the Athenian graduates, the doctors and lawyers of 'unredeemed

Greece,' that the flame of patriotism burns more brightly" (1905: 27). The rupture of this irredentist dream in the war of 1897 and its complete dissolution in 1922 dispossessed Greek society of a valuable ideology. The aborted attempt to integrate nation and state, that is, the ethnoreligious identities of the millet with the modern secular entity, exposed the very contradictions upon which Greece was built.

Conservative forces responded by establishing the dictatorship of General Ioannis Metaxas in 1936, which ensured control of the state by those politically on the right. Their answer to the debacle of 1922, as well as to political disunity and the rise of socialism, was the creation of a "Third Greek Civilization," based on classical culture and fortified with Orthodoxy and the Byzantine heritage. Metaxas's Third Greek Civilization escaped the present by returning to a glorious and piety-filled past.

The liberal bourgeois elements, on the other hand, proposed an aesthetic consciousness. Having forfeited the state, especially the education system so crucial to their mission for a national homogeneity, they intensified their efforts to maintain their authority over culture. They proposed an autonomous aesthetic as a cure for failed irredentist aspirations and wrecked hopes for a modern, democratic, and liberal state. The indispensable tool in their aestheticization of culture was the notion of Greekness (*Ellinikotita*).

Dimitris Tziovas has shown in his investigation of this concept that, although *Ellinikotita* had already appeared by 1851, it reemerged in the literary criticism of this generation as a concept endowed with reconciliatory capacities (1989: 31-38). Always a utopian notion (Vakalo 1983: 10), Greekness was now temporalized. It signified not only an imaginary place, a territory that could not be, but also, and more important, a time projected into the past and the future. Its literary history was synchronic, spanning the eras from Homer to the present (Leontis 1990). Unlike the Hellenism of the purists, which strived for resemblance, Greekness sought continuity. It longed for a familiar story and anticipated a more positive future. As the poet George Seferis put it: Greekness "will only show its face when the Greece of today has acquired its own real intellectual characters and features. And its characteristics will be precisely the synthesis of all true works of art which have been produced by Greeks" (1966: 95). Greekness was an aesthetic, synthesizing agent that amalgamated the unique features of Greek culture. This singularity of Hellenism, Odisseas Elytis contended, always lay in its "assimilating energy, which, with material taken from East and West, necessarily fashioned models of civilization different" from those it borrowed. Throughout its history, the Aegean, the sea bordering three continents, has given forth a third world, whose "originary" power and truth rivaled the other two (1974: 424).

Greekness was an attempt to determine an authentically Greek nature in the overwhelming presence of European modernity, experienced by Greeks in terms of insufficiency and inferiority. Greece, Yiorgos Theotokas complained, never offered anything of cultural value to Europe (1979: 37). It simply copied without creating. Furthermore, the glories of ancient Greece could no longer compensate for feelings of belatedness. Modernization put Greek culture on a path of perpetually catching up with Europe. Theotokas and others concluded that, one hundred years after independence, Greece was still in a derivative position. In place of sterile imitation Theotokas proposed an active engagement with European thought, the importation of models in a context of "national tradition" and "national character." He proposed a fusion of the classical and the modern:

> This would be really something special and new, something Greek; it would be finally a Greekness which would really transcend the miseries of localism; it would have contempt for all the phony provincialisms and Hellenocentrisms of the café and would have the hope (distant certainly, but not groundless) to acquire sometime an international significance. (cited by Tziovas 1989: 123)

Greekness embodied the foreign and the local, the traditional and the new. It harmonized modernity with indigenous traditions. It represented an autochthony without the ethnocentrism of the demoticists or the Hellenolatry of the Metaxas dictatorship (Tziovas 1989: 5, 38). The poet Elytis wrote: "This was the only way for Greeks to become again Europeans; by contributing and not just borrowing" (1974: 572). Greekness enabled the reconciliation of the contradictions defining Greek identity since the original encounter with modernity: East and West; local and cosmopolitan; religious and secular; traditional and modern; state and nation, Romeic and Hellenic. Although the second unit of each opposition was privileged particularly in high culture, Greek society could now be experienced not just as one or the other but, in many cases, as both. Greeks could claim their traditions but still be Europeans; they could be faithful to their heritage yet be modern. Greekness promised a perfect union of otherwise self-eroding antinomies.

Insofar as Greekness facilitated the overcoming of these differences in an imaginary realm, it operated aesthetically. In western Europe, as I shall discuss in the next chapter, the autonomous aesthetic constituted a redemptive space in a differentiated society, compensating for the side effects of modernization. Paradoxically, as Schulte-Sasse points out, this longed-for space was located within modernity, which generated it, and outside it, as it was the object of desire, the Other of modernity (1989: 90). The aesthetic in Greece also appeared as modernity's solution to the problems it created. But the problems in a peripheral country like Greece were a result not of industrialization but of its absence. Alienation was caused by belated and hence "imperfect" modernization, rather than by the fragmentation of society. In other words, the purposeful introduction of cultural and political institutions was not accompanied by similar transformations in society and the economy. A parliamentary democracy was installed and an autonomous literature constructed without a bourgeois civil society. Greek culture internalized this incongruity between imported institutions and indigenous reality in the form of the oppositions I enumerated above.

The *Megali Idea* was an attempt to mediate one of the most irreconcilable of these conflicts, that between ethnicity and state, by incorporating the Greek populations of the Near East in one political entity. It failed. Instead of expanding, the Greek kingdom had to accept instead two and a half million refugees, many of whom had little or no sense of Greek consciousness. Far from resolving the tensions in Greek culture, the *Megali Idea* violently brought them to the fore as never before. The explosive revelation of these dichotomies as well as the wreck of the national project made the necessity for an aesthetic concept urgent. Greekness opened up a space for the experience of an integrated national consciousness beyond the bad antinomies of modernity. The territory of Greekness was the archipelago of the Aegean, the last land before the lost Orient, the transcendent place of sun, light, and sea, a utopian time that could not be (see Leontis 1991).

Greekness manifested the aestheticization of the politics of national identity. It was the culminating stage in the grand plan to fabricate a social solidarity through a common language and on a foundation of shared narratives, opinions, beliefs, and habits. The imaginary finally became the source of national unity. Here indeed lies the success of nationalism. Culture, as Eagleton has shown (1990), infiltrates the texture of peoples' lives, enforcing social cohesion without the necessity of laws. While in the initial phase of nation building, sectional interests must be neutralized (sometimes brutally), after the establishment of the nation identity can be experienced spontaneously. People are rarely compelled to identify with the nation because their own personal stories have become linked to the national narrative.

In the case of Greece nationalism has produced one of the most culturally homogeneous states in Europe. "It is remarkable," writes Kitromilides, "how areas as different in their historical experience and political development as the Ionian Islands and the islands of the eastern Aegean, or western Thrace and Crete, came to look so much alike once integrated into the Greek state" (1989: 177). While minorities such as the Macedonians and Turks exist, on the whole ethnic groups have been effectively socialized so as to bind their fate with that of the nation. What is more remarkable is that this identity has been internalized by the citizens of the state so that it seems to stem from within, to be an expression of their own inner being. This is precisely the *beauty* of national culture. It compels identification with the homeland paradoxically without compulsion because it becomes part of people's lives. Patriarch Anthimos, in his attack on the idea of the state, wondered how this entity could exist without coercion (see chapter 2): "What order can then remain in such a government, and what morality, when the passions rule?... How can they live without any civil discipline, those who despise unsullied marriage, and harm the whole state? How can they live without the reproach of conscience, those of them who, won over by gain, can lightly cheat the civil law; when the fear of God and the threat of eternal punishment is not a bridle against wrong-doing?" (Clogg 1969: 106). The fear of God is not required because national culture, working surely as a substitute religion, enforces loyalty to the state. When culture ceases being visible, no longer a construct to be fought over but an ideology concealing its operations, it functions aesthetically.

The aestheticization of culture is a product of modernity. This is, in a sense, the case made by Zissimos Lorentzatos in his essay "The Lost Center" (1961). Once Greeks decided, he argues, to answer Europe and Fallmerayer by proposing their descent from classical Hellas they desecrated their "spiritual heritage" and began to strive for that "famous aesthetic goal:... the poetic *individualismus* and the accompanying theory (and practice) that proclaims there is nothing higher in the world than art for its own sake" (1980: 120). When we speak of poetics in Greece, he writes, we mean European poetics. "Europe has always been the model we have followed in our arts, and therefore the crisis of Europe, the metropolitan problem... is a thing we share in common" (106). It is not surprising, he concludes, that the answers provided by Cavafy and Seferis to the crisis in poetry never go beyond poetry itself. "They never for a moment put into question poetry itself" (111).

Cavafy and Seferis could not put poetry into question because they both regarded the aesthetic as the panacea for the "crisis in poetry," and more important, for the general malaise of culture. Although Lorentzatos himself anathematized aestheticism—"Let art for its own sake go to hell"—in favor of the Orthodox identities, Greek culture itself had by this time internalized the European problematic of modernity. The Generation of the 30s simply gave the autonomous operations of art an indigenous respectability. It aestheticized the socializing mission of the Enlightenment, with the result that, while in the past the politics of this culture were made explicit, now they were forgotten or not acknowledged.

The suppression of politics can be seen in the anthologies of the period, particularly the one edited by Kleon Parashos and Xenofon Lefkoparidis. The volume, tellingly entitled *Ekloyi apo ta Oreotera Ellinika Lirika Piimata*

(Selections from the most beautiful Greek lyric poems, 1931), illustrates the prominence given to aesthetic value. The editors write in the prologue that their collection has an "aesthetic character," comprising poems that display "authentic" and "true lyricism." Pure lyricism rather than, say, national value, constituted the decisive criterion in the editorial process. And in order to accentuate the lyrical properties of the poems they felt justified in doctoring them. They extracted, for instance, a certain "rhetorical load . . . incompatible with the purity of the poems' lyrical tone." They also printed segments of poems, because the inclusion of whole poems "would have undermined the beauty of the [selected] passages." This violation of the texts' integrity for the sake of lyricism is similar to Hantseris's strategy ninety years earlier. But a major difference exists between them: while Hantseris's Procrustean methods were motivated by his position in the language question, Parashos and Lefkoparidis's editing was inspired by aesthetic considerations. Parashos and Lefkoparidis had no anxieties about national language and felt little need to prove the viability of Greek literature, since the liberal bourgeois intellectuals had contrived a consensus on these matters. The law of art had become internalzed in the Greek experience, that is, made implicit. An aestheticized culture, to paraphrase Kant, functions purposefully without expressing its purpose.

Parashos and Lefkoparidis published their anthology at a time when literature was emerging as an autonomous entity. Their collection no doubt contributed to this development. During this period editors, critics, students, journalists, and publishers were undertaking a task that would have been theoretically and practically impossible a century earlier, when neither the discourse nor the social apparatus existed to support autonomous art. The anthologists of the nineteenth century were learned men concerned with Greek writing. They compiled anthologies with the aim of fabricating a national homogeneity rather than collecting beautiful verses. An aesthetic orientation separates Parashos and Lefkoparidis from their precursors. Their anthology was made possible by the transformations in Greek society that had opened up a space for Greek literature in the public sphere. But the humanists Parashos and Lefkoparidis, for whom politics and aesthetics seem incompatible, acknowledge neither the past struggles nor their own exercise of power. Incognizant of their position in the institution of literature and its history, they adopt an objective demeanor, communicating in the shared discourse of literary criticism.

When we look at prose anthologies of the twentieth century we see that they followed a similar course, though, as pointed out earlier, this genre was incorporated into literature later than poetry. Even in 1928 Konstantinos Skokos complained in *To Ellinikon Diiyima, iti, Apanthisma Eklekton Diiyimaton tis Neoellinikis Logotehnias* (The Greek short story, or, selection of choice short stories of modern Greek literature) of the public's indifference to prose writing. With this publication Skokos hoped to provide an "authentic" picture of its development by choosing the best and most "beautiful" works. His criteria here, as in the first edition of the volume (1920), were aesthetic: "coherence of ideas," "representational facility," and "simplicity of the sentences" (1920: 285).

Originally demoticists promoted the short story for their sociopolitical ends, as a form of writing recounting the story of the Greek nation. After the aestheticization of literary practice, anthologists began to see it as a purely literary genre. A. D. Papadimas's anthology (1923) and the special issue of the literary magazine *Kiklos* (4, 1934), devoted to the "best prose writers after the war," introduced new authors to the official lists. Both publications worked within the consensual space of demotic criticism. They aimed to revise the canon but not, as in the past, to replace it with an alternate discursive practice.

Within the institution of literature there existed no major competing discourses since purist writing had been denied any literary merit. G. Valetas was concerned in his collection (1947-49) with charting the evolution of demotic prose from 1345 to the present. He openly acknowledged that his interest lay exclusively in the "best and most representative pieces of popular prose writing" and thus did not include examples from the purist tradition since the majority of its works had no "aesthetic worth." Valetas demoted purist texts from their former rank as literature. Significantly, he did not simply designate it bad literature but denied it any literary status whatsoever so as to ignore it completely.[26] A passage of demotic prose had for him inherent literary qualities as well as a distinguished tradition; texts of *katharevusa,* on the other hand, lacked both a past and, more important, any literary value. Valetas and other anthologists simply selected the "best and representative" examples of the demotic tradition with a few patronizing references to the purist school. In M. H. Ikonomu's collection of short stories (1951), as in his anthology of poetry, there is no place among the classics of Greek prose for purist authors. This holds true as well for Apostolidis's authoritative anthology of short-story writers (1953-54).

The "Neutral" Canon

Attempts at either the consolidation of the canon or its revision occurred within the realm of shared assumptions established by demoticism. The canon eventually accommodated women writers, the anthology by Dimitris Lambikis (1936) being an early example. Constantine Cavafy's poetry, previously considered anomalous, was acknowledged in the 1920s as a high point of Greek literature by Grigorios Xenopulos, Tellos Agras, and Alkis

Thrilos.[27] I have already alluded to the elevation of Kalvos into the pantheon of Greek poets. Also worth mentioning is Seferis's success in classifying the nearly forgotten memoirs of General Ioannis Makriyiannis as a prototype of Greek literature. In a similar move Apostolidis incorporated into the fifth edition of his anthology the previously despised *rebetika,* the popular songs produced by the lumpenproletariat of Athens and Pireas. The rediscovery of a text, its resurrection, or its reclassification from non-literature to literature, does not, as I argued earlier, alter the canon's nature or direction. These changes simply indicate shifts in value assigned to specific texts or genres as they move from the durable to the transient category.

The struggles of the past to form a national culture were transformed within the institution of literature to debates about textual exegesis. Though critics chose different methods of interpretation (whether Marxist, humanist, or formalist) they did not differ about the centrality of (demotic) literature in culture. For this reason critics could adopt an objective and disinterested position since they were working within the consensus of demotic humanism. In perhaps the most influential poetic anthology of Greek poetry, the *Antholoyia* of Iraklis Apostolidis, published in 1931 and subsequently reprinted in twelve editions, the authoritative voice of the anthologist almost completely disappears. Apostolidis, who wrote the prefaces in the third person and signed them as "the anthologist," disclaims in them all axiological motives, emphasizing that his task is not to judge or evaluate but rather to choose the most "representative" poems. Neither his personal preferences nor his ideological presuppositions enter into this process, since "the anthologist erases himself and, as a third person, classifies [his poems]." He does nothing but present "a bouquet of a variety of flowers" to his readers. This is all the information Apostolidis provides in his terse prefaces, apparently not wanting to influence the reader. According to a contemporary reviewer of this volume, Apostolidis teaches us that "the poem has no need of discussion or interpretation"; it passes through all boundaries and "enters the heart" (Panayiotopulos 1936: 352).

Apostolidis and Panayiotopulos present the anthology as an autonomous and unpremeditated entity, thereby giving the impression that its contents are not selected but rather immaculately conceived. It is as if the canon had always been demotic. Indeed, readers not aware of the struggles conducted to establish it would be persuaded that this anthology really constitutes *the* canon for all periods. Those without a knowledge of purist anthologies could not, on the basis of this volume, know the extent and significance of purist writings. In collecting all these "representative" texts Apostolidis provides a history of demotic poetry but, of course, disregards the very genealogy of this anthology. In other words, he historicizes his collection but not his own critical discourse. What Jane Tompkins (1986: 88) says of anthologists of American literature holds true for Apostolidis: believing in the inherent nature of literary value, he can not see his own role in shaping the list of great authors. Having adopted the language and strategies of aesthetic humanism, he, like subsequent anthologists, sublimates the physical and discursive violence waged in the past. The aesthetics of the new order suppresses the politics of exclusion. Despite the editor's claims of objectivity and comprehensiveness, his collection, like the New Testament and the discourse of philosophy, represents only one version of the canon: the winning side. Apostolidis's *Antholoyia,* like K. Th. Dimaras's *Istoria tis Neoellinikis Logotehnias* (History of modern Greek literature), both products of the Generation of the 30s, constitutes a crystallization of the modern Greek literary canon. It is the master narrative of Greek culture, a unilinear story of the progress toward demotic truth.

This version of the Greek canon cannot accommodate the verses of Ilias Tantalidis, the prose of Alexandros Rangavis, the theatrical writings of Rizos-Nerulos and the tradition they represent. The system of values supporting these works has been suppressed. Though pushed aside, purist texts nevertheless retain their significance as the elitist, archaistic, and revivalist Other of demotic populism. As Stallybrass and White observe, what is socially peripheral is often symbolically central (1986: 20). Thus, literary culture invokes purism as an unfortunate accident in tradition, a slipping away from national truth, a digression from the authentic development of Greek literature that sprang forth with the *Erotokritos* and the Cretan Renaissance, blossomed with Solomos and the Heptanesian School, reappeared in Athens with the writings of Palamas and the Generation of the 80s, and matured with the writers of the 1930s. Demoticist humanism, as the privileged discourse of public culture, has the authority to define the canon and hierarchize all other sites of discourse.

Aesthetic and linguistic value have been conflated. The beauty of the text seems to determine an editor's decisions. E. Hrisanthopulos explains in his anthology (1937), for example, that he has selected only poems with poetic worth. Like Parashos and Lefkoparidis he even edited passages that, in his view, compromise the aesthetic integrity of individual poems or the entire anthology. Whereas in the nineteenth century editors altered poems to accommodate them to their position on national culture, after the aestheticization of culture they change texts to make them more beautiful. In the nineteenth century a rival discourse could have challenged an editor's view by providing a different conception of language, the nation, and literature. In the twentieth century, however, disagreements are voiced according to the norms of demotic culture. Critics may condemn an anthologist's violation of the author's original intentions but they do not question the notion of aesthetic (that is, national) value.[28]

By the 1950s anthologies claimed to offer not just beautiful poems, but the best poems.[29] Yioryis Simiriotis (1952) promises his readers good and beautiful verses that would entertain them and cultivate their taste. The canon had by this time acquired a tradition of masterpieces expressing the individuality of the Greek nation. M. Ikonomu states that his collection (1952) contains only classics of modern Greek literature. He has included, Ikonomu writes confidently in his preface, "the most representative poems of those poets who are no longer alive but whose names have an undisputed place in modern Greek poetry and whose work transcends time." Of course there is a place here for a few of the most famous purist authors, but as in earlier examples, they are added more for historical reasons than any other. The classics of modern Greek poetry are without exception demotic. But since the demoticism of the canon is now beyond question, it would be more accurate to say that the canon is simply composed of great national texts. To become timeless, these great works of literature, like all classics, must suppress their historical origins. Whereas at the height of the struggle between purism and demoticism a text spoke only to specific communities, in the consensual space of national culture it addresses itself to all. It "transcends" politics and eschews every ideological position.

In the 1960s the Greek canon had achieved "self-realization," and from this point onward its development followed a predictable pattern of consolidation and revision. Anthologies appeared that either confirmed its greatness by cataloguing its classics or demonstrated its poverty by pointing to suppressed works. From the perspective of the canon the major struggles have ended, as debates concern the order of the hierarchy. Critics jostle to have their favorite authors admitted to the hallowed list. The notorious controversies conducted in the public sphere of the previous century about national identity have evolved into debates about literary meaning. No matter what form it takes, the Greek canon will remain demotic until the demotic view of literature, tradition, and Greece is challenged, which means, of course, until the position of literature in the invention of the nation is significantly questioned.

Chapter 4
The Emergence of Art and the Failures of Modernization

In the previous chapter I demonstrated how modernization eventually pushes peripheral cultures into an aesthetics of autonomy. Literature's original function of introducing Greeks to a catalogue of national virtues became compensatory during the 1930s. The socializing mission of literary culture was aestheticized when the notion of Greekness began to reconcile the ideological antinomies embedded in Greek identity. The imperfect integration of imported institutions, in this case literature, with the infrastructural realities of Greek society meant that these institutions functioned differently from their prototypes in western Europe. In this respect Greek literature is neither an ethnographic aberration nor a European imitation. Having emerged in a negotiation between local necessity and European imposition, it is similar to yet unlike the literary paradigms of western Europe. The compensatory role of literature, for instance, developed not in response to social fragmentation created by industrialization, as in western Europe, but in reaction to the ideological contradictions in Greek culture that emerged after its confrontation with modernity. An autonomous literature enabled readers to transcend the incongruity between western constructs and indigenous practices.

I wish to explore the reasons for this lack of fit between foreign products and Greek society by examining some forces hostile to modernization. In this chapter I will investigate the institutionalization of an autonomous literature while looking into agents frustrating its establishment in Greece. By examining cases of resistance to western culture, I intend to demonstrate the Other of modernity. A word of caution is in order, however, on my use of such terms as *European tradition* and *western European,* particularly as I have been insisting all along on specificity. In one respect these designations are inaccurate, insofar as they imply a cultural homogeneity among nations that does not exist. The genesis of literature or the system of the arts, for instance, cannot be ascribed to one national tradition. From another point of view, however, say the Greek, European culture did (and does) make felt its overwhelming presence. It could not be ignored and indeed was simultaneously admired and despised, emulated and feared. Greek intellectuals imported into Greece concepts they felt belonged collectively to Europe. Although they discriminated between individual literary traditions, they considered such supracultural notions as literature or art to have a European source. When I refer to the European tradition, therefore, I do not mean a unified consciousness or a metaphysical structure but rather a set of cultural discourses and institutions that Greeks recognized as European and with which they felt they had to come to terms.

The Development of the System of Arts

By contending that art, literature, and criticism are of recent origin, I am not suggesting that painting, poetry, dance, or their treatises did not exist in previous ages, but rather that our understanding of them differs from those of former periods. Clearly, the *Iliad* performs functions in the 1990s substantially different from those in the archaic age. For modern readers it occupies a prominent position in "western literature" as a celebrated masterpiece. The ancient Greeks, however, could not have thought of it as "literature" since the category was not conceptually available to them. This epic poem, far from being cordoned off as a unique class of writing by virtue of its fictional nature, was intimately integrated within the social praxis—recited at celebratory occasions, taught, or often used in the adjudication of legal disputes. In the same way, ancient Greeks would not have referred to a piece of sculpture as art. While appreciating the beauty of the work, they would not have characterized it as a distinctly aesthetic object. The notion of art presupposes a critical orientation, discourse, and system of values that emerged only in the modern age.

What we understand as art—that is, the system comprising all the fine arts such as literature, architecture, sculpture, dance, drama, and opera—is a product of the eighteenth century. *Techne,* the nearest ancient Greek equivalent—and modern Greek translation—of this term, signified simply craftsmanship, in an extended sense, rather than a system of arts. Indeed, *techne* covered a broad range of creative capacities. There was, for instance, the *techne* of sculpture, medicine, agriculture, carpentry, and so on. *Techne* suggested a skill or a group of skills that could be applied to all human activities, from the crafts to the sciences, and that could be taught to others. It meant, according to J. J. Pollitt, an "organized procedure for the purpose of producing specific preconceived results" (1974: 32). Aristotle discusses *techne* in *Physics,* defining it as a purposive process that produces a final form out of preexisting matter. "In the products of art [*techne*]," Aristotle observes, "we make the material with a view to the function (194b, 7)."[1] The arts make their material serviceable, he argues.

Classical philosophers such as Aristotle did not distinguish beauty (*kalon*) from the moral good and did not always conceive of it in relationship to "art." In the theory of beauty, consideration of art was absent in Plato, and played a secondary role in Plotinus and Augustine (Kristeller 1965: 168). Indeed, none of the classical philosophers discussed art as a problem in its own right. Furthermore, they did not (as we do) separate the aesthetic quality of objects from their intellectual, moral, religious, and practical functions and hence did not group the arts under one principle such as disinterestedness.[2] Since philosophers did not consider the fine arts a unique and autonomous genus, sharing common characteristics, they did not reserve for them a separate space in the classical episteme but rather classified them along with sciences and crafts. The earliest such system was the list of the seven liberal arts: grammar, rhetoric, dialectic, arithmetic, geometry, astronomy, and music (Kristeller 1965: 173). Significantly, of the seven only music is now regarded as an art, yet in antiquity it was thought to have a greater affinity to mathematics than, for instance, to poetry or dance.

The Middle Ages inherited the scheme of these seven liberal arts but did not develop a comprehensive theory of the arts. *Ars* in the Middle Ages signified a body of knowledge; *artista* meant an artisan of any kind; the painter was often grouped with the druggist and the sculptor with the goldsmith or stonemason (Barasch 1985: 45). Art, in other words, was incorporated in daily practice instead of being isolated as a separate sphere of human activity. Although issues regarding representation were discussed in the debate over the image during the Byzantine period, these questions were raised inadvertently, not in their own right, but in the context of theology (46). Similarly, workshop texts prescribed models to be followed. Like Vitruvius's *The Ten Books of Architecture,* they were largely manuals discussing technical and material matters rather than treatises on the nature of the beauty of art.

During the Renaissance a theory of visual arts emerged, but it was neither comprehensive nor systematic. Art still carried a vague connotation of skill or knowledge. In the sixteenth century scholars began to group together painting and other visual arts and to separate them from the sciences

(Kristeller 1965: 181). Comparisons were drawn, for instance, between painting and poetry, and their distinguishing features recorded. This period also witnessed the appearance of treatises on the arts and the artist, such as those by Vasari, Danti, Armerini, and Pino. All of these developments were instrumental in the foundation of the modern system of fine arts.

Charles Batteux took the first decisive step in this direction in his *Les beaux arts réduits à un même principe* (The fine arts reduced to a common principle, 1746) where he set out, as his title tellingly indicates, to classify the fine arts in one category. Batteux isolates three distinct groups of arts: first, the mechanical arts, which have the satisfaction of a person's needs as their object; secondly, the beaux arts such as music, poetry, painting, and sculpture, which take pleasure as their end; and finally those arts, such as eloquence and architecture, which combine the objectives of utility and pleasure (27). While the first and third categories employ nature to achieve specific ends, the fine arts do not refer to nature but rather copy it: "the Arts are the imitation of beautiful Nature" (82). Taste, the capacity to distinguish the good, bad, and mediocre, is to the arts, according to Batteux, what intelligence is to the sciences. The law of taste, he observes, necessitates the imitation of nature. The concept of imitation enables Batteux to establish a unifying link between seemingly unrelated activities. The fine arts share a single bond and differ only in the expressive medium they employ in their respective fields, such as color (painting), sound (music), gesture (dance), or speech (poetry). With Batteux there appeared a recognizable system of the arts "reduced" to a common principle. But since this system was still oriented toward the outside world (which it sought to depict), it had not yet developed into an autonomous entity.

The conceptual isolation and institutionalization of art reached its completion in Germany, where Batteux's ideas found fertile soil, especially in the newly created branch of philosophy, aesthetics (Woodmansee 1984: 26). Alexander Baumgarten first used the term *aesthetics* in the *Reflections on Poetry* (1735) where in his discussion of perception he observed *"things known* are to be known by a superior faculty as the object of logic; *things perceived* of the science of perception, or *aesthetic"* (1954: 116). Aesthetics for Baumgarten was the science of sensuous knowledge. Although he considered this realm a separate philosophical discipline, he still placed it in the context of epistemology. Furthermore, he limited his discussion to poetry and eloquence instead of expanding it to the other arts. Moses Mendelssohn was the first among German writers to formulate a systematic theory of the fine arts. In his essay "Betrachtungen über die Quellen und die Verbindungen der schönen Künsten und Wissenschaften" (Reflections on the sources and relations of the fine arts and letters, 1757) he poses a question similar to Batteux's (to whose work he refers) regarding the similarity of the arts: What is the common factor, he asks, of the arts such as poetry, painting, dance, music, architecture, which allows them to achieve their shared end (1929: 168)? The unity of the arts, he answers, lies not solely in their reflection of nature, as Batteux believed, but in their tendency to please and move us through the sensuous representation of perfection, in other words, beauty (171). All the fine arts have as their central component beauty, which is created by the harmony of the internal relationships in the rendered object. His lesser-known pupil, Karl P. Moritz, took the idea of the common principle uniting all the arts, stripped it of its instrumentalist framework, and proposed in his "Versuch einer Vereinigung aller schönen Künste und Wissenschaften unter dem Begriff des in sich selbst Vollendeten" (Attempt at a unification of all the fine arts and letters under the concept of self-sufficiency, 1785) that works of art are self-sufficient entities, the perfection of which the observer contemplates disinterestedly, that is, for their own sakes (1962: 4). The unity of all the arts, Moritz argued, consisted of their self-sufficiency, autonomy, and inner harmony.

Kant's work appeared in this intellectual context. His task was to systematize the ideas on aesthetics and grant them the privilege of an independent place in a philosophical system. One of Kant's specific aims in the *Critique of Judgment* (1790) was to prove, first the uniqueness of the judgment of taste, that it differs from purposive acts, and second its universality, that the judgment of an object's beauty is a common human property and hence has a *Gemeingültigkeit* (universal validity). His intent was to explore the inherent features of the aesthetic experience. Taste, as Kant defined it, is the faculty of estimating an object or mode of representation by means of delight without any interest. The object of such a delight is called beautiful (1952: 50). Taste, furthermore, is the faculty of estimating what makes our feeling in a given representation universally communicable without the use of a concept (153). In order to avoid the empiricism that the study of taste had taken in philosophers such as Hume, Kant sought to ground the judgment of taste on an a priori principle and incorporate it within the framework of his transcendental method. To justify taste Kant had to prove its intersubjective validity by showing that this validity is not based on a concept but on a common human response to beauty. This common response to the aesthetic was a major component in the sphere of shared sentiments and affections being devised by the bourgeoisie as a source of social bonding.

When reflecting on a beautiful object, Kant believes, one does not seek knowledge about it; that is, one is judging it with respect to the pleasure it produces, rather than in relation to any definite concept. The aesthetic for Kant concerns not knowledge of objects but the pleasure of the subject (Guyer 1979: 71). This pleasure is pure since it is based on the formal purposefulness of the object, free from individual needs and tastes. In the experience of the beautiful a person's faculty engages in a harmonious play with the imagination and continues to exist in that state not through will or interest but through the formal beauty of the object, its unity, totality, and the harmony of its parts. This idea is succinctly summarized by Kant's paradoxical phrase *Zweckmässigkeit ohne Zweck,* translated as "purposefulness without a purpose" or "finality without an end," which means that an object does not have a purpose though its formal harmony convinces us that it has been purposefully made as a result of a plan or rule. It is as if it were conforming to a law without a law. This lawfulness without the law, Eagleton observes, describes the way the bourgeois public sphere functions. The success of this society lies in making ethical ideology appear less a coercive force than a "principle of spontaneous consensus" (1990: 41). The purpose of the public sphere was the fabrication of such a consensus so that moral imperatives would be internalized in the daily lives of individuals, without an air of compulsion or duty. "In the aesthetics of social conduct . . . the law is always with us as the unconscious structure of our life" (42). The aestheticization of social practices is also the ultimate goal, as I argue in the previous chapter, of the project of statism: the maintenance of national unity through a network of linked experiences. The westernized Greeks strived for such an imagined community so that (secular) culture instead of religion would determine identity and cement social harmony.

In the aestheticized order subjects obey the invisible law because it is disinterested. Beauty, for Kant, is the form of finality in an object perceived by a subject without the representation of an end. "The *beautiful* is what pleases in the mere estimate formed of it (consequently not by intervention of any feeling of sense in accordance with a concept of the understanding). From this it follows at once that it must please apart from all interest" (1952: 118). Without any exterior goal the judging subject is incited to remain in the state of contemplating the beautiful object strictly for the pleasure it affords. The suppression of the notion of interest is perhaps one of the most masterful strokes of aesthetic ideology, because it permits an individual or a class to exercise power while denying participation, belief, and investment. Kant argues that a subject making an aesthetic judgment neither finds this activity worthwhile nor ascribes value to it. It is as if, in calling an object beautiful, a person passed out of this world into a dimension of pure forms inhabited by people with noble intentions. Aesthetic ideology treats art as a sacred realm where ordinary norms of culture do not apply. In this sphere individuals are released from epistemological, economic, and political constraints so that they can experience an undifferentiated identity and escape the enervating antinomies of modernity.[3] A concept like Greekness is aesthetic because its promised unification of differences occurs in this imaginary space.

The criteria of disinterestedness and form of finality are important to Kant's argument, since they justify the universality of the judgment of taste. The pleasure produced under these conditions through the harmony of the faculties is globally communicable. In calling an object beautiful, according to Kant, one does not merely report an experience of pleasure but claims intersubjective validity for the statement. For this reason one may say that "this object is pleasing *to me*" but not that "it is beautiful *for me*" since, insofar as it is beautiful, it must be beautiful for everyone. Since we all respond to the beautiful in similar ways we can demand assent from others. The terms with which Kant expresses the criterion of universal validity, Paul Guyer notes, "suggest not so much *expecting* the occurrence of a mental state in another person, or *attributing* a state to another, but rather *demanding* or *requiring* something from someone, or even *imposing* some kind of obligation on another" (139). The word Kant most often uses in this context is *Anspruch* (demand). Grammatical analysis of the text shows that the third critique remains in the register of *Sollen* (ought); the statements of taste are written in the imperative (Bourdieu 1984: 489). According to Kant, however, there is nothing wicked for people engaged in aesthetic judgment to demand agreement from others because, far from acting egotistically, they participate in a universal process shared by all. They can expect unanimity because everybody feels and thinks the same way. The supposedly common response to beauty is but one experience linking the subjects to one another. In the enforced consensus of the public sphere the judgment of taste becomes one of the shared sensibilities defining bourgeois identity.

The universality of the aesthetic judgment and the obligations it imposes on people is the basic point of the third critique. Kant's argument may be summarized as follows: 1) pleasure in beauty must be based on a universally communicable mental state, since this is necessary to the ability to share knowledge; 2) this state must be based on the cognitive faculties being engaged in free play but not determined by concepts, and hence uninfluenced by practical goals and interests; 3) the reflection of the formal features of an object affords us a pleasure that is pure and disinterested; 4) this pleasure in beauty is based on a common human sense; 5) we therefore have the right to demand agreement from others for our aesthetic judgments.[4]

With Kant there appeared for the first time a systematic theory that sought to demonstrate the distinctive properties of the aesthetic and its autonomy from practical needs and wants. Kant demonstrated that the aesthetic judgment was conceptually isolatable. In this respect, *The Critique of Judgment* is a "treatise on the unalterable necessity of a realm in which humans can practice their innovative mental powers without being delimited by the utilitarian necessities of everyday life and logical thinking" (Schulte-Sasse 1986–87: 41). His work exerted great influence on other German philosophers such as Friedrich Schiller, and also on such popularizers of German thought as Mme. de Staël, Victor Cousin, E. A. Poe, Thomas Carlyle, and Samuel Taylor Coleridge, who diffused these theories in their own countries. Although Kant devoted the majority of the third critique to an analysis of the aesthetic judgment rather than art in general or the specific fine arts, his ideas were used to underwrite the autonomy, uniqueness, and purity of art. "On a tide of vaguely simplified Kantian thinking," William Wimsatt and Cleanth Brooks state, "such terms as 'German Aesthetics,' 'Kant's aesthetics,' 'freedom,' 'disinterestedness,' 'pure art,' 'pure poetry,' 'form,' and 'genius' were floated into currency" (1957: 477). The distinctiveness, independence, and integrity of art had received a philosophical underpinning.

Our understanding of art as a functionless, autonomous, and perfect form is a result of such philosophical speculations. But autonomous art is not a product simply of philosophy. It arose in response to the differentiation of social practice, one of the chief characteristics of modernity. Indeed, the separation of reason into the autonomous systems of art, science, and morality is what for Max Weber constituted the essence of modernity. Jürgen Habermas has argued that the project of modernity, as formulated by the Enlightenment, consisted of the attempt to develop an objective science, a universal morality, and an autonomous art according to their own inner logics.[5] Art emerged along with these two other systems with its own proper claim to reality. It evolved into an institution after it separated itself from other practices in the festival, aristocratic court, and church.

From Aristocratic Arts to Bourgeois Art

As art no longer partook in the religious ritual of the Middle Ages or the public festivals of feudal or courtly society, it lost its aura and began both to accumulate an aesthetic discourse and to acquire the status of an institution. In the bourgeois era art emerged as a historical category, with rules governing the production and reception of individual works. The transition from the courtly-aristocratic arts to the bourgeois institution of art witnessed not simply a modification of aesthetic function but the appearance of a distinct social site. In courtly society arts such as music and dance formed part of the festival and courtly culture. They were considered mimetic and served to glorify the prince; their primary task was political, "the legitimation of absolute rule" (Christa Bürger 1977: 10). The arts constituted public events celebrating absolute power; but they also entertained. But by the time of Goethe and Schiller the arts entered a process of formalization through which, dissolving their connection to courtly society, they formed an autotelic sphere of practices. Whereas the arts had been valued for the effects they had on an audience, bourgeois art was an instrument of self-understanding. Art became a private, individual affair, having withdrawn "from the space of public performance into the immanence of the representational sphere" (Wellbery 1984: 71). Poetic language, no longer a matter of eloquence or rhetoric, response or effect, as it had been seen from classical antiquity, evolved into a privileged form of transparent representation. As a representational practice, art did not simply entertain but moved, and the audience derived pleasure from both a well-executed performance and the intrinsic features of the represented object (45).[6] Because it was believed to have social effects, literature began to be regarded during the eighteenth century as the foremost representational art. In the Enlightenment project of social engineering literature emerged as the most effective means of socialization—the induction of people into bourgeois culture.

The Bourgeois Public Sphere

The bourgeois public sphere, as explained by Jürgen Habermas, arose in the attempt of the middle class to restrict the power of the absolutist state; it replaced the realm of monarchical authority over subjects with a sphere in which authority was determined by critical discussions. Consisting of institutions such as the press, schools, museums, theaters, and concert halls, the public sphere was created in the tension between the private and public realms; it mediated between civil society and the state apparatus. It was composed by private people with no official power who joined together as a public (1989: 27). Having arisen first in England at the end of the seventeenth century, it developed in France and Germany at the beginning of the eighteenth century.

This dimension of human activity had a discursive as well as social character. It comprised institutions such as coffeehouses, salons, newspapers, clubs, reading circles, and journals, which served as places of conversation and aided the dissemination of views on politics, literature, art, and philosophy. These spaces were occupied by individuals who believed that access to the arts should be determined by one's interests and education rather than social position. Indeed, they claimed to disregard social status; admission to the discussions was open to all educated property owners (Habermas 1989: 36). The aim of the new citizens—the civil servants, doctors, officers, teachers, priests—was to gain social acceptance, acquire political power, and to enlighten the general public through education. The topics under discussion eventually became part of the general exchange of public opinion. Since the debates had an ostensibly rational and universal aspect, judgments expressed within their framework reflected ideally not individual beliefs but the view of the majority. Public opinion, supposedly articulated through consensus, came to represent the views of all members in society.

In its early phase the bourgeois public sphere was rooted in the world of letters. The reading public for literature in England, for instance, was formed in the coffeehouse milieu of the late seventeenth century, in which there reigned a mixture of news and conversation, fiction and fact, informed opinion and baseless speculation (Hunter 1988: 503). The men who joined in the conversations were readers of journalism, didactic works, biography, travelogue, and history, becoming a generation later consumers of novels. Literary culture served as an important realm in which the bourgeois gained self-understanding and devised a repertory of shared opinions and beliefs. "Literary discussion," Eagleton says, "which had previously served as a form of legitimation of court society in the aristocratic salons, became an arena for political discussion in the middle classes" (1984: 10). There was a drive, Rolf Grimminger argues, to "literarify" society; that is, to educate it through the publicly available medium of literature (in Bürger et al. 1980: 118).

This tendency has not abated in our time; it is now called textualization, both in the literal and the metaphorical or Derridean sense. In the wake of modernism's apotheosis of the text modern culture has proposed the literary as its model and hermeneutics as its paradigm. Our thought, as Fredric Jameson has argued (1972), has a linguistic if not a textual obsession. Everything seems to come down to the sign or the text; nothing exists beyond language and its margins. Structuralism and deconstruction, acting on Mallarmé's cue, have taken it upon themselves to textualize the world and turn it into a book. *Text* in Derrida, like his notion of writing, takes an extended signification: the text is "henceforth no longer a finished corpus of writing, some content enclosed in a book or its margins, but a differential network, a fabric of traces referring endlessly to something other than itself, to other differential traces. Thus the text overruns all the limits assigned to it so far . . . all the limits, everything that was to be set up in opposition to writing (speech, life, the world, the real, history, and what not, every field of reference—to body or mind, conscious, or unconscious, politics, economics, and so forth)" (Derrida 1979: 84). Modernist and post-modernist textualization is a product of the Enlightenment valorization of literature.

Literary value in the public sphere was incorporated into the educational system as one of its fundamental elements. Literary writing (the telling of stories, teaching by example) was indispensable in the education of the public, which was thought to be incapable of unmediated rational thought. Literature became the most effective means of socialization, as it was thought to foster the collective internalization of socially important norms (Schulte-Sasse 1985: 109-10).[7] Writers such as Johann Christoph Gottsched recognized the value of all narrative discourses in social engineering; with his *Critische Dichtkunst* (1730) Gottsched intended to establish an enlightened literary culture in Germany. The cultural institutions of the public sphere served as a way of validating the newly acquired authority of the bourgeoisie. The middle classes could point to the existence of their arts in order to gain self-esteem in an absolutist state and a hierarchical society. The cultural goods of the public sphere, no longer the private property of the court or church, were becoming available to all citizens—to all readers, listeners, and observers (Habermas 1989: 40). In practice, however, the masses, half of which were illiterate, had neither the money nor the education to participate in this bourgeois market. The arts remained the venue of the bourgeoisie.

The middle classes gained access to dramatic productions only after the courtly theaters opened their doors to this new audience. In the Renaissance and the baroque, theaters were part of royal or noble residences, hidden from everyone but the prince and his guests. This isolation proclaimed, albeit implicitly, that the drama within, like the physical structure itself, belonged to the aristocrats. With the construction of commercial theaters in the bourgeois era dramatic art reached a mass audience. Theaters became significant elements of urban design as they changed from private possessions to public monuments (Carlson 1989: 73). They began to be erected on a grand scale: the Opera House of Frederick the Great (1741), the national theater (1766) in Berlin; London's Covent Garden was redesigned in 1809. These cultural monuments also served as symbols of national unity.

Until the eighteenth century music had definite ritualistic or celebratory ends and could be heard either in church or in the residences of princes. It was useful in maintaining power and prestige, inscribed within the systems of power (Attali 1985: 57). For the lower classes in Europe music was an ubiquitous phenomenon (Leppert 1989: 28). In the concert halls of the bourgeoisie, however, freed from the purposes of social representation, music was transformed into a separate sonoric entity. People paid for it as for any other commodity. It became autonomous and secular when, separated from the background noise of the festival, court ceremony, or church, it emerged as an autotelic form to be appreciated for itself. No longer in the air, part of the life-praxis, music became an art.

Painting followed a similar development. In earlier centuries works of art were displayed primarily within the private holdings of the aristocracy, royal families, and the church. It was only after paintings were publicly exhibited in the salons of the eighteenth century that lay people had the opportunity to view these works in any numbers. Painting entered the lives of Parisians in the salon exhibitions first organized by the Academy in 1737 (Crow 1985: 1). These pioneering public exhibits attracted a great number of viewers from the middle classes whose opinions and verdicts began to determine taste. Eventually they were able to appropriate the visual arts. At the beginning of the nineteenth century the salon was theoretically open to all artists, not just those selected by the Academy. Universal access was the single principle of the public sphere. As the critic La Font put it in 1747, "a painting on exhibition is like a printed book seeing the day, a play performed on stage—anyone has the right to judge it" (in Habermas 1989: 40). In 1818 the Luxembourg Museum was created for the exhibition of works by living French artists. Although the aristocracy and government still commissioned artists, by the nineteenth century popular taste, represented by the private gallery and the art dealer, replaced the authority of the elite. Popular opinion demanded smaller genre pictures as opposed to the grand historical paintings of the Academy. After 1855 members of the manufacturing classes began buying pictures in larger numbers not only for aesthetic but also, and significantly, for financial reasons (Mainardi 1987: 33). The purchase of paintings for investment deprived art of its aura and transformed it into a commodity.[8]

The arts were progressively wrested from the control of the court and brought under the authority of the bourgeoisie. This class erected theaters, libraries, opera houses, concert halls, museums, and art galleries in order to see itself represented artistically. The institutionalization of the arts began in these public places around the end of the eighteenth century. In time a specialized discourse—disseminated through journals and taught at schools and centers of higher learning—organized around each art, thus giving rise to art history, music appreciation, and literary criticism.

Literature, as mentioned earlier, emerged as one of the most significant cultural forces in the public sphere of the eighteenth century. While music and painting existed before the public sphere as the arts of the nobility, literature was valorized by the middle class in its creation of a national culture. This class invented literature by transforming practices of reading and writing, and by circumscribing the term's range to include only fictional texts.

Previous ages did not posit such a stark division between imaginative and discursive writing. The word *literature* itself, for example, stemming from the Latin *litteratura* (a translation of the Greek *grammatike*) meant, in its most basic form, grammar.[9] *Litteratura* had multiple uses: it signified variously writing, grammar, instruction, education, or the use of letters. In antiquity the term *litterae* was coterminous with *humanitas* and *paideia*. During the High Middle Ages *litteratura* referred to anything written, a usage English and German have retained, as when printed brochures from a travel agency are called literature (Godzich and Spadaccini 1986: x) or when bibliography is referred to as *Literatur* in German. In the Renaissance *litterae* was combined with *humanae* to distinguish secular writing from sacred texts. In the seventeenth century it was coupled with *belles lettres* and used in the extended sense of literary culture, erudition, or knowledge of classical languages (Wellek 1978: 18). This modern meaning of literature, conveying an idea of an individual's literacy and educational status, was a more general term than poetry or poesy, the words then current for imaginative composition. But *literature* did not suggest at that time active composition, as did poetry, but simply reading. It was a category of use rather than of production (Williams 1977: 47).

At this stage, however, the word *literature* indicated the reading experience not simply of imaginative writing but of all kinds of texts, including philosophy, history, poetry, essays, and theology.[10] In the eighteenth century *literature* began to shed this extended meaning and refer to a core of imaginative writings. No longer a quality of the reader, it was the creation of the author's imagination. Furthermore, literature, comprising only fictional writing, was incorporated as an art within the new system of arts. Texts within its domain demanded special treatment. Under the imperatives of the new interpretive modes literary texts required silent reading. Consumers of literature did not concern themselves with the veracity of its statements nor did they regard it relevant for specific practical purposes. They responded to the texts irrespective of their communicative and purposive ends. Literature came to represent a specialized form of writing in a sphere of human activity defined by the imagination and beauty.

The Dissolution of the Public Sphere

The elevation of literature to the privileged realm of aesthetics also led to its commodification. While in the early public sphere literary discussions promoted mutual understanding among citizens through a realm of shared cultural assumptions, literature after the capitalization of the book industry (which in Germany began in the 1840s) became a consumable good. The progressive capitalization of the book trade resulted in the subjugation of literature to the profit motive. For much of the nineteenth century the English novel, for instance, was produced for financial profit even though its aestheticization as the dominant literary form in the 1840s concealed its commodity status (Lovell 1987: 74). While in previous decades literary discourse had been put in the service of political enlightenment, under the new order it became attached to the apparatus of competitive capitalism. Reviewers, having abandoned broader pedagogical goals, addressed a cultural elite as their audience; they guided educated readers—with the help of a canon of respectable texts—through the excessive supply of an expanding market. Their critical oeuvre, informed by the aesthetics of autonomy, saw its task as the interpretation of individual works. It was devoted to art rather than to the public (Hohendahl 1989: 122).

Even as early as 1770 the German bourgeois avant-garde began to dissociate itself from its class and to divorce its aesthetic taste from that of the reading public (Hohendahl 1982: 54). The cultured, largely male readers appropriated the classics and contemporary "serious" authors while the anonymous and relatively uneducated consumers turned to the literature of entertainment. The contradictions inherent in the dichotomies of pleasure/enjoyment, pure taste/impure taste, high/low literature, and connoisseur/consumer exposed the lack of consensus in the public sphere. Ideological claims regarding the universal validity of and global access to the aesthetic simply could not hold. Though in principle art and literature were available to all, only the educated could really appreciate and understand them.[11] In effect art belonged to them. Since the mass consumer was thought to possess an inadequate aesthetic sensibility, and since only a minority participated in literary discourse, literary practice could no longer be validated by the public sphere. In the early stages of the Enlightenment critics spoke among equals as people versed in literature, but by the romantic period they had turned into specialists bearing privileged knowledge.

The commodification of the other arts followed literature's lead. During the late seventeenth and early eighteenth centuries paintings began to be produced mostly for a market instead of for a single patron or the church. They acquired the status of wares in the capitalist system of exchange, defined by their prospective sale to a new class of buyers rather than by commissions. Intermediaries, acting either as agents for the artists or for the consumers of art, facilitated the distribution of products (Wartofsky 1980: 245).[12] Similarly, music became a consumable good when it was deritualized, sold as spectacle, and stockpiled. After the musician was enrolled in the division of labor, Attali argues, bourgeois individualism began to be enacted; instead of legitimating absolute order, music made people believe in its existence and in its impossibility outside of exchange (1985: 57)

In the commodification of art bourgeois culture confronted one of its latent contradictions, the conflict between its idealistic-pedagogical and its economic interests. This, according to Jochen Schulte-Sasse, had the effect of imposing upon the book, the most significant instrument of Enlightenment social politics, a precariously double existence as commodity (*Ware*) and spirit (*Geist*) (in Bürger et al. 1980: 99). Art could not sustain this tension. It therefore invoked the Kantian injunction against interest of any kind to distinguish itself from mercenary practice and thereby preserve its sacred nature. Art differentiated itself from the crafts as literature moved apart from sentimental writing. High literature claimed to be free from the mechanism of the market while low literature was by definition a product of that market. Real literature, unlike commodity literature, was not subject to the laws of supply and demand but to its own aesthetic standards. Indeed, one of the projects of aesthetics had been to separate pure creation from vulgar production so as to promote the vitality of real art. Kant and Moritz attempted, with the notion of *Ding an sich*, to save the inner value of the work from the threat posed by its relationship to utilitarian products and the mechanical arts. Aesthetics insists that the value of the work lies in the thing itself rather than in socially determined needs or norms. This theory, in effect, represses the mediation of the market. By ascribing to works spontaneity, individuality, and autonomy it conceals their commodity status.

The distinction between the pure pleasure of the few and the crude enjoyment of the masses is founded on the refusal of impure sensation.[13] In order to bolster high culture, pure taste required its dialectical opposite— impure taste. Aesthetics postulated coarse taste as a negative comparison to pure sensation in order to empower the latter with cultural authority. Pleasure, disinterestedness, and refinement needed enjoyment, seduction, and vulgarity to distinguish themselves (in the same way that affluent neighborhoods require impoverished residential areas as a comparison). In postulating a distinction between aesthetic and ordinary consumption the discourse of aesthetics valorized the aesthetic experience over other experiences. As capitalism began to subsume most areas of life, high art presented itself as one of the last refuges, untainted by market instincts, where the individual could find peace, transcendence, and universal communicability.

Social Differentiation and the Aesthetics of Autonomy

The separation of art from other practices led to a specialization of its function. Art exploited its unique potential to demonstrate that the experience it provided could not be obtained from other activities.[14] To claim authority, art had also to claim an exclusive role, separate from those of politics and religion. Although it freed itself from the interventions by the state and church, art could not forget the ambition of the Enlightenment— it still aspired to some sort of social effect. Herein lay the paradox: art aspired to both aesthetic autonomy and social consequences. On the one hand it was functionless; on the other, it sought social relevance.

The formalization of art formed part of the general differentiation within modern societies during the seventeenth and eighteenth centuries as the subsystems of politics, economics, science, law, education, and religion became dissociated from one another and organized in relatively autonomous frameworks. Functional differentiation, according to the German sociologist Niklas Luhmann, "organizes communication processes around special functions to be fulfilled at the level of society" (1982: 236). This phenomenon is a feature of modern societies, which are also characterized, as I mentioned earlier, by secularization, nationalism, industrial capitalism, bureaucraticization, parliamentary government and universal suffrage, individualism, the privileging of the future, and the dissociation of the aesthetic from moral and political realms. A society shifts in the direction of functional differentiation if it "introduces compulsory education for everyone, if every person (whether nobleman or commoner, Christian, Jew or Muslim, infant or adult) has the same legal status, if 'the public' is provided with a political function as an electorate, if every individual is acknowledged as choosing or not choosing a religious commitment, and if everybody, given the necessary resources, can buy anything and pursue any occupation" (243). Differentiation begins as a specialization of roles, when at least two distinct roles are organized around a specific function: for instance, clerics and laymen, politicians and the public, teachers and pupils. Usually the political function is the first to split off from kinship organization (Hoogvelt 1978: 28). While in stratified systems the extended family performs a variety of activities, such as providing political authority, ensuring economic productivity, and transmitting cultural information, in a differentiated society many of these functions are taken over by specialized institutions. The household is separated from business as personal wealth is demarcated from business finances.

As regards the aesthetic we have seen that in stratified societies of western Europe, organized into unequal and hierarchical strata, the arts were integrated in the praxis of the court, church, or festival. Under the general process of differentiation, however, the arts were unified under one concept (aesthetic autonomy) and ascribed a compensatory function: to provide a space of deliverance from the consequences of social fragmentation. Art, as Schulte-Sasse observes, emerged in the second half of the eighteenth century as a privileged sphere of cultural activities; it was increasingly seen "as a realm of reconciliation and redemption that was able to suspend the negative side-effects of the functional and social differentiation of society" (1989: 87). Paradoxically, art evolved into an autonomous institution yet was assigned the task of transcending social differentiation by devising unalienated experiences. "As a functionally differentiated space, art under modern conditions is at once structurally equivalent to other differentiated activities and burdened with the primary function of sublating differentiation in a reconciliatory manner" (87). It is thus a product of modernity but also desires the Other of modernity, an undifferentiated totality. Art both affirms the structures of modernity and criticizes them.

The functional dissociation of art undermined the sociopolitical project of the Enlightenment. The times were right not for political revolts but, as Friedrich Schlegel observed, for an "aesthetic revolution, through which that which is objective in the aesthetic education of the moderns could become dominant" (1795-96 1947: 101). The Enlightenment cause of political emancipation became aestheticized. In *On the Aesthetic Education of Man* (1794-95), Friedrich Schiller proposed art's most salient feature, aesthetic autonomy, as the basis for human freedom. The prime mission of art, Schiller wrote, is not to entertain but to edify, civilize, and ennoble. If "man" is to solve the "problem of politics in practice he will have to approach it through the problem of the aesthetic, because it is only through Beauty that man makes his way to Freedom" (1967: 9). Beauty, Schiller claimed, offers us the possibility of becoming human beings (149). Taste alone brings harmony in society; while other forms of communication divide society, the aesthetic mode unites it, "because it relates to that which is common to all" (215). Beauty provides not only an undifferentiated identity but also the hope for a more just society, especially at a time of social unrest and failed revolutions. The aesthetic is universally valid and democratically attainable; each person under the right conditions has the right to contemplate it. Schiller underscored its egalitarian nature: "In the Aesthetic [but differentiated] State everything—even the tool which serves—is a free citizen, having equal rights with the noblest" (219). Schiller ascribed to the aesthetic a mediating function, to reconcile the interests of the individuals with those of the collective.

The Greek Difference

The appearance of an autonomous aesthetic in European society and the institutionalization of the arts did not occur in Greece in the manner outlined above. It becomes necessary to make such a statement only because, as I argued in the first chapter, contemporary criticism still believes that art and literature are universally available creations. The imported concept of autonomous art did not function in Greece as might have been expected; that is, it did not follow the history of its European prototype or perform the same role. The principal reason for this "imperfect" integration is the absence of a social and cultural context for its reception and future development. It was imposed from above through centralized planning rather than having emerged in response to changes in Greek society.

The bourgeoisie of western Europe privileged literature in their construction of a shared culture. This sociopolitical project became aestheticized when literature took on a compensatory function. The autonomous aesthetic arose as a consequence of social differentiation. It delivered the citizens of modernity into a utopian realm of undifferentiated unity where they could transcend the problems of their fragmented society. But how could literature or the aesthetic fulfill these tasks for people whose society had not been compartmentalized into separate zones or who had not experienced the personal and social alienation of industrialization? They obviously could not, as my analysis of the Greek canon has shown.

In this chapter I will discuss the factors responsible for the Greek difference by focusing on resistance to modernity. I will examine the genealogy of the concept of literature, particularly the tension between aesthetic autonomy and local exigency, in order to study the modifications in its form and function as it adapted to the Greek situation. I will deal here with the "failure," the Other of modernity, and the agents that obstructed the seemingly linear effort to westernize Greece. I begin with the local elements that frustrated differentiation and hence undermined some of the most fundamental features of bourgeois society.

In Greece, as in other Balkan countries, clientelistic networks developed immediately after the introduction of a centralized state, extending family and kinship ties into the body politic, and thereby denying the pretensions of government and bureaucracy to be autonomous institutions. These networks were the result of the imposition of bourgeois political institutions upon a stratified society. Before 1821 political, economic, social, and religious activities were not dissociated from one another. Although, as I indicated in chapter 2, society under the Ottomans was separated into occupational groups, the peasants, the bulk of the population, did not participate in the exercise of political authority. In the local communities individuals performed one or any number of roles. The priest served as village leader; likewise a religious assembly could have also functioned as a political body. With the introduction of autonomous constructs these traditional patterns of interpersonal relationship did not disappear; they penetrated the parliamentary and bureaucratic systems. In a sense they served as extended families, offering protection to their members at all levels of society. Spreading both vertically and horizontally, they became the "central mechanism of social integration and political organization" (Diamandouros 1983: 45).

Although the networks frustrated social differentiation, they were in fact a product of modernity, since they appeared as a result of political modernization without industrialization, the incorporation of bourgeois institutions without a polity of citizens. The strong central state in a rural agrarian society unprepared for bourgeois political and administrative structures became the only vehicle for political power, social mobility, and distribution of wealth. The state, as is true in countries of the Third World (Roxborough 1979: 142), dominated civil society. Peasants related to the state largely through their patrons, who helped them evade the law, seek redress, or manipulate authority; the peasants in turn voted for their patrons (Legg 1977: 285). These links between bearers of unequal social and economic power (Tsoucalas 1978: 5) served to integrate the peasants into the state, a factor that inhibited the formation of strong peasant movements like those in other Balkan countries (Mouzelis 1986: 44, 73).[15] The importance of the state made it necessary for all citizens to participate in relationships that would guarantee access to the economic surplus. This phenomenon, according to Tsoucalas, explains the "over-politicization" of Greek society. "The majority of the ruling strata were driven into the exercise of 'politics' as a profession . . . and the mass of the population attained their most immediate interests in relation to their access to protection by the organized political power" (11).[16]

The clientelistic networks are good examples of the structures produced by the imperfect integration of western prototypes and the autochthonous infrastructure. They show that traditional kinship patterns, far from being eradicated, transformed themselves in the new context. Equally important, they point to the absence of a differentiated social structure like that out of which autonomous institutions emerged in the West. The building of liberal and egalitarian institutions without a bourgeois public sphere and industrial capitalism principally accounted for the failure of modernization during the nineteenth century, particularly Trikupis's program in the 1880s. The client-patron relationships, for instance, undermined even the idea of universal male suffrage—guaranteed by the constitution of 1864—because people felt they did not all have equal access to government. Since they did not believe in the supposed neutrality of the body politic, they tried to circumvent it. Indeed, the idea of disinterestedness was as foreign to the political as to the literary practice of the nineteenth century. These networks blurred the fundamental bourgeois demarcation between the private and public realms.

A bourgeois public sphere, as a cultural and social foundation for modernization, could not emerge under these conditions. Though individual institutions were imposed from the top, modernity could not be imported as a totality and without obstruction from below. The modernizing process did not lead to the duplication in Greece of European history. The newspaper *Neologos Athenon* (Sept. 6, 1874) addressed with mocking humor the uncomfortable fit between new constructs and the country's infrastructure: "We have neither ships, nor an army, nor roads but in a short time we will have an Academy. Let Turkey tremble! Let the Byzantine Empire rejoice! The Academy is being erected" (cited by Skopetea 1988: 76). While the westernizers built an academy, they could not establish the social, economic, and political base to support and ensure its successful integration in society.

A Not-So-Autonomous Literature

Literature provides another example of the tensions in Greek society. Although literary writing was dissociated in the 1920s and 1930s from the general field of textuality, this new construct did not win wide acceptance even among intellectuals and writers. While certain cultural elites promoted an autonomous literature encompassing fictional texts, others continued to conceive of literary writing in a nonaesthetic manner.

This was the case in the nineteenth century when four designations for "literature" were in circulation: *filoloyia, grammatoloyia, grammatia,* and *logotehnia.*[17] The classical philologist Ioannis Sikutris contends that nineteenth-century Greek scholars could not arrive at a common appellation for what in western Europe—where they all were studying or living—they understood as "literature," "littérature," "Literatur," and "letteratura" (1956: 120). I. Pantazidis, also a philologist, had made this very same argument many decades earlier in an article "Filoloyia, Grammatoloyia, Logotehnia " when he sought Greek terms to render the meaning of the French *littérature* or the German *Literatur.* After explaining to his Greek readership that the German *Nationalliteratur* signified creative writing only, he proposed that the most appropriate Greek word to translate this meaning was neither *filoloyia,* nor *grammatoloyia,* nor *grammatia,* but *logotehnia* (1886: 545, 547). Pantazidis's suggestion did not seem to have had any effect, even though his article was published in *Estia,* one of the most influential magazines of the day. Indeed, *logotehnia* was not listed in Stefanos Kumanudis's *Sinagoyi Neon Lexeon* (Collection of new words, 1900), a catalogue of neologisms from 1453 till 1900. The four terms, particularly *filoloyia* and *logotehnia,* continued to be used interchangeably up to the first two decades of the twentieth century.

The lack of unanimity as to a Greek word for "literature" points to a central problem expatriate scholars were facing: they were importing a terminology unsuitable or irrelevant not only to Greek writing but to Greek society as a whole.[18] They were seeking a Greek word to denote a group of texts whose coexistence had not been deemed necessary. *Logotehnia* comes to approximate the European concept of literature—the goal of these scholars—only in the early twentieth century. Indeed, Kostis Palamas, a distinguished poet, foremost representative of the Generation of the 1880s, and one of the first "critics," did not use the word in his critical oeuvre (Ditsa 1988: 124). The lack of consensus compelled Sikutris in the 1930s to introduce some regularity to the discussion. In his article he suggested that *grammatia* refer to the whole body of written texts of a nation, *logotehnia* to creative writing, and *filoloyia* to the study of the two (121, 125).[19] Sikutris's own writing clearly demonstrates the existence of a separate category for fictional texts. But his work belongs to the modernizing program of the 1930s, which sought a functionally differentiated aesthetic realm. There were isolated cases before him, such as Pantazidis's article and Cavafy's poetry,[20] which promoted literature as an autonomous sphere of textuality. But by and large "literary" texts were not regarded in the nineteenth century as an exceptional category of writing. Indeed, no space was assigned to the literary in those treatises from the late eighteenth and early nineteenth centuries that addressed Greek writing. Scholars of that period neither treated literature as an isolated subject of knowledge nor conceived of genres such as poetry and drama as distinct from other types of textuality.

Literary History as National Politics

The differences in taxonomic criteria between the 1930s and the early 1800s can be seen in Yeoryios Zaviras's (a merchant from Macedonia) *Nea Ellas i Ellinikon Theatron* (written in the latter part of the eighteenth century and published posthumously in 1872), an influential work that covered the entire expanse of Greek writing. The author's purpose, as set forth in his title, was to compile a catalogue of Greek authors and their works since the capture of Constantinople by the Ottomans in 1453.[21] His interest lay unambiguously in Greek writing of every kind: philosophy, theology, mathematics, natural sciences, rhetoric, and medicine. Interestingly, among the scholars in these fields he included poets such as Yeoryios Hortatzis, Vitzentsos Kornaros, Rigas Velestinlis, and Kesarios Dapontes—writers who a century later would be dissociated from this context and placed in the autonomous category of literature. Zaviras simply felt no need to differentiate between the poet and nonpoet.

Although Zaviras addressed himself to all forms of Greek writing, Iakovos Rizos-Nerulos characterized Zaviras's book in his *Cours de littérature grecque moderne* (1827) as a "revue critique des principaux ouvrages de la littérature grecque moderne" (134)—a critical review of the principal works of modern Greek "literature." The meaning Rizos-Nerulos assigned to *littérature* is broad. His book dealt with the literary, in the modern understanding of the word, no more than did Zaviras's. It was subsequently translated into Greek in 1870 as *Istoria ton Grammaton para tis Neoteris Ellisi* (History of modern Greek letters). The French *littérature* had been rendered as *letters,* broadly meaning education and culture, a close approximation of Rizos-Nerulos's usage. He had examined extensively the development of the Greek language from classical times to the present under the heading of *grammatoloyia.* He then moved to an analysis of the first stages of Greek *filoloyia* (written culture), as manifested in the building of schools, the rise in the number of translations, and the transference of European learning to Greece. His interest here was in the enlightenment of the Greeks. He concluded with a list of renowned Greek authors in the categories of theology, rhetoric, history, philosophy, philology, translations, narrations, stories (*mithistorie*), and lyric poetry. Writing in general, although denoted *littérature,* was Rizos-Nerulos's true concern.

Andreas Papadopulos-Vretos, a librarian of the Ionian Academy on Corfu, conceived of writing similarly in his encyclopedic catalogue of books (1854-57) printed in either vernacular or archaizing Greek from the downfall of the Byzantine Empire to the founding of the Greek nation.[22] His aim, as stated in the prologue, was to instill in Greeks an awareness of their own cultural productivity, to teach them their written tradition. Realizing the need for catalogues of modern Greek letters (*grammatia*) in such an enterprise, he published his book with the intention, he wrote, of introducing readers to "the progress [made] by our national culture and language." Believing written culture to be "the true picture of the intellectual, moral, and political condition of literate [*pepedevmenon*] nations," he hoped to demonstrate that even under the "barbarian yoke" Greeks never ceased cultivating letters. His purpose was to use literature, in the extended sense, as a means of socializing Greeks into the values of the nation. Writing constituted an important part of the Enlightenment project to educate people and produce a collective culture—a "picture" of the nation—in which they could envision their national solidarity.

Papadopulos-Vretos divided his work into two parts: *vivlia ekklisiastika* (ecclesiastical books) and *vivlia filoloyika ke epistimonika* ("literary" and scholarly books). The second section is of particular interest here because in this inventory of secular texts Papadopulos-Vretos's taxonomic criteria become apparent. Predictably, he records grammars, classical texts, lexica, scholia, translations, books on philosophy, history, geography—but also "literary" texts such as the *Erofili, Thisia tu Avraam, Erotokritos,* and the *Sholion ton Delikaton Eraston* by Rigas. The author clearly did not consider these latter texts sufficiently distinct to classify them separately. Whereas he distinguishes between the ecclesiastical and the secular, between the sacred and the profane, he does not separate the literary from the nonliterary. His object of study is *filoloyia,* in both its extended sense as written culture and the more limited meaning of philology.

Konstantinos Sathas turned his attention to compiling a catalogue of all available Greek texts written between 1453 and 1821. His tome is a comprehensive register, as the subtitle announces, of the "biographies of Greeks who have distinguished themselves in letters" (1868, Preface).[23] He too did not allot a separate space to creative writing. Sathas placed poets such as Yeoryilas, Kornaros, and Foskolo among grammarians, translators, philosophers, theologians, and historians. The poets were included simply because they wrote in Greek.

All these compilations partook in the enterprise of establishing a national identity. Their authors, most of them purists, uncritically interested themselves in all texts, literary or not, that could be said to contribute to a grand narrative that, when rehearsed in the consciousness of all Greeks, would foster the collective internalization of nationally important norms and values. Such texts would enable identification with the nation and help designate patterns of social conduct. "Literature" would thus serve multifarious purposes of social engineering in the construction of cultural identities, an effort succinctly summarized in a statement describing Dimitrios Vikelas's goal in writing his own work: to outline "the intellectual state of the nation, the history of its letters and education" (1871: 2). Having posited a direct relationship between the political history of a nation and its "literature," Vikelas went on to prove a continuity in Greek written culture from the classical, through the Byzantine, to the modern period, uninterrupted by four hundred years of Ottoman rule (29). This was to be the textual heritage of the Greeks. Though a gap existed between ethnicity and state, insofar as the majority of Greeks still resided outside the kingdom, Greeks everywhere could find in the written tradition a common fund of experiences. For the scholars of the period the collection of Greek texts was their investment in this fund. Such an enterprise did not presume a dissociation of the political and aesthetic spheres.

A Differentiated Space for Literature

A site for literary writing was opened up in Alexandros Rangavis's study (1887), a shortened version of his *Histoire littéraire de la Grèce moderne* published in Paris a decade earlier. In the first and second sections of this work, in which he discussed Greek letters from 1453 to 1821, Rangavis dissociated ordinary from "poetic" writing. Although not classifying Cretan drama, the poetry of Rigas Fereos, Vilaras, and Iakovos Rizos-Nerulos as literature, he recognized it as a unique group, distinct from prose.

In the last part of the book, covering Greek writing from 1821 to his present, Rangavis expanded on this simple distinction between prose and poetry by further distinguishing scholarly *(epistimonika)* books from those belonging to belles lettres *(kalliloyia).* Drama, poems, short stories, and novels form a genus quite separate from translations and lexica, and from works on philosophy, history, political science, and the natural sciences. Rangavis insisted that in the broad range of Greek writing *(filoloyia)* discursive and belletristic works should be divorced from one another. Without dwelling on this division, Rangavis proceeded to discuss some authors, primarily poets, whose work fell in the domain of creative writing: Kalvos, Solomos, Valaoritis, the Sutsos brothers, Lefkias, Ioannu, Zalokostas, Markoras, Kallivursis, Kalligas, Parashos, Drosinis, Surris, and Palamas. It is important to note that Rangavis saw these writers as poets rather than "literary" figures. Rangavis carved out a separate space for literary writing without necessarily conceiving of this category as functionally autonomous. His aim was still to outline the tradition of Greek writing. Like his predecessors he strived to trace for the nation its grammatological heritage. In contrast to his precursors, however, and in spite of his purist ideology, his book acknowledged a more prominent position for fiction than ever before.

The isolation of fictional texts from the general class of writing and the contraction of literature's semantic potential from the total field of Greek textuality to belles lettres and "imaginative" writing can be witnessed in literary histories written by non-Greeks: Rudolf Nicolai (1876),[24] Karl Dieterich (1909),[25] and D. C. Hesseling (1924).[26] The first self-consciously historical account of Greek literature to appear in Greece was the *Istoria tis Neoellinikis Logotehnias* (History of modern Greek literature) by Ilias Vutieridis (1924–27).[27]

Vutieridis, himself aware of the gap separating him from his precursors, discussed the differences between his work and previous histories. His history of modern Greek literature, he noted, was limited to imaginative and creative works and thus excluded philosophical, theological, and scholarly texts. An examination of those works, he observed, does not belong to a history of literature, since modern literary history chiefly addresses "genuine literary works" (14). He conceded that this was not the practice of his predecessors, who, as philologists, regarded all texts as "literary." His volume, however, was concerned not with *filoloyia,* writing in general, but with *logotehnia,* the accepted modern term for literature, which was used by Vutieridis in his title. Although Vutieridis did not consistently distinguish *filoloyia* from *logotehnia,* he kept within the boundaries of the new definition. Throughout his study he repeatedly reminded readers that his subject was literary, noting, for instance, that he discussed the demotic songs "as literary works [*logotehnimata*] rather than monuments of folklore," (23) contrary to the usual approach of his precursors and most contemporaries. He also referred to the Renaissance epic *Erotokritos* as a "literary" work, the beauty of which had been appreciated by countless readers (179).

Vutieridis took a prominent role in the mission to consolidate the position of demoticism in Greek society. His concept of a differentiated literature was an attempt to appropriate literary practice from the purists by inventing a new entity along with folklore. The appearance of Vutieridis's *History* shows the extent to which the literary had been rarefied. But this view was still in the minority. At the turn of the twentieth century literature was still discussed from the perspective of national identity. Critics were drawn to literary texts primarily because they could use them in the ideological battles of the day.

We can see this in Aristos Kampanis's *Istoria tis Neoellinikis Logotehnias* (History of modern Greek literature, 1925). For the most part the author concentrated on literature that he understood as incorporating imaginative works. Nevertheless, he smuggled in such nonliterary texts as a modern Greek grammar by Sofianos (1534), the *Turcograecia* (1584) by Martin Crucius, the works of the French scholar Du Cange, as well as those of Korais and Psiharis.[28] On the whole Kampanis remained faithful to the modern notion of literature, but his aims were not purely literary. While he hoped to delineate the development of Greek literature, his more pressing goal was to intervene, by means of this history, in the linguistic controversy, for Kampanis's overriding concern lay with "demotic literary production" (9) rather than with the general field of Greek literature. As a demoticist, he composed a very selective history, discussing solely those authors who wrote in the vernacular. He hailed, for instance, the demotic epic *Erotokritos* as the most significant linguistic and literary monument of the prerevolutionary period, and characterized its author Kornaros as one of the most influential in Greek literature (65). On the other hand, he condemned purist poets for having introduced a "Byzantine scholarly tradition" into Athens. Specifically, he dismissed the work of Alexandros Sutsos as of little interest to literary study (112, 116).

Although Kampanis thus limited the concept of literature, he positioned it within the social conflicts of the day. His book was very interested, its ideological position unambiguous, and its politics unabashedly explicit. One cannot speak here of an aesthetics of autonomy. Vutieridis and Kampanis conceptually isolated literature but did not aestheticize it. Writers, particularly those like Kampanis, imported the modern notion of literature in order to consolidate a popular national tradition. They saw in such a concept another possibility of maintaining their hold on culture, given that it was the only realm available to demoticists. The difference in degree of formalization, however, between Vutieridis's and Kampanis's conceptions of literature indicates the lack of consensus even within the demoticist movement. Vutieridis's notion of a literature radically dissociated from other writing remained an anomaly even in the context of literary history. Indeed, his efforts were undone, as I shall show, by K. Th. Dimaras, who expanded Vutieridis's contracted concept in order to incorporate more easily the revaluations of the canon by the Generation of the 30s.

Critique of modernity

Dimaras's attempt in *Istoria tis Neoellinikis Logotehnias* (History of modern Greek literature, 1948), the most influential literary history in Greek criticism, to broaden the signification of literature offers an example within literary discourse of Greek opposition to European models. In resisting the functional differentiation of literature, he argued for its continued integration in social and political life. Even within demoticist discourse there was no absolute unanimity; constructs introduced by one group were rejected or modified by another. Purposeful modernization thus developed unevenly.

As the clientelistic networks obstructed the liberal institutions of government and administration, so in the realm of culture Hellenocentric forces struggled against the influx of western goods. At roughly the time of the histories by Vutieridis and Kampanis the antiwestern strains in Greek society, always present in one form or another since the second crusade in 1204, were articulated by Ion Dragumis (1878–1920). The main conflict running through Dragumis's oeuvre is the opposition—defining Greek society since its encounter with modernity and central to modernization theories—between, on the one hand, the foreign and modern and, on the other, the indigenous and traditional. The worst calamity befalling Greeks was, according to Dragumis, their imitation of European culture, which extinguished their demotic and Byzantine traditions (1978: 51). Modernization initiated two tendencies: *xenolatria* and *arheolatria*—the worship of the foreign and the ancient. Of the two he considered the former more destructive to Hellenism, which, according to him, is opposed to cosmopolitanism and "les idées modernes" (73, 79). Dragumis also rejected bourgeois political institutions. It would have been better for the Greeks, he wrote, to have chosen "Athenian democracy or the Spartan form of government" instead of the constitutional model (1976: 68). The best solution, however, would have been neither the western nor the ancient but the Byzantine and religious heritage, and the local form of self-government practiced in the Ottoman Empire.

The Greeks, he insisted, dazzled as they are by western ways, ignore their own culture and accept a way of life incompatible with authentic

Greek society. His arguments, powerfully articulated, pointed to the misfit between western and Orthodox culture. "The English, French, and Germans wrote scholarly books about their states. And the Greek scholars took these books and translated them literally into Greek, saying: 'This happens in England. Therefore . . . this should happen in Greece as well" (108-9). They failed to see, however, that Greece does not resemble England, which developed "naturally" out of its own traditions, but instead is an "artificial construct by foreign diplomats."

The importation of statist ideology, Dragumis contended, destroyed autochthonous political practices. In place of local communities (*kinotites*) the westernizers established municipalities; in place of the bishop and the patriarch they installed the prefect (*nomarhis*), the secretary/minister, and the king. Modernization led to a greater revolution than that against the sultan (23), for not only politics but culture had been also affected. The German-trained architect introduced new designs, the tailor imported new fashions, the poet published "romantic verses" (1978: 57). Everything now was mixed with not completely digested "new and Frankish [western] ideas" (1976: 24).

Dragumis's critique of modernity resembles recent arguments against modernization theories (see Introduction). Greek culture, he claimed, a product of both the East and West, cannot be rebuilt according to the criteria and standards of the West only (104). In questioning the introduction of ideas and institutions that are irrelevant, superfluous, or dangerous to Greek culture, he strived to undo some of the side effects of modernization, chief of which was the separation of the Greeks from their homeland. The Greek state would remain for him artificial until it encompassed all of Hellenism. But the irredentist dream to expand the boundaries of the state and reconcile the conflict between state and nation had failed in 1922. The Greeks of Asia Minor arrived in the kingdom as refugees with memories of lost homes and fallen empires. His image of a national home, founded on Byzantine and Orthodox principles, a plain (*kampos*) small but beautiful, sweeter than the rest, rich in memories, lively and many-colored (61-62), was never attained. Dragumis longed for a society untainted by western ways. This vision of an undifferentiated space prior to modernity was to be fulfilled in the 1930s by the aesthetic notion of Greekness.

The challenge facing critics of modernity was how to define the Hellenic difference, given the overwhelming influence of western culture. Recognizing that the military structure, legislative system, educational institutions, art, architecture, and lifestyle had western prototypes, they often resorted to the discourse of romantic nationalism to preserve the integrity of Greek culture. Their arguments advocated both resistance to foreign ways and the rediscovery of the tradition destroyed by the Enlightenment. Periklis Yiannopulos (1869–1910), a prominent opponent of modernization, denounced emulation of the West, and advocated reliance on indigenous models. Greek culture, he insisted, must "flourish again and create a new civilization" (1963: 84).

The resurgence of Hellenism quite often involved a return to popular practices traced back to Byzantium. Tradition for many writers usually represented the Byzantine inheritance as transmitted through the Orthodox Church and the scholars living under Ottoman rule. Against the hegemony of the West these critics proposed the culture of the East. By the East they meant the culture of Orthodoxy rather than the Orient, for the Orthodox Church had defined itself as eastern, a characteristic inherited from the Byzantines, who constituted the Eastern Empire, in contradistinction to Rome and the Western Empire.

Opposition to the West had a long history. The Church itself had been militantly antiwestern since the sack of Constantinople by the Crusaders in 1204. Witnessing western aggression, Nikitas Honiatis was reported to have said that "even the Saracens are merciful and kind compared to these men who bear the cross on their shoulder." The French Crusaders of Angers sang triumphantly "Constantinopolitana civitas diu profana" (City of Constantinople so long ungodly) as they carried off relics from the City (in Ware 1963: 69). The feelings of hatred and revulsion at the sacrilege of the Crusaders reinforced in the Byzantines the long-standing doctrinal differences. After 1204 the schism over dogma between the eastern and western churches was recognized as irreconcilable. Some Byzantines, deeply suspicious of the pope and hating the West, actually preferred an Ottoman to a Catholic conquest. Indeed, the Grand Duke Lukas Notaras declared that he would rather see the Muslim turban in the midst of Constantinople than the Latin miter. The failure of the West to send help before 1492 exacerbated the antagonism of the Byzantines toward their coreligionists.

In the last century perhaps the most profound rejection of modernity, particularly its doctrine of statism, was the irredentism of the *Megali Idea,* which infused Greek national ideology from the moment of its declaration in Parliament by Ioannis Kolletis in 1844, until 1922. Although the doctrine was officially announced in 1844, its beginnings can be traced to the late Byzantine Empire and the idea of imperial destiny held by Byzantine Greeks (Runciman 1968: 378). Essentially it fused messianic Byzantinism with romantic Hellenism. But while the Byzantine Empire was multiethnic, the *Megali Idea* was nationalistic, prescribing the dominance of the Greeks over the Near East (Mango 1965: 40).

The *Megali Idea* was really a product of the Greek encounter with modernity. It resulted from the manifest difference between ethnicity and statehood: the plain fact that the Greeks as a people did not all reside within the Greek state. In a sense it sought to recover the premodern and prestatist ethnic identities of the Ottoman and Byzantine empires (see chapter 2) but, paradoxically, on a national scale. Though the territorial ambitions of the *Megali Idea* were modified with each military success or failure, one common aim remained—the liberation of Constantinople/Istanbul and the triumph of Hellenism in the East (Skopetea 1988: 325). For many Greeks the essential goal of 1821 was the recapture of the City, which since 1453 they had yearned would become "ours once more." Sokolis in his *Aftokratoria* (Empire) maintained that the revolution was fought for empire, with Constantinople as its spiritual center, rather than for an autonomous Greece. "The revolution of 1821 was a completely religious struggle," he argued (1916: 135). The concept of a Hellenic empire prevailing in the East counterbalanced the aspirations for a centralized state oriented toward the West. On one level irredentism subverted modernity by rejecting the opposing elements of the east-west dichotomy. Yet, at the same time that the *Megali Idea* attempted to reconcile the prestatist identities and the Greek state in a national empire, it embraced the ideological oppositions of the modernization project. It failed, beaten by the emerging Turkish nationalism—which disbanded the Ottoman Empire in favor of a Turkish nation— but also under the weight of its own contradictions.

The antinomies in Greek culture were resolved not militarily but aesthetically; they were projected into the utopian space of Greekness, which permitted Greeks to be both Hellenic and Romeic, to christen their children Pericles as well as Maria, to waltz with pleasure but not to be ashamed of the *kalamatiano*. While the idea of Greekness (and its compensatory function) came to define Greek identity, the aestheticization of literary practice was not universally accepted. Lorentzatos, as we have seen, denounced autonomous art as another foreign import destroying the "spiritual tradition" of Greek culture (see Leontis 1987). He enjoined Greeks to recapture the "lost center" of a society before differentiation. As an example of authentic Greek art he pointed to the altar of the Monastery of Lavra on Mount Athos (circa 1530), painted by artists with no knowledge of western artistic techniques (1980: 116). He urged Greeks to open their eyes to their true heritage, "the ever-living spiritual tradition of the East" (110). But they should achieve this, he added, with "non-aesthetic criteria"; since autonomous art has destroyed its metaphysical center "there is no point in going to art in order to regain it" (118, 121).

In "The Lost Center" (1961) Lorentzatos mourns the aestheticization of artistic practice in Greece. The solution, he says, lies in reintegrating the arts into the social praxis from which they were dissociated, in returning to the center prior to its dissolution. The center acts for Lorentzatos as a redemptive realm outside modernity where people can experience an undifferentiated being. Paradoxically, however, this is a very modern strategy, for his projection of the lost center as a utopian space of unalienated wholeness has an aesthetic aura. Lorentzatos endows the center with the reconciliatory capacities of modern art. Did the paintings in the Monastery of Lavra promise contemporaneous believers such an aesthetic transcendence? They did not, but they are made to function in this way by modern critics feeling cut off from the culture the paintings represent. The return to that space and time, when these paintings were integrated in the life of believers as part of their religious ritual, can only be experienced aesthetically. It will remain an imaginary event. This perhaps explains the elegiac tone pervading Lorentzatos's essay. Nonetheless this text illustrates another point of antagonism to the autonomous aesthetic. That Lorentzatos's answer is ultimately aesthetic does not detract from its critical potential. This and the other examples of resistance to western culture appropriate western modes of thought. Perhaps, barring complete isolation, critique as internal transgression—the use of strategies from the dominant to undermine its power—is the only way peripheral cultures can subvert the hegemony of western discourses.

Though such cases of inversion have become less frequent after the 1960s, especially within official culture, they nevertheless occur. One recent example is the controversy concerning the publication of the collected works of Greece's national poet, Dionisios Solomos, financed by a major bank, which identified this venture as part of its cultural politics. It advertised the publication as a celebration of the national and "spiritual contribution of our great poet." In his literary column of January 1, 1989, in the highbrow newspaper *To Vima,* the eminent professor of Greek literature George Savidis noted that one of the volumes comprises the poet's dramatic works. As everybody knows, Savidis reminded his readers, Solomos never wrote a single play. The volume in question contains dramas on the life of Solomos actually written by the editor, Yiannis Nikolopulos, who had published his own theatrical pieces to dramatize the role played by Solomos in the "national struggle of our people." Savidis protested this "fraudulent" scholarship and called for the destruction of the books. His review provoked a response (Feb. 5) from the bank's director, who rejected Savidis's injunction as medieval. Of more interest, however, is the letter of Nikolopulos himself (Feb. 12), which, by defending his project and attacking Savidis for his "reactionary" politics and "Hitlerian" censorship, brought to the fore the gap between the academic discourse of the professor and the populist language of the editor. Rejecting Savidis's disinterested posture, Nikolopulos invoked personal narrative in his argument, calling his work a product of dedicated reading and study under "harsh conditions of persecution, exile, imprisonment, and death sentences," conditions that Savidis, as a representative of the country's "spiritual and cultural corruption," could never understand. His enterprise, politically committed and "national" in scope, he argued, cannot satisfy Savidis's "metaphysical and idealistic" criteria, so incompatible with his own dialectic of "historical materialism." As a representative of the country's elite, Savidis is thus unable to accept that a Communist, imprisoned for his beliefs and granted a war pension for his efforts against the junta, could be qualified to offer "spiritual, national, as well as ideological nourishment to our struggling people and to our much-betrayed native land."

This debate is relevant here as an example of friction between academic and popular approaches to literature. That an editor in Greece may deem it proper to publish his own texts on the national poet as part of the poet's actual collected works points to separate discourses, independent of academic humanism, which, in regarding literature as "national nourishment," reject the assumptions of official culture and refuse its aesthetic claims. Indeed, the two combatants neither speak the same language nor share the same presuppositions about the meaning and uses of Solomos's texts. While Savidis condemns the violation of professional standards and authorial integrity, Nikolopulos defends his credentials as editor on the strength of forty years' research and, not least, his struggles and suffering for his homeland. For him notions of aesthetic autonomy and authorial integrity are irrelevant in comparison to his fight for national liberty and social justice. With his own personal story Nikolopulos frays the grand narrative of the aesthetic, unraveling some of its universalist claims.

The debate between Nikolopulos and Savidis indicates how a high discourse attempts to distinguish itself from practices it designates low. As I argue in the last chapter, there cannot be a split between high and low before the formation of professional elites and the aestheticization of the arts. Purism did not so much reject the popular as try to co-opt it through education. It compiled a catalogue of national virtues it hoped would be incorporated in the daily life of individuals. This is not Savidis's concern; he aspires to cultural capital rather than a national culture. In charging Nikolopulos with fraudulent scholarship and in calling for the edition's destruction, Savidis denies it legitimacy as literary criticism. High discourses, associated with powerful socioeconomic groups, possess the authority to draft rules of exclusion and prohibition. But at the very moment of negation the low can invert the commonly held codes, values, and norms, and the hierarchy itself. For a couple of weeks in *To Vima* an alternate, nonacademic, nonautonomous form of literary practice penetrated the realm of high culture. Ridiculed by mainstream scholarship and criticism, Nikolopulos's arguments nevertheless highlight sites of opposition to the dominant aesthetic ideology.

Still a National Literature?

As I have often argued, resistance to the introduction of foreign practices modifies the expected function of the imported structures. In terms of literary practice this has meant that Vutieridis's conception of literature as a dissociated body of textuality has not been adopted by subsequent histories of literature. To be sure K. Th. Dimaras's *History of Modern Greek Literature* (1975), which established a paradigm for future work, is not a history of literature in the sense that Vutieridis's is. Dimaras's work is informed by a definition of literature open to many types of writing . While twenty years earlier Vutieridis limited the range of literature to purely imaginative texts, Dimaras extended it again to encompass the "totality of all written monuments" (1975: i). The term *literature* for Dimaras covers fictional as well as scholarly or theoretical works, a fact that makes his history, as he himself admits, overlap the history of culture. Unlike Vutieridis's conception of literature, Dimaras's neither signifies one isolated group of texts nor occupies its own exclusive space. It constitutes a branch of writing, a dimension of grammatological history. In a sense his work resembles the histories of letters published in the nineteenth century, as much of the volume is devoted to nonliterary issues such as scholarship, education, rhetoric, the church, printing, and historiography.

Dimaras's expanded concept indicates that literature was not recognized by all critics as an isolatable category of culture. Although such a conception of the literary had been proposed by a few scholars such as Pantazidis and Vutieridis, assumed by modernist poets like Cavafy and Kariotakis, and promoted by some critics such as Thrilos and Agras, it was far from being universally accepted. Furthermore, many poets and critics of the Generation of the 30s worked with a more formalist understanding of the literary. Yet the presence of such an expanded conception of literature, in the most authoritative Greek literary history, shows that only a certain elite regarded Greek literature as one of the arts. In Dimaras's time the dominant question still seems to have been not "What is literature and how can we best compile its history?" but rather, "What does the Greek written tradition contain and how can we make it reflect the individuality of the Greek nation?"

This seems to have been the case with subsequent volumes. The influential *History of Modern Greek Literature* (1973) by Linos Politis, for instance, still posits the literary experience in a sociopolitical context. It follows Dimaras's precedent in expanding the grammatological horizons of literature to such an extent that it develops as much into a history of written culture as of literature. Politis, as he states in the preface, is a demoticist. Even as late as 1973 the literary historian still insists on acknowledging his position in the linguistic question. His view of the development of modern

Greek literature is determined by the presuppositions of this discourse. This holds true for two earlier histories by Yiannis Kordatos (1962) and by Spiros Melas (1962). Both feel it necessary to affirm the existence of demotic culture. Although the issue of language was not as urgent in the 1960s as it had been at the turn of the century, the positions of all three critics suggest that the question of national individuality continued to shape the configuration of literary history. Even during the last two decades literature was still a by-product of the ideological foundry molding Greek identity.

The situation differs with those texts written by foreign critics and published abroad: André Mirambel's *La littérature grecque moderne* (1953), Bruno Lavagnini's *La letteratura neoellenica* (1969), Börje Knös's *L'histoire de la littérature néo-grecque* (1962), and Mario Vitti's *Storia della letteratura neogreca* (1971), translated into Greek in 1978. These texts are of course products of western European literary criticism, in which literature has for more than a century been differentiated from other discourses. The four critics remain faithful to the assumptions of aesthetics: they isolate literature, treat it as art, analyze the literary qualities of the texts, and trace the evolution of Greek tradition. The Greek critics may also have had these aims, but for them literature, in the extended or limited meaning, was still part of the nation's politics.

Unlike other spheres of culture in which literature had been aestheticized, literary history remained a conscript in the service of a nationalist ideology. In this task it shares many similarities with the original mission of literary history that arose in Europe in the nineteenth century. The aim, as Hans Robert Jauss puts it, "to represent in the history of literary works the idea of a national individuality on its way to itself," may be seen in one of the most influential histories of a national literature, Gervinus's *Geschichte der poetischen Nationalliteratur der Deutschen* published between 1835 and 1842 (Jauss 1982: 3). The fear that German literature lagged behind other traditions prompted Gervinus to chronicle the long development of German writing. A feeling of cultural belatedness (just as in Greece) motivated the purposeful introduction of cultural identities to give the German people a canon of texts demonstrating their legitimacy as a civilized nation. The word *national* appears conspicuously in the title, emphasizing Gervinus's belief that national individuality informs the facts and events that the literary historian collects and studies. Gervinus made literary history a participant in political discussions.[28] He systematically excluded aesthetic consideration from literary history (Hohendahl 1989: 218). The result of this and other canonizing efforts was that the German Reich under Bismarck (around 1870) possessed a collective literary heritage.

Central in the work of Gervinus and other philologists of the nineteenth century such as Scherer, De Sanctis, and Lanson, stood the conviction that national identity was the invisible part of every fact and that this idea could be represented in a series of literary works. The notion of a national self-image unfolding in its literature was the thread connecting all the literary works in a grand narrative. The succession of texts was mediated by the idea that they all reflected the quintessence of a nation. These literary historians selected a series of indigenous texts, sanctified them into a canon, and then proclaimed them the embodiment of a people. Their central objective was to determine the essential qualities of a national literature by differentiating such literatures from other traditions.

This original sociopolitical mission was eventually aestheticized. The study of English literature in the nineteenth-century curriculum "meant committing to memory the components of a historical map of the National Literature and Language, while the work of scholarship was largely directed towards the production of a suitably detailed documented chart of the English cultural tradition" (Doyle 1982: 25). Literary studies renounced their early role in the configuration of national character when they evolved into an autonomous discipline almost exclusively concerned with the study of literary texts. Consequently the role played by literary history in the creation of a national identity seems to have been forgotten. Indeed, the more literature and literary studies consolidated their place in society, the more their originally political goals were suppressed.

Greek literary history has not forgotten these goals. Even the modernists of the Generation of the 30s, despite their formalist experimentations, aspired to create an authentic Greek art. The surrealist poet Odisseas Elytis, for instance, dreamed of a day when an array of people "armed" with an international consciousness would lean toward the "native soil," adapt the "pure Greek substance," and create "a new and truly national culture" (1974: 366). The dominant figures of this generation and their heirs have shown that even when literature had been subsumed in aesthetics, it could still provide a forum for deliberations of Greekness, but with a difference: whereas in the past Greece was understood as content, now it is appreciated as form.

Chapter 5
Spaces of a Public Culture

The invention of the nation-state in eighteenth-century Europe coincides with the fabrication of a new type of civil society, a domain of private interests separate from the state, which legitimated the state and was protected by it. In this realm individuals were constituted as citizens of a union whose language and identity distinguished them from members of other states. Their identity was constructed in the social spaces of the bourgeois public sphere: the coffeehouses, salons, art galleries, theaters, concert halls, publishing houses, social clubs, academies, and universities. If national culture was created as a means of contriving a social consensus by imprinting itself upon the sensibilities of citizens, the imprinting took place in these sites. There individuals mastered the stories of the nation, identified with its meanings and symbols, and acquired guidelines of conduct. They became in a sense national subjects. Culture enabled the mediation of their specific interests with the general, connecting their individual identities to a vaster unity.

Literature, the art of telling stories, was valorized in the English, French, and German public spheres as an effective means of socializing people into the values of the middle class and national culture. Literature promoted the collective internalization of public norms, conventions, and symbols. It also brought individuals together into a common social experience, thereby enabling them to discover their shared identity. Because of its privileged position in the Enlightenment project of culture-building, literature was the first art to evolve into an autonomous institution in the general process of functional differentiation. It became a social component among other components, bearing both symbolic and economic value. Although aesthetics and romantic criticism tried to deny the latter, literature before any other art was subjected to the laws of the culture industry through mass production, the serialization of novels, and publication of inexpensive books.

In the context of social differentiation literature emerged as an autonomous system, still involved in education but given a new function—compensating for the fragmentation of society. As in other autonomous spheres of modernity, boundaries were drawn around it, distinguishing the practice within from that without. (It is this border between it and other social domains that the historical avant-garde, by designating ordinary objects aesthetic, tried to break.) It developed its own rules of entry and exclusion, patterns of discourse, and definitions. The production, organization, and evaluation of works were conducted according to internal norms rather than, say, the rules of the church or state. The literary institution developed as a system of interconnected sites and a set of discourses, functionally defined, but related to other institutions in society. It was both a spatial structure and a praxis, an edifice and a series of activities. It represented a cluster of spaces where it was written, discussed, printed, sold, transmitted, taught, and canonized. In this chapter I wish to discuss some of the places where literature is produced and consecrated as a cultural good.

Literature as Institution

Recent attempts to regard the literary institution simply as shared knowledge and conventions ignore both its complexity and its specifically modern nature. Frank Kermode, for instance, defines it as the medium of pressures and interventions that may facilitate or limit the individual's manner of reading. The literary institution is for him the professional community that interprets secular literature and teaches it to others, and which has the authority to define the limits of its subject, impose valuations, and validate interpretations (1979: 72). It exercises both canonical and hermeneutic restrictions in that it determines both the object of interpretation and the method (74). Kermode's view ignores the social context of literature and, by using the department of literature as its defining metaphor, emphasizes one site of cultural legitimation over others. The publishing house and the classroom do not have the same function. The institution of literature cannot be identified with only one of its sites.

The conception of the institution as a set of conventions conflates diverse practices into a vague idea of production. This is the major shortcoming of Stanley Fish's notion of interpretive community. Literature for Fish becomes a conventional category: "What will, at any time, be recognized as literature is a function of a communal decision as to what will count as literature" (1980: 10). This is an important critique of humanism's cele-bration of the author as the central agent in literary culture, but Fish just shifts the emphasis from author to readers who "make" literature. These readers are members of a community that constrains their subjectivist pro-clivities by its assumptions and strategies for reading or "making" literature (11). The questions readers pose, the practices they adopt in interpreting literature, are not their own but the property of the community to which they belong.[1] Fish defines the interpretive community as being "made up of those who share interpretive strategies not for reading but for writing texts, for constituting their properties" (14). Readers write, not read, texts because the strategies exist prior to the act of reading and therefore deter-mine the shape of what is being read. Fish fuses discovery and interpretation and then concludes that "interpretation is not the art of construing but the art of constructing. Interpreters do not decode poems; they make them" (327).

Fish's terms, such as *making* and *constructing,* may have shocked tra-ditionalists with their economic connotations, but they have little to do with the production of literature as a commodity.[2] In fact, their use actually suppresses any perception of the mediation of the market in literary pro-duction. When Fish says readers produce poems he remains at the level of reading, and he means by production the new interpretation and hence the new poem that arises. But readers in the classroom do not make poems in the same way that publishing houses manufacture books. Fish's description of interpretation as a form of production only borrows a capitalist term, and conceals this difference. His work is an extension of the aesthetic strategy originated by Moritz and Kant, which protects the inner value of art from the culture industry. Whereas they situated value in the *Ding an sich,* Fish posits it in the reader's interpretive strategies. Interpretation is the "only game in town" he says (356), played by those writing articles, attending conferences, sitting on review or tenure committees, and studying literature (343). His notion of interpretive community, insofar as it describes only the workings of an English seminar, denies literature its history, sub-limates the struggles waged in its name, and reduces all conflicts to dif-ferences in literary meaning. Hermeneutics is the modus vivendi here; all acts are leveled to this single plane. This is hardly a comprehensive account of the institution of literature but it is an excellent strategy, as has also been shown by the rapid expansion of deconstruction, for maintaining the primacy of interpretation in literary criticism. Interpretation may be the only game in town now, but it has been played for only two hundred years, a result of social differentiation, the emergence of new reading practices, and the transformation of criticism from a prescriptive, expository activity to an analytical practice.

Fish's notion of conventions and shared knowledge describes only one aspect of the literary institution, the specialized discourse that accumulated after the initial dissociation of literature from the social praxis. The symbols, norms, information, standards, and reading strategies reproduce on a discursive level the initial differentiation of the literary zone from the social environment at large. They are the ideological markers separating literary from nonliterary practice, the criteria governing exclusion and prohibition, the capacity of the autonomous field to determine the rules by which works are produced and legitimated. This body of conventional understanding is situated in identifiable social spaces, not cloistered interpretive communities. Similarly, production signifies not just reading practices but the actual work carried out in the creation of literature. Poets, for instance, compose poems according to a set of currently available conventions, but they require the networks of printers, editors, and publishers to circulate these texts, and reviewers, critics, and teachers to consecrate them as art. These cooperative unions, as Howard Becker observes, make conventional knowledge available to their practitioners, and integrate them into the economy through a distribution system (1982: 93). Since the key to survival is distribution, groups and individuals compete for access to this system. Whether a work or style gains acceptance as art has both economic and aesthetic consequences.

Networks enable the production and dissemination of works of art, artistic styles, and forms of knowledge. German Idealist philosophy, for instance, was produced by such a coalition of professors, located primarily in the reformed universities of Jena and Weimar between 1780 and 1820. The Idealists, closely connected as colleagues, isolated a paradigm in the 1780s, organized themselves and propagated their work, trained their own students, established new research centers, and generated secondary material until their work, having attained the level of normal science, became routine (Collins 1987: 55). The Idealists made philosophy a respectable academic subject and endowed the philosophical faculty with a prestige comparable to that of the faculties of law, theology, and medicine. It is doubtful that, in the absence of this intellectual alliance, these theories would have been designated significant cultural products.[3] Individual texts or schools survive by joining these cooperative networks. But access to them is governed by rules of exclusion and prohibition.

Entry into an institution depends on knowledge of its conventions, which are not available to the uninitiated. These conventions ultimately create abstract form and pure theory or refined, nonrepresentational art, both requiring interpretive expertise.[4] An acquaintance with art history and theory, for instance, permits the analysis and discussion of even the most abstract modernist painting. "Works of restricted art," argues Bourdieu, "owe their specific cultural rarity to the rarity of the instruments with which they may be deciphered" (1985: 23). Modern society sanctifies objects as art by distinguishing them from ordinary goods. Works are consecrated, as Bourdieu states, by two types of institutions, those that preserve art and those that train people in the appreciation of art. "These consist, on the one hand, of sites which conserve the capital of symbolic goods, such as museums . . . and on the other hand, of institutions (such as the educational system) which ensure the reproduction of agents imbued with the categories of action, expression, conception, imagination, perception, specific to the 'cultivated disposition'" (23). While all institutions invest works with cultural meaning—endowing them with aesthetic properties, canonizing them—some induct people into their values, thereby ensuring the survival and transmission of these values.

Although there exist numerous cultural sites for the production and evaluation of aesthetic products, they have a common principle—the autonomous aesthetic whose primary function is to provide compensatory experiences. The theater, music store, classroom, and literary magazine play their own specialized roles in culture but they all share the notion of autonomy. In other words, the ideology of art's function defines the institution of art. The idea of aesthetic autonomy has governed, from the eighteenth century to the present, the way individual works of art are produced, understood, discussed, and legitimated. The norms, conventions, criteria, judgments, and opinions of aesthetic theory are derived from this concept of autonomy.[5]

It is important, however, in an investigation of aesthetic practice not to remain exclusively at the level of ideology—the ideas about art circulating at a given time—at the expense of the social sites generating this ideology. Peter Bürger, for instance, defines the institution of art as "the general definitions of art in their social determinacy" (1979: 174). By examining art's function in society Bürger is able to determine its specificity and analyze historically the transformation of that function. He fails, however, to establish a connection between social spaces and the institution of art, thereby giving the impression that the institution consists only of notions about its function. He postulates ideas about the purpose of art without fully connecting those ideas to the social process and without relating the actualization of art to the differentiation of modern societies. Bürger conceives of the institution as an independent system functioning on the basis of its own laws. In describing the institution Bürger succumbs to the aestheticist ideology this institution promulgates about itself. His notion of art as institution not unsurprisingly resembles the work of art itself: self-regulating, autonomous, and self-reflexive.[6]

This aestheticism becomes quite evident in Bürger's discussion of the avant-garde. Although he provides a brilliant genealogical analysis of the phenomenon, when he describes individual works he returns to the critical and hermeneutic assumptions that the avant-garde sought to subvert. Bürger, for instance, speaks about John Heartfield's photomontages aesthetically, from within the institution of art and with its language. This is of course inevitable; in choosing to analyze individual works, he can do nothing else but interpret them. Interpretation, the search for deep meaning, is really the only methodology sanctioned by the institution of art. Bürger acknowledges this when he admits that "the avant-gardist work is still to be understood hermeneutically" (1984: 82). The avant-gardist work is still art and thus demands interpretation; it becomes an occasion for a "critical hermeneutics." In other words, as long as it is treated as art it will have to be interpreted.

Interpretation, however, is also a cultural practice, bearing its own history inseparably linked with the institution of art. One cannot subvert art without questioning this practice. By so readily becoming art, by being so effortlessly absorbed into the institution it had sought to desacralize, the avant-garde failed to shatter art's autonomy and reconcile it to the social praxis. In providing the avant-garde with an exegetical underpinning, Bürger seems to affirm this failure. Despite his historical analysis of the institution of art, he still believes in the transgressive and ultimately redemptive powers of art. In his article "Literarischer Markt und autonomer Kunstbegriff," Bürger points to individual works of postmodern art, specifically Peter Weiss's novel *Die Ästhetik des Widerstands* (The aesthetic of resistance, 1975), as a way out of art's present impasse. The current task, he argues, is to transform the radicalness of the avant-garde into the "intensity of a critique" of aesthetic autonomy (Christa Bürger et al. 1982: 11). In his search for the radical potential of contemporary art, he sees Weiss's novel as almost a paradigmatic work that proposes a nonauratic use of art: the novel is neither totally isolated from everyday life nor is it completely subsumed by it (190). In the moment of its exhaustion, it seems, art still seeks relief from art. Bürger treats the aesthetic as a privileged realm where utopia can survive.

Bürger's aestheticism can be avoided by historical investigations. Literature is a modern construct, a result of the transformation from a stratified to a differentiated society. It emerged as a unified system when it carved out a social space and fashioned an independent discourse. No longer part of other social practices, it constituted its own sphere of activity governed by its own dynamics and internal laws. It is a historical category structurally equivalent to other institutions but also entrusted with the task of over-coming the problems of social fragmentation. Despite its claims to the contrary, art is never independent from its social space. It consists of norms, conventions, and ideas about its function that determine the way individual works are produced, appreciated, understood, and criticized. The system of beliefs cannot be schematically separated from its social organization. By the same token, these practices are neither autonomous nor immanent but function at specific locations.[7] Like all institutions, literature supplies appropriate rules for conduct by sanctioning certain truths about itself and reality while prohibiting others. It determines human activity by ingraining patterns of behavior in readers.

The institutionalization of literature can be said to have been realized when a certain field of textuality has been isolated and designated literary, a system of norms and conventions established, and a material organization erected. Such a formation prescribes a specific Weltanschauung as it also designates rules of practice—rules, that is, not only for the reading of texts but also for entry into the institution itself. What will be admitted as literary and what rejected, and who will be permitted to interpret authoritatively these works, is determined by implicitly acknowledged rules of exclusion and prohibition.

Literature in western Europe emerged in the bourgeois public sphere, which was rooted in new kinds of social sites: coffeehouses, clubrooms, spas, salons, reading societies. The new literary practice, the codes and conventions of reading, the aesthetic judgments, the opinions on taste developed in these spaces, which mediated between domestic privacy and public institutions. These places produced not only discourse but also bour-geois subjects. They regulated bodies, morals, and manners. The rational, well-mannered, and civil citizens of the coffeehouse differed substantially, Stallybrass and White write, from the grotesque bodies of the alehouse (1986: 96). Swearing, gambling, or rude behavior was not permitted in the sites of the bourgeois public sphere. Discourse and practice were purified in the interests of rational discussion. The bourgeois public sphere rejected the carnivalesque (though it incorporated it in the form of masks and symbols as its Other, its negative representation) for the refined arts that occupied a dominant position in middle-class homogeneity.

In nineteenth-century Greece it is not possible to speak of a bourgeois public sphere as it existed earlier in western Europe. This is why, as I have argued throughout this study, modernity "failed." One of the structures most indispensable to the duplication of western models was absent. The demoticists did attempt, however, to establish such a realm toward the end of the nineteenth century. They sought to appropriate existing places of discourse and create new ones as a way of consolidating a national imaginary. Each social space became a locus for the production and the experience of the values, norms, idioms, and sentiments of the new identity. In the following pages I will investigate representative institutions of this public culture. Specifically, I will analyze sites in which literature, so important in the project of social engineering, was invented and legitimated as a cultural good. My aim will be to show that, though initially the literary and political projects overlapped, eventually literature evolved into an autonomous system.

The Press and Magazines

The press played a significant role in the early European public sphere. Originally, taking the form of leaflets and broadsheets, the press reported on public affairs to the emergent public of doctors, pastors, officers, professors, scholars, and jurists (Habermas 1989: 20). The press transmitted information to the cluster of private (i.e., nonadministrative) people coming together as a public body.[8] It was the training ground for critical public discussions. As there was initially no major difference between literary criticism and political journalism, both were placed in the service of political enlightenment. "Since its genesis in the eighteenth century," Hohendahl writes, "the liberal model of literary criticism had been inseparable from the bourgeois public sphere. Indeed the category of the public sphere itself created the framework for the concept of literary criticism" (1989: 119). Literary criticism abandoned its political function in Germany, according to Hohendahl, after the political disappointments of 1848. From this point on literature was discussed separately, and from 1870 criticism became feuilletonistic; no longer meshed with political writing, it occupied a separate section of the newspaper that concerned itself with literature.

The early Greek newspapers and journals displayed many such characteristics of literary culture. The first Greek-language newspaper, the *Efimeris,* published in Vienna between 1790 and 1798, was established to transmit French revolutionary ideas to Greeks in the diaspora and the Greek territories of the Ottoman Empire.[9] Although these early newspapers carried texts about cultural events, they devoted no specific space to literature. After the 1820s, however, the political and the literary overlapped in newspapers appearing in Greece. Announcements of the publication of a novel or of a collection of poetry usually were made in newspapers in which reviews of these publications would later appear. In most cases these took the form of personal statements about the author, either libelous attacks or sycophantic panegyrics. Newspapers serialized novels, translations initially, Greek later on.

Newspapers abounded throughout the country. In Athens alone, with a population of 35,000 in 1842, nineteen presses were turning out fifteen newspapers. An even greater explosion in the number of newspapers and periodicals was soon to follow. In 1883 fifty-two newspapers were being published in the country, and Athens, now with a population of around 84,000, supported twenty-two; in that year alone six new magazines appeared (Papakostas 1982: 15). By 1890 the number of newspapers grew to 131 (Tsoucalas 1981: 145). Tsoucalas reckons that by 1886 a thousand newspapers had been started, a number corresponding roughly to about one newspaper for every 150 to 200 literate people living in urban centers (146). Most of these were short-lived and characterized by what Tsoucalas calls a hyperpoliticized orientation; they were established, as in the the early European public sphere, to promote the ideological position of individuals or groups rather than as financial ventures. By the end of the nineteenth century newspapers and magazines absorbed a significant part of Greek literary prose writing (Drakoules 1897: 66). Contemporaneous sources point to the prominent role played especially by magazines in the formation of literature. The magazine, and not the book, according to Ilias Vutieridis, acted as a "mirror of spiritual life" and an indicator of the development of art and learning (cited by Papakostas 1982: 17).

The proliferation of newspapers disseminating a diverse range of ideologies points to an active political culture and to the absence of a homogeneous public sphere. At the end of the century the struggles over national culture had reached their peak. The discussions of language, tradition, and the nation were conducted from sometimes irreconcilable positions (staked out in the original encounter with modernity) rather than from assumptions held in common. There was no unified public, and consequently no "objective" and "unbiased" public opinion to which the press could refer, and through the supposed neutrality of which a consensus could be fabricated and articulated as truth. Indeed, conflicts were waged over the very criteria needed to form a sphere of shared opinions, values, dispositions, and judgments. The victory of demoticists enabled them to consolidate their culture as the national one. At the end of the nineteenth century, however, no single community could engineer a national homogeneity even though this had been the goal of nationalist discourse for over a hundred years.

Magazines, in the very early stage not easily differentiated from newspapers, figured prominently in this mission. Greek magazines began to circulate in various European cities around the beginning of the nineteenth century. Almost all were short-lived, usually remaining in press only for a couple of years, as a sampling shows: *Athena* (Paris, 1819-?), *Kalliopi* (Vienna, 1819-21), *Mellisa, i, Efimeris Elliniki* (Paris, 1819-21), *To Mussion* (Paris, 1819-?). Although these pioneering publications were referred to as "literary periodicals," none had a decidedly "literary" orientation. They were concerned on the whole with general cultural matters such as pedagogy, translations, and philology.. Their sponsors, Enlightenment scholars of the diaspora, hoped to introduce Greeks to the new stories of their national culture.

The most influential was *Ermis o Loyios* (The scholarly Hermes) published in Vienna between 1811 and 1821. Not a literary periodical in the modern sense but a publication of general learning (Koumarianou 1964: 26), this magazine spearheaded the Greek Enlightenment project. Indeed Korais believed that its publication would make a significant contribution to the liberation of the Greeks and the creation of an independent nation on the French republican model. Its editors aspired in their commentary to promote the rebirth of Greek letters by informing Greeks of the latest developments in European culture (see issues 1818: 274; 1820: 336). The philological search for authentic meaning and the reconstruction of origins informed editorial policy. In its columns there appeared articles covering a broad range of cultural interests: reports on schools in Greece and abroad, articles on philology, ancient Greek philosophy and rhetoric, announcements of new books, reviews, news about the founding of Greek journals, newspapers, theaters, and printing presses. The magazine also published a lexicon of classical Greek and texts of ancient Greek authors. Conspicuously absent from its pages, however, were references to modern Greek writers. The 1814 volume, for instance, contains a number of articles on classical Greek and Latin authors, but none on modern Greek writing.

In its inaugural issue *Ermis o Loyios* identified itself as a "literary [*filoloyiki*] newspaper" whose purpose was to publish material on *filoloyia*—that is, on knowledge and learning, on the Greek language (particularly the comparison between the modern and ancient languages), and on Greek books (1811: 1). Six years later (1817: 1) the editors reaffirmed this goal by reminding their readers that, as a "literary" magazine, they deemed it necessary to publish a treatise on *filoloyia*. In reality this turned out to be about classical philology, for they understood *filoloyia* as written culture rather than literature. Their interests may be compared to the attempts of contemporaneous scholars to document the totality of Greek books. In both cases literary writing gave one account, though not a privileged one, of the emerging Greek myth.

The absence of essays on or even references to modern Greek texts in this and other magazines shows that literature had not been an object of primary concern but was included in the political endeavor to compile a repertory of national stories. Publications such as *Ermis o Loyios,* often conflating statist and orientalizing rhetoric, were the first to tell Greeks about the central themes of their modern narrative: Greeks constituted a homogeneous ethnic and linguistic community; they had a glorious past; they were (the original) Europeans; they belonged to the West as opposed to the East; their interests lay in rebelling against the Ottoman Empire and building an independent state.

In the first thirty years of independence many periodicals appeared in Athens. One of the earliest, *Efterpi,* circulating in the years 1847–55, was a cultural magazine, though it had an expressed interest in "literary" matters, especially in indigenous writing. Along with translations of foreign works, it printed poems and prose pieces of Greek writers. The most influential was *Pandora,* founded by the scholars Alexandros Rangavis, Konstantinos Paparrigopulos, Nikolaos Dragumis, and Grigorios Kamburoglu. In the period between 1850 and 1872 it occupied a central place in the intellectual life of Athens, established a pattern for future magazines, and served as one of the most important media for education, general learning, and entertainment (Sahinis 1964: Prologue). Its circulation stood at 1,100 issues, though it is estimated that as many as 10,000 people read it regularly (Margaris n.d.: 44). *Pandora* was closely connected with the University of Athens as many of its contributors were professors. On the whole it remained a highbrow, conservative journal, often reporting on and publishing reviews of winning poems from poetry contests. In its columns appeared articles dealing with philology, archaeology, and philosophy; reviews; and translations of European literature. Since the editors wished the magazine to become an effective conduit for cultural information, they gave much space to reviews of current books, mostly general or scholarly works but also poetry and prose. From the perspective of future literary developments, one of *Pandora*'s most lasting contributions was its promotion of Greek poetry and prose. Although a magazine of general learning, it offered to poets, and not necessarily the most renowned ones, the possibility of publishing their works in its pages. It supported *katharevusa* and, with the exceptions of the demotic poems of Solomos, Tertsetis, Markoras, and a few others from the Heptanesian Islands, accepted only texts in the purist idiom. In its columns there also appeared texts from prose writers of the period, such as those of Konstantinos Ramfos, Spiridon Zambelios, and Angelos Vlahos, including the two most successful novels of the period: *O Afthentis tu Moreos* by Alexandros Rangavis and *Thanos Vlekas* by Pavlos Kalligas. *Pandora* constituted one site of discourse in the purist public sphere. The magazine's close affiliation to the university shows the interdependence of these sites and the situatedness of discourse in specific social spaces. It is because political, aesthetic, and moral judgments are produced and legitimated in this network of social spaces that they become the objects of struggle.

The majority of the prose texts appearing in *Pandora* were translations rather than original works. Greek readers of the latter half of the nineteenth century consumed an enormous quantity of translations. Contemporary writers like Alexandros Rangavis remarked on the preference Greeks had for foreign prose; they read translations, he observed, but write poetry (1877, 2: 269). Greek prose, still considered inferior to that of Europe, was treated as a secondary form of writing, as "light literature" (*elafra filoloyia*). The preponderance of translations indicates that prose did not have legitimacy as a literary genre. *Pandora,* nevertheless, contributed to the formalization of a national literature insofar as it printed original works, occasionally texts of criticism (see, for instance, issue XX, 1869–70), as well as biographies of writers, and some reviews of recent publications. It was a site for both the production and the consecration of literary writing as a cultural good.

Pandora's prominent position was superseded by *Hrisallis* (1863–66). In the inaugural editorial Irineos Asopios promised his subscribers *filoloyia, kallitehnia* (art), and variety. For him *filoloyia* encompassed "everything capable of being said in a tasteful way (*pan pragma legomenon kalos*) either in prose or in meter" and consisted of the novel, short story, and travelogue. *Filoloyia,* Asopios wrote, is the flowering of each living or dead language, but he noted that his magazine would restrict itself to the modern "literatures." His emphasis on the modern departs from his precursors' neoclassical celebration of philology. His conception of *filoloyia,* incorporating several literary genres, was less inclusive than that found in the catalogues of printed Greek books.

Yet significantly Asopios applied this term only to European writing. When he referred to modern literatures in the prologue, for instance, he listed foreign authors only, as though Greek writing was not a legitimate form of *filoloyia*. Since *Hrisallis* aspired to publish works of and on literature, it was compelled to adopt not only a western European perspective but also its discourse and texts. Here we encounter again the discrepancy between imported models and Greek practice. Since Greek literature had not yet developed into a differentiated body of genres and texts, the magazine had in effect introduced a concept to refer to a nonexistent reality. As a result *Hrisallis* was compelled to use it with regard to European literatures only. In striving to convey its readers to the "metropolitan centers of the West, the museums of Europe, the international exhibitions," *Hrisallis* was in effect transporting them to the source of its own ideas on art and literature.[10]

Western material, however, was imported not just for its own sake but for use in the construction of a Greek culture. This can be seen in the policies of *Estia* (1876–95). The magazine contributed to the cause of modernization by promoting a unified discourse to serve as a basis for discussions of all topics, ranging from literature to politics. To this effect *Estia* was marketed as a family magazine of general learning with an encyclopedic and historical orientation; it attained a circulation of 3,000 by 1892.[11] Its active participation in the production of a shared identity is demonstrated in the competition it launched in 1883 for an "original" short story describing scenes from the "life of the Greek people." The editor, Nikolaos Politis, confessed that the short story was the least developed genre in Greek literature (*filoloyia*), with the result that few Greek short stories could be compared with examples from western Europe. Nevertheless, he acknowledged the influence this genre could exercise upon "national character," since the depiction of scenes from Greek history and social life "pleased" readers and excited in them "love for the nation" (Bulletin of *Estia*, May 1883, no. 333, p. 1). These competitions, unprecedented since only poetic contests had been organized until then, had such a positive effect on the social recognition of the short story as serious writing that since then the magazine has been closely identified with this genre's genesis. Furthermore, it published in 1896 the earliest, and hence very influential, anthology of short stories (see chapter 3).

The short story competition provides another example of the forced attempt, initiated by feelings of belatedness, to establish cultural identities. The absence in this case of a European literary genre prompted calls for its creation. The editor considered the legitimation of the short story a "national enterprise" because literature served as a medium of communication allowing individuals to experience their nationhood. *Estia*'s support of the Greek short story points to the development and proliferation in Greece of social spaces for the consecration of cultural material, another clear manifestation of modernity. These sites formed the realm where demotic culture was being produced. If the major aim of demoticism was the formation of a shared identity as a means of promoting a national/ popular homogeneity, this entity had to be situated in specific institutions. The short story competition demonstrates the interrelationship between discourse and social coordinates, in this case a magazine with its own print shop and the short story. More often than not these institutions of the demotic public sphere were separate from the state apparatus.[12]

The magazines of the nineteenth century attempted to construct a broad literary culture. Their collective efforts contributed to the legitimation of writing as literature and paved the way for the transformation of this literature into an object of analysis. By supporting indigenous writing they demonstrated that not only German, French, English, and Italian but also Greek texts could become worthy of scholarly concern. These periodicals represent specific and discernible sites, connected to the university, the newspaper, and the publishing house, in which literary issues were discussed. The cultural magazines of the nineteenth century were also vehicles for the transmission of European literary notions, on the basis of which the institution of Greek literature was being erected. The Europeanized Greek middle class could then point to the institution as demonstrable proof of its modern and cosmopolitan orientation. Greek literature, as the Greek-American editors of an anthology remarked, could take its place in the world "pantheon" of literatures. Only unfamiliarity with the Greek language, they insisted, gives the impression that Greece has not created a literature (*filoloyia*) (Anon. 1913: Prologue). Even after the turn of the century a sense of delayed development determined discourse on culture.

Criticism

For much of the nineteenth century and in the early part of the twentieth, critical practice coincided with cultural politics. Poetry, short stories, novels, popular songs, tales, were discussed in relationship to language, nation, identity, Europe, the classical past, tradition. There was neither criticism per se nor critics engaged professionally in the study of literary texts. Those concerning themselves with poetry, the novel, or drama were men of letters. As in the early phase of the European public sphere, professors, philologists, poets, diplomats, and lawyers wrote essays or reviews of literary works in addition to their principal occupations. With their writing they partook in the ideological battles of the day. For instance, the questions of language and of a national poetry made their presence perceptible in Emmanuil Stais's analysis (1853) of Solomos's poem "Lambros" (in Kitsos-Milonas 1980). Subsequent essays on Solomos by Polilas (1859 and 1860) and Zambelios (1859) also explored the national character of this poetry (in Kitsos-Milonas 1980). Both Zambelios and Polilas viewed literature from the perspective of national culture. So did the demoticists in their struggle to secure demotic as the language of the state and to demarcate its literature. The first and inevitable step in their campaign to canonize the folk songs, the *Erotokritos*, and the Akritic cycle of poems was to demonstrate their "authentic" Greek qualities (Tziovas 1986).[13]

Critical practice was so entangled in linguistic debates that it cannot be separated from them (Vayenas 1986: 50). Even contemporaneous commentators, such as the littèrateur and professor Dimitrios Vernardakis, observed that Greek criticism had not developed in his time (1884). Aristos Kampanis, looking back at this period in his study of Greek criticism, remarked that the critical capacity of nineteenth-century scholars was "exhausted" by the debates over language (1935: 145). In consequence, as Dimaras argues, Kampanis's own book serves as simultaneously a history of criticism and the language question (1939: 1499). Even fifteen years after his easay the editors of the volume on criticism for the *Vasiki Vivliothiki* (1956) wrote of their difficulties in distinguishing works of criticism from texts on the linguistic controversy. Their task was almost impossible because criticism was an extension of the general project of political and cultural unification.

Some writers, such as Emmanuil Roidis, attempted to transform criticism into a professional discipline along European lines. A supporter of demotic, but compelled to write in *katharevusa,* the language of prose, Roidis fought, as in "On Contemporary Greek Poetry" (1877), for the establishment of the popular idiom as the national language and for the acceptance into the canon of the work of the demotic poets Vilaras, Hristopulos, and Solomos (Roidis 1978). In the poetic competition of 1877 he rejected all the submitted works, stressing in his report that poetry had not existed in Greece. Influenced by the ideas of Hippolyte Taine on milieu, Roidis believed that Greece lacked the appropriate context to produce an authentic poetry.

Roidis also addressed the state of contemporary criticism, particularly the adjudications of the poetic competitions, condemning judges for their sycophancy, lack of system, and their indifference to theoretical problems. Roidis proposed an interpretive and analytical criticism to replace philological practice. He denounced reliance on plot outlines and the explication of grammatical, syntactical, and metrical features (Dimiroulis 1984: 146). In short, Roidis wanted criticism to formalize itself into a modern discipline. Both his philosophical ideas and their application in his work were attacked, particularly by the scholar Angelos Vlahos. Roidis's plans for an interpretive criticism based on French models were thwarted by the tendency, still dominant in Greece, to use poetry and prose in a socializing enterprise. The reception of Roidis's theories was not favorable because there was no context for them. An independent criticism was impossible at that time for exactly the same reasons that, according to Roidis, Greece was incapable of producing a poetry; namely, the social conditions enabling the emergence of a specialized language and knowledge about literature were absent. The rejection of Roidis's ideas reveals one more time the incongruity in Greece between modernizing aspirations and its sociocultural infrastructure.

A systematic criticism appeared in Greece in the discursive space carved out by demoticism, which "freed" the study of texts from the necessity of philology (K. Th. Dimaras 1939: 1498–99). To be sure, demoticism enabled the rise of criticism—but not because, as the demoticist Dimaras believes, demoticism represented the truth. Rather, it fostered the creation of an autonomous national literature with criticism as its custodian. But much of this criticism has been journalistic: what in Germany is called *Literaturkritik* (the criticism of literature in the press) as opposed to *Literaturwissenschaft* (the academic study of literature). Typical were the essays of the poet Kostis Palamas (1859–1943), the first literary author to treat literature as his primary vocation rather than as an avocation (Dimaras 1975: 415). But Palamas could not be considered a professional writer within a differentiated society, since poetry was still integrated in the social praxis. The prestige of his craft enabled him to write authoritatively on matters beyond poetry and prose. He used this privileged position to make pronouncements on any matter of national significance. His function as unifying national symbol was made manifest even at his death in 1943. The funeral was held under German occupation, a time of famine and shortages. Although communication was difficult, news of his death spread by word of mouth, and despite the prohibition on public gatherings thousands congregated at the cemetery. As the coffin was lowered into the grave, the mourners violated the German order against any manifestation of nationalism by spontaneously breaking into the national anthem. The poet Angelos Sikelianos captured the significance of the event in a line from a poem he recited for the occasion: "on this coffin rests the whole of Greece." It would be difficult to imagine such an event in a society that conceives of poetry as an esoteric and elitist activity.

Later critics continued to write criticism as a form of cultural study. Though Fotos Politis (1890–1934) was considered in his own time a critic, his three-volume collected works contains many texts that do not concern literature specifically. In his essays, almost all of which were published in the daily press, he wrote on poetry, but also on the nation, the War of Independence, language, the Greek intellectual, folklore, and translation. Of his contemporaries only Yiannis Apostolakis (1886–1947) can be regarded a professional academic critic.[14] As the initial holder of the professorship of modern Greek literature at the University of Thessaloniki from 1926 to 1940, Apostolakis was the first Greek scholar to bring attention exclusively to modern literary matters. Apostolakis represents the inaugural step in the professionalization of Greek criticism, a development reinforced by the installation in 1925 of a professorship of modern Greek studies at the University of Athens (though until 1976 this chair was closely associated with Byzantine literature).

The transformation of criticism into a social practice, whose principal duty was the analysis of literary texts, took place in the work of the poets, novelists, critics, editors, and publishers who made up the Generation of the 30s—the most powerful literary alliance of twentieth-century Greece. Its most lasting contribution to modern Greek culture was to aestheticize literature by converting it into an object of critical study. Although few members were academics, many were professional critics devoted to the systematic study of modern Greek literature (Kriaras 1964: 13). In contrast to the scholars of the period, who concentrated primarily on post-Byzantine writing, they wrote on recent and even contemporary literary texts. While the universities were grudgingly recognizing the literary production of the last two centuries, these critics sanctified the poems, short stories, and novels of living writers as literature. Andreas Karandonis, editor of the magazine *Nea Grammata* (1935–45), which promoted work of this generation, wrote critical essays on Greek poetry, particularly that of George Seferis and Odisseas Elytis. His writing testifies to the configuration of an aesthetic in Greek culture. About Seferis's poem "Turning Point" he had this to say [1931]:

> I saw "Turning Point" both as content and form, I examined its
> [internal] elements, the numerous relationships between them, and
> their final expression; I attempted to determine the type and
> number of influences [upon it], explaining the significance of true
> and creative influence, and differentiating it from the thoughtless
> and pointless imitation of each foreign and parasitical modernism.
> (1976: 94)

As a New Critic, Karandonis believes the literary text to be a self-contained whole, composed of internal components alluding to each other and to other texts. The poem is a thing-in-itself to be analyzed and enjoyed as an object of beauty.

The Generation of the 30s provided an aesthetic underpinning to the efforts of its demotic precursors. This development, however, did not destroy the demotic public sphere as it did not compartmentalize culture into high and low. The aestheticization of cultural practice was a consequence of the ideological turmoil introduced by modernization in Greek society. But this project did not end here, for it had not led into the seizure of the state. Demoticism conquered and refashioned culture but could not appropriate the state mechanism. The criticism of the Generation of the 30s pressed on with its agenda of consolidating its gains beyond culture. This entailed the further expansion of the demotic public sphere, leading ultimately to a reconciliation of civil society with the state. Critics continued to write for a broad public of educated consumers rather than for an elite composed of other critics. By midcentury a body of critical knowledge on modern Greek literature had accumulated, much of it of a journalistic variety. During the last three decades an academic criticism has differentiated itself from its journalistic counterpart, but the division between them is still not as stark as in western Europe and North America.

The professionalization of criticism is taking place in the spaces of the demotic public sphere, with its texts and its language. Even in the 1980s, after profound social and political transformations in Greek society, it is still possible to detect elements of the national and popular culture fostered by demoticist discourse. People with minimal education still read the Renaissance epic *Erotokritos;* poetry readings until recently have filled entire stadiums; the awarding of Nobel Prizes to Greek authors (Seferis and Elytis) became occasions of intense national pride; the views of writers are often sought in newspapers and magazines, and not always for literary matters; Theodorakis's musical settings of "serious" poems such as Elytis's *To Axion Esti* have become modern classics. This was the aim of the demotic modernizing project—to create a sphere of shared experiences where Greeks can communicate in a standardized language and participate in a unified literary culture. Although these practices are disappearing or are deemed low by an increasingly differentiated official culture, they are recalcitrant reminders of demoticism's success.

The centrality literature can still have in society is demonstrated by the events following the death in August 1988 of Kostas Tahtsis, one of the country's leading novelists. Tahtsis was buried in the official cemetery of the state, where Members of Parliament, heroes, and persons of national renown lie. His funeral became a public event; among the leaders of the art world in attendance was the minister of culture, representing the state— a sign of the appropriation of the state mechanism by demotic culture. For days the electronic media and the press carried broadcast documentaries or printed articles on Tahtsis and his work. While this may seem remarkable enough when compared to the marginal position occupied by writers in western cultures, it becomes even more so in light of Tahtsis's widely known transvestism. (He was strangled by one of his clients.) Tahtsis was not just the darling of a radical chic but a national figure accorded the authority to make pronouncements on topics of social concern. While high culture may have been officially disgusted by Tahtsis's life (though unofficially fascinated), it could not dismiss him, given the prominent role occupied by literature in the public sphere. Though Tahtsis as transvestite may have been symbolically peripheral, literature as public discourse made his writings socially central.

The marking in 1983 of the fiftieth anniversary of Cavafy's death provides another illustration of literature's capacity to transmit public opinions and shared values. In western Europe and North America an anniversary of such a difficult and demanding poet would probably attract the attention only of specialists. In Greece, however, it was turned into a public phenomenon, with special programs on television and radio, public readings of his poetry, symposia, the publication of many critical studies, the reissue of his collected works in popular editions, and the erection of statues of Cavafy in public places. Most important, almost all literary and some nonliterary magazines circulated special issues on Cavafy. Many of the contributors to these magazines were students, poets, novelists, journalists, teachers, historians, lawyers, physicians, economists—in fact, all types of "critics" taking an interest in Cavafy's poetry. Their texts appeared in cultural magazines such as *Nea Estia, Hartis, Politis, Lexi, Semiosis, Nea Poria, Andi,* and *Diavazo,* the very same periodicals regularly hosting the critical work of scholars, since there is to date no academic journal specializing in literature or literary theory.

Academic criticism still does not possess sole and exclusive authority to utter statements on literature. Amateurs with a certain level of education enjoy rights to critical discourse. As early as 1917 Fotos Politis referred to this phenomenon, noting that "every Greek who barely knows how to read considers himself competent to judge artistic works" (1938: 88). Politis, like Roidis before him and Sikutris after, seems to complain that nonspecialists gain access to criticism. In varying degrees they have sought to restrict entry into this discourse but have failed, thwarted by other groups, a development pointing again to the "failure" of modernity. The universal accessibility to literary practice was a cardinal feature of the European public sphere before its dissolution. In Greece, as my previous examples indicate, literature continues to be integrated in the social practices of certain communities, even though its function was aestheticized in the 1930s. The authority to speak on literature is dispersed throughout many sites: university, secondary school, newspaper, magazine, public lecture, literary society, art gallery, library, broadcasting, foundation, ministry of culture. Literary criticism is only recently developing into an independent profession.

The Teaching of Literature

The educational system was finally incorporated into the demotic public sphere after the retreat of extreme right-wing interests in 1974 and the declaration of demotic as the language of pedagogy and the state in 1976. Only after this period did the spheres of state and culture in some ways converge. For the past two centuries education, the crucial mechanism for the socializing process, functioned outside of the national popular culture produced by demoticism. The three major liberal reforms of 1899, 1913, and 1964 to modernize it along bourgeois liberal lines failed, blocked by forces consolidated in the state apparatus. If the demotic public sphere created a national culture as a source of social solidarity, educational institutions, particularly at the postsecondary level, did not figure prominently in this development. The first chair of modern Greek studies, for instance, was established only in 1926 at the University of Thessaloniki (a supporter of demoticism); at Athens no such chair existed until 1976.[15] Although it is commonly held that "the canon is what gets taught," the Greek case indicates that the official pedagogical system does not always play a direct role in the formation of the canon. Greek schools and universities during the nineteenth century and much of the twentieth provided a largely humanistic education based on classical Greek rather than on modern literature.

The university in Athens was established quite soon after independence. The erection of the university in 1836, of the national library in 1834, and of the academy in 1839, all grand projects for an impoverished nation, reflect the force of the modernizing program and the role expected of culture in this process. As I have argued, national integration was experienced in the realm of culture before it was achieved territorially and politically. Since there was no precedent for such institutions, the models were European. The university, for example, was named after Prince Otto of Wittelsbach, son of King Ludwig I of Bavaria and "hereditary monarch" of Greece, who arrived in February 1833 accompanied by a regency council of three Bavarians (since Otto was only seventeen) and an army of 3,500 Bavarian soldiers. The university's neoclassical architecture reflected the style in Munich. Its constitution was based on that of the University of Göttingen and in its early years seven of thirty-four professors were German. The university was divided into four faculties: theology, philosophy (humanities), law, and medicine. In its first year fifty-three students and seventy-five auditors were registered, coming from the three secondary schools operating then in Greece: Athens, Nafplion, and Siros (Pantazidis 1889: 29).

Like other cultural institutions it was appropriated by the purists. Their obsession with the classical tradition is reflected in the subjects offered by the philosophical faculty in its first decade. The lectures were almost exclusively devoted to the study of (classical) Greek and Roman history, literature, and archaeology.[16] There was no mention of modern Greece in the titles of the courses or any attempt made to differentiate between modern and ancient Greece. When professors referred to "Greek poetry," "Greek history," or "Greek grammar" they meant classical Greek as a matter of course. The term *filoloyia*, signifying toward the end of the century "literature," at this time meant simply philology, the study of classical texts.

This classical bias ran through the history of the university well into the 1920s, when modern Greek chairs were finally introduced. In the 1860s the university recognized the modern language in some way with two courses on the history of modern Greek *filoloyia*.[17] This coincided with the university's interest in contemporary Greek poetry, as reflected in its sponsorship of poetic and philological competitions. But, as I shall show in the next section, the university's principal aim in supporting these competitions was the composition of modern Greek poetry—originally in the purist language. As far as the poetic competitions were concerned, the university served as a site for the production rather than the legitimation (study, analysis, criticism) of modern poetry. The lectures in the philosophical faculty were almost exclusively oriented toward the classics and were conducted in an archaistic language closely resembling the ancient. In tutorials students analyzed Greek and Roman authors and composed (classical) Greek and Latin passages. New regulations passed in 1868 called for modern Greek exercises to be done in the philological tutorials but no papers in the modern language were ever submitted (Pantazidis 1889: 235). The orientation of the syllabus toward the classics, the exclusion of courses on modern texts, and the absence even of chairs of Byzantine culture reflected the authority of the reigning purist ideology, which sought the reconstitution of Hellas and the reconstruction of an old myth. By contrast, demoticist discourse claimed to fashion a new story relevant to modern reality.

The humanistic curriculum in elementary and secondary schools was also based on a heavy staple of classics and theology. During the early years of the Ottoman occupation the schools were few and run largely by the church. In the sixteenth century centers of Greek learning began to appear in various European cities and by the seventeenth century Greeks began to evince an exceptional inclination for education (Tsoucalas 1977: 449). This tendency, as I noted in chapter 2, shows the prosperity of Greek merchants within the Empire and in the diaspora, and the high priority they attached to education in their modernization project. Greeks of the diaspora proved extremely generous in the funding of the pedagogic institutions. The gifts of just ten benefactors made before 1870 equaled 25 million drachmas, a sum higher than the budget of the Education Ministry for that period (Tsoucalas 1977: 488). Not only schools and gymnasia but also the university, library, academy, polytechnic, and stadium were financed at least in part through contributions from wealthy Greeks residing abroad. Often simple and impoverished peasants donated a few drachmas, sometimes their entire fortunes, to the cause. In their case it is not the amount that is significant but the ideology that their gifts reflect. The fact that illiterate peasants, often geographically removed from Greece, regarded the financial support of national education, instead of other institutions, a patriotic duty, indicates the success with which westernizers managed to connect the national interest with culture. The ideological identification of modernization with education is borne out by statistical evidence indicating that, despite the new nation's crippling burden of poverty, the number of students in comparison with the general population was higher than Greece's neighbors and equaled or surpassed the industrial states of western Europe (Tsoucalas 1977: 431). In 1885, for example, the number of students studying at the university (but excluding those attending foreign institutions) on a per capita basis was the highest in the world. An American diplomat observed in 1873 that Greeks tended to be overeducated in relationship to the country's economic state and that even the poor displayed a pronounced interest in education (Tsoucalas 401). The lower classes, convinced of the value of education, were able to send their children to school in large numbers because tuition was free. Indeed, Greece led most of the world by a hundred years in providing universal access to education.

Although education was initially perceived as a prerequisite of economic progress, the pedagogy it ultimately provided on all levels was largely nonproductive (Tsoucalas 1981: 116). Given the absence of industrialization, it trained students for the service and professional sectors. Overeducation coincided paradoxically with industrial underdevelopment, another consequence of modernization in the cultural field without comparable transformations in the economy. The state had no choice but to incorporate educated peasants in the inflated public service sector. The remainder joined the Greek comprador bourgeoisie outside the kingdom: in Rumania and southern Russia until the middle of the nineteenth century, Asia Minor for the entire century, and Egypt, Sudan, and Ethiopia since 1880 (Tsoucalas 116–17). Expanding capitalist activities in these regions demanded merchants, agents, lawyers, civil servants, and speculators. When these enterprises were disrupted and access to the areas denied, especially after 1922, the liberal Venizelos government introduced reforms in 1929 to orient the education system toward the sciences and technology. But this met with only limited success, since Greeks still preferred to send their children to the humanistic gymnasia despite the diminution of professional outlets. The prestige attached to nonproductive education persists. Large numbers of underemployed professionals and experts emigrate now to West Germany, North America, and Australia.

Humanistic learning characterized elementary education in Greece immediately after independence.[18] These early schools emphasized ancient Greek with no instruction in the modern language. The 1836 program set aside on the average twelve hours a week for classical Greek at the elementary level and six at the secondary level, three and five respectively for Latin, and four and two for French (A. Dimaras 1973: 66). Interestingly, French was taught as a modern language whereas Greek was not. This holds true for the curricula of the years between 1864 and 1867. The secondary school course prospectus of 1867 shows that seven main subjects were taught: classical Greek, Latin, mathematics, history, science, French, and religion; twelve hours were devoted to Greek, compared with four to Latin, three to mathematics, three to history, three to science, three to French, and two to religion (Chassiotis 1881: 251–52). Pupils spent most of their time in detailed grammatical explication of classical texts; they read long passages of one author for the expansion of their vocabularies and composed essays in the classical languages. Reading was an exercise in textual analysis; an attempt to find authentic words and to reconstruct origins. Classical Greek dominated the curriculum, not as a dead language but as a substitute for the modern one.

Modern Greek (*katharevusa*) was introduced in 1876 but its instruction was classified under ancient Greek. The parliamentary bill of 1877 prescribed for the secondary school eight to ten hours in classical Greek but only two for the modern language (A. Dimaras 1973: 228–29). The bill did not recognize the autonomy of *katharevusa* but specified that students translate from the classical to the modern language and write essays in modern Greek on the basis of classical texts. Students spent months on one short classical work, analyzing its linguistic aspects without ever examining its content. The modern language consumed 7 percent of school time and was taught in only three of the seven grades.

All the authors of the 1884 elementary school syllabus belonged to the purist school (in A. Dimaras 1973: 256–60). Significantly, the syllabus was divided equally between "literary" and "nonliterary" works. Passages were taken from such scholars as Korais, Asopios, Paparrigopulos, and Zambelios, as well as from such poets as Sutsos, Zalokostas, Parashos, and Vikelas. With the exception of Valaoritis, demotic poets were not included. Purism, as my examination of the histories of Greek writing shows, promoted a literary culture in an extended sense. Interestingly, however, the poets in this syllabus correspond quite closely to the ones anthologized in the major collections of the period, a fact indicating the correlation in the purist public sphere between cultural and state apparatus. This convergence was undone with the demoticist appropriation of culture.

The hours assigned for classical studies continued to outweigh those for modern Greek. Even as late as 1899 *katharevusa* represented one-third of the course load for the classical language and was taught only in the elementary school. In the new program drafted by the board of education in 1914 the classes prescribed for modern Greek corresponded to half of those for the ancient language. Provisions were also made for instruction in the modern language at the high school level. By 1931 modern Greek studies became firmly established in the secondary school. Classical Greek, still privileged even as late as 1961, consumed twice as many teaching hours as the modern language. In 1964 the centrist government of Yeoryios Papandreou introduced reforms to strike a balance in the instruction of the two languages. This legislation was nullified by the dictatorship of 1967, which reaffirmed the dominance of *katharevusa* and ancient Greek, two components of its ideological program. Modern Greek language and literature were once again made out to be the poor relations of Greece. Their status within education was ensured only by the bill passed by the Karamanlis government in 1976 legalizing demotic as the official language of the state.

Not only in Greece but in many western nations the classics formed the stock program of humanistic education. In the German gymnasium German literature was subordinate to classical studies and was taught until the 1840s for rhetorical analysis only (Hohendahl 1989: 246). Until the latter decades of the nineteenth century in the United States American literature was treated as ancillary to the study of Greek, Latin, rhetoric, and oratory, and was used instrumentally to illustrate grammar, elocution, and civil and religious ideas. English literature was introduced "as a means of reinstating cultural uniformity and of controlling unruly democratic elements entering higher education after the Civil War" (Graff 1987: 12). English literature was regarded in egalitarian America as a more democratic and more appropriate means to achieve this than the elitist classics.[19] Philology was dominant in the English universities as well. English studies was eventually established as the poor man's classics, the liberal substitute for those unable to gain access to the reigning canonical texts (Eagleton 1983: 27). Since the classics held full sway in Oxbridge, English literature was first taught in London, in the urban universities of Edinburgh and Glasgow, and in the technical institutes of the industrialized cities. English studies as a discipline was instituted during the second half of the nineteenth century in the technical colleges and the newly built universities, where it was regarded as a humanistic supplement to the steady diet of practical knowledge (Baldick 1983: 62).[20]

It is only to be expected that Greek education would follow the European example in giving primacy to philology. But Greeks, as I have argued, had a problematical relationship with the classics. Once Greeks were convinced that the pagan architects were their forefathers, the ruins of Athens (along with the wonders of Europe) were transformed into a source of anxiety, subsumed into the oppositional framework defining Greek identity. The modern Greeks were expected by Europeans and themselves to emulate, if not excel, the classical Athenians. Typical of these philhellenes were the French travelers Pouqueville and Firmin Didot who, on their visit in 1817 to the famous academy of Ayvalik (Kydonies) in Asia Minor, persuaded the pupils to abandon their vernacular in favor of ancient Greek. If students failed to keep their agreement they were compelled to recite a page of Homer publicly. The students were also required to replace their Christian names with classical ones (in Clogg 1972).

The Greeks appropriated the ideology of Hellenism to gain favor from Europe and to counterattack its discourse of orientalism, which portrayed them as barbarians. The Greeks' appropriation of the original European civilization enabled them to answer accusations of backwardness and despotism by claiming a cultural and racial propinquity to Europe. Hellenism, however, necessitated the rejection of their most familiar and immediate

cultural characteristics, recognized as oriental (see Herzfeld 1982). The
students of the academy of Ayvalik, for example, had to forsake their
demotic language and Christian names to satisfy the expectations of their
French visitors. The adoration of the classics came also at the expense of
modern Greek literature. The valorization of the classical texts, once a
revolutionary idea in the creation of a secular culture, developed into an
orthodoxy that stifled the reforms of 1899 and 1913.

Because the University of Athens recognized modern Greek literature as
a subject of study relatively late, academics from related disciplines (philology, archaeology, Byzantine studies, folklore, and linguistics) turned to
modern Greek literary works during the 1930s. Not being students of a
modern literature, however, they scrutinized the texts at hand with the
philological vigor reserved for the classics. Above all, the works they chose
came from the post-Byzantine period and from the Cretan renaissance.[21]
With the possible exception of Apostolakis, no scholar during this decade
chose as his realm of expertise the literary texts of the last two centuries
(Kriaras 1964: 14). It was to be expected that these scholars would analyze
modern Greek texts from the perspective of their own disciplines. This was
true from the beginning. Modern Greek literary texts came first to the
attention of scholars as linguistic documents. Korais, for instance, published
many works with the view to examining the history of the language. For
many scholars since Korais literary works served as texts for the study of
the Greek language (Vranusis 1971–72: 43–45). While a distinguished academic tradition existed in Greece, as well as in Europe, for the study of
Byzantine and Renaissance writing, including the popular songs, no comparable discipline had been formed for modern literature.

Although professors did not regard Greek literature as an object of
knowledge, the poets, novelists, editors, and journalists of the 1930s did.
Their criticism, as stated earlier, was of a journalistic variety which Ioannis
Sikutris, the German-trained classical philologist,[22] considered unsuitable
for the university. In an article (1932) concerning the teaching of modern
Greek, he referred to the lack of a technical discourse and conceptual
apparatus for the analysis of modern literary texts. He deplored the absence
of standard academic practices, such as the provision of footnotes and
bibliographies, and the shortage of complete editions and reference works.
Since modern Greek literature, he noted, was studied primarily by poets,
critics, local historians, and journalists, research in this area would remain
in the "prescientific" stage (1956: 242). After appraising the situation, he
concluded, like Roidis some fifty years earlier, that under the circumstances
then current modern Greek criticism could not develop into an academic
discipline. This would occur only after it acquired its own specialized vocabulary and the secondary tools involved in the critical enterprise: introductory

books, grammars, histories of modern Greek literature, critical editions of texts, interpretive analyses, and theoretical texts (243). But all of this, Sikutris stressed, still depended on the full acceptance of modern Greek literature as a subject of study.

In short, Sikutris sought professional criticism, produced by a coalition of experts at the university rather than by amateurs and dilettantes. But, as he himself admitted, there was no context for such a practice. Professionalization of criticism is a function of the general process of social differentiation in modern society by which subsystems dissociate themselves from the social milieu to become autonomous entities. It occurs when a community of specialists distinguishes itself from other groups, develops a discourse, establishes rules for exclusion and admission, and organizes and disciplines its members. It forms its own code of ethics to guide behavior and to ingrain its praxis in practitioners.

Professionalization itself is a process, Magali Larson states, "by which the producers of special services [seek] to constitute and control a market for their expertise," an attempt to translate one order of scarce resources, special knowledge and skills, into another, economic rewards (1977: xvi). Individuals belonging to a profession command authority and accrue privileges for their expertise. The professionalization process, Larson states, binds a body of abstract knowledge to a market. Indeed, the standardization and codification of professional knowledge is the basis on which a professional commodity is made and recognized as distinct (40). Each profession considers itself the appropriate organ to study or speak about its domain. It claims the exclusive right to practice within its designated area. The profession is also a self-policing entity insofar as it possesses exclusive authority to determine the content of its knowledge and the conditions for access to it.

Academic literary criticism may be considered a profession, inasmuch as it is an autonomous self-regulating body, affiliated with the state but possessing a distinct discourse, and producing its own subculture. Since it depends on external funding, it does not have direct control over its market as the medical and legal professions do nor does it enjoy the same monetary rewards. Nevertheless, it has exclusive authority over its own sphere of practice which is sanctioned by its specialized knowledge. Entry into the profession is dependent on mastery of this knowledge. While everyone may appreciate literature, only those having undergone rigorous training may be considered specialists of literature. Scholarly criticism's success in gaining professional status is its persuasive claim to deal exclusively with literary texts. Having appropriated literature as its sole object of study, criticism parades as its sole custodian, all the time denying the involvement of other agents in the collaborative enterprise of literary production.

Greek criticism even at this day cannot be considered a professional discipline because the necessary differentiation in literary culture has not taken place. Professors of literature have not constituted themselves producers of special services, since they have not codified their form of literary knowledge as distinct from journalistic practice. The right to critical discourse remains dispersed over several institutions. Many university critics still act as public intellectuals, regularly writing in the press for a broader audience and on matters not, strictly speaking, literary. There is to date no professional association that would promote the interests of the community. The only regular "literary studies" meeting is, significantly, the Poetry Symposium held annually in Patra since 1981. The title of the symposium, indicating once more the prominent place of poetry in literary production, places the emphasis on literature rather than its study. The meeting is attended by professors of literature but also by poets (who read their work), and anyone else interested in literature. A panel thus may be composed of persons representing disparate levels of critical knowledge and competence. This is also true of literary magazines. In the absence of an academic journal devoted to the study of literature, scholars publish their criticism in literary magazines where their work appears alongside poetry or prose and essays composed by journalists or lawyers. In such a context of heterogeneous interests and professional affiliations the authority of the professors to speak exclusively on literary matters is not recognized. The controversy between Savidis, a professor of literature, and Nikolopulos, the editor of Solomos's collected works, is an example of how alternative practices can violate the norms of the academy and its claims to speak exclusively on literature.

Poetry Competitions

Although for much of its history the university did not participate directly in the configuration of modern Greek literature, it promoted its production in the third quarter of the nineteenth century largely through its sponsorship of annual poetry and philology competitions.[23] They were made possible through gifts from wealthy expatriate Greeks who wished to foster the development of a national poetry and *katharevusa*. The first, established through a benefaction by Ambrosios Rallis, was held annually between the years 1851 and 1861 on March 25, the national holiday of Greece. It was succeeded by a competition endowed by K. I. Vutsinas in 1862 which took place annually until 1876. In addition to these, less well-known poetry contests were organized.

The effect of these competitions extended beyond the bookish halls of the university to people on the street. Ordinary individuals took an interest in their outcome because poetry to a greater or lesser extent was part of their lives, as a private pleasure but, most important, as a reflection of their national self-image. Poetry facilitated a communion between an individual and the national consciousness. The day of the competition was turned into a public celebration. Contemporary accounts, such as the following by the French consul Eugène Yemeniz, testify to both the theatricality and the communal aspect of the event:

> On this day the whole of Athens is on the move: all social classes show the same eagerness; the cafés and markets are empty; the squares are full with the crowd which gesticulates, shouts, and debates with the fervor typical of this people. After reading the report on the various works submitted to the competition, the president proclaims the winner, congratulates him in the name of the nation, recites his verses at the top of his voice, and crowns him with laurels. Upon leaving the ceremony the crowned poet, received with the acclamations of the crowd, is carried to his house as though in triumphal procession. It is not possible to conceive the disputes and arguments animating this great literary debate to the very end. (Yemeniz 1862: 216)

There could be no more striking testimony than this to poetry as a phenomenon of the street, an activity integrated in society, an event of public consumption. Although professors selected the successful poem, they had no exclusive right to it. The university, a stronghold of purism, opened its door to nonmembers because it sought to introduce them to the shared imaginative repertoire of the dominant culture. In such circumstances the poetry competitions facilitated a commingling of social and cultural groups united by the experience of national poetry. Poets, academics, and lay individuals participated in a process mediated by poetry. But the overlap promoted during these events, between the national and popular realms, could not be reproduced in many other sites of the purist public sphere because purism, as I noted in chapter 3, either dismissed popular culture or sought to reform it entirely.

The judgment and the successful poem were published in one of the Athenian periodicals. These documents make the politics of the selection process clear. Since the aim of the competitions, especially the Rallis, was to underwrite the authority of the purist language, and since they were affiliated with the university, it was understood that the main criteria in the selection process were linguistic. The poems were judged primarily for the degree to which they expressed the reigning purist ideology. Pure literary value could hardly have been a dominant consideration of the judges when many of the submissions were dismissed outright because of their language. Although they often praised the poems submitted in the vernacular, they inevitably chose those written in *katharevusa*. Supporters of the demotic attacked the competitions for their exclusiveness and often published their dissenting opinions. Eventually, resistance to demotic weakened and by 1873 prizes began to be awarded also to poems written in the vernacular.

During their approximately twenty-five-year duration the university competitions consecrated poems as texts of a national culture. Tellingly, the patrons did not endow chairs for the study of modern Greek poetry. Neither they nor the judges regarded the poems—to which they awarded prizes—as fitting objects of research, on a par with the classics. Clearly they wanted poets, not critics. As the poet Karasutsas stressed in the prologue to his collection *I Varvitos* (The lute), poets were the spiritual guardians of the nation, inspiring love for the country, consoling Greece, and preserving hope for the future (1860: iv–v).

With the gradual legitimation of demotic national poetry, the task of supporting the production of poetry, as opposed to other genres, was less pressing. The literary society Parnassos and the periodical *Estia* launched a short story contest. The poetry competitions, identified with purist poetry, were replaced by literary societies and magazines as centers of literary activity. Demoticism either seized spaces of the purist order in the formation of its public sphere or designed new places of assembly and discourse. It preserved the prominence of poetry as a mediator of national experiences, though it supplanted purist writing with vernacular texts that it assigned to the genres of literature. Literature remained public property in the demotic public sphere.

But the aestheticization of literature and the professionalization of criticism are leading to the emergence of specialized communities that forsake the public function of literature and criticism. Many features of the agora culture are coming to an end. People are not likely to come out into the streets to celebrate poetry if it has been appropriated by specialists who produce criticism in a language they do not understand. By the same token a culture divided into upper and lower compartments cannot serve as a space for the resolution of social and political problems. The process of occupational differentiation within culture and state intervention in this area may well lead to the dissolution of the demotic public sphere, as has happened in western Europe. Though this development is likely, given the appearance of specialized discourses, it will not necessarily result in the complete destruction of public culture as a realm of shared values, sentiments, and beliefs. There are instances of opposition that, in frustrating the formalization of the literary into a refined form, attempt to preserve the linkage of individual identities with the national one as the task of literature.

Literary Cafés and Societies

Since demotic culture was effectively disenfranchised by its exclusion from the state apparatus, it had to construct alternate hubs of literary activity.[24] Prominent among these sites were the literary cafés, which between 1880 and 1930 served simultaneously as retreats of leisure and as meeting places for poets, prose writers, artists, scholars, and intellectuals. Among the dozen or so most frequented, the best known was the Mavros Gatos (named after the Parisian Chat Noir), which welcomed the Athenian intelligentsia from 1917 to 1922, whereupon it was replaced by the Etoloakarnania (Papakostas 1987, Papadimas 1976: 21, 54). Mavros Gatos gave the impression of being less a café than a cultural center where discussions took place, magazines were planned and promoted, lectures given, and even secret political meetings held. Indeed, the Athenian chapter of the socialist party met regularly in Mavros Gatos until its members were arrested there in May 1917. The café's double function as an assembly space for political and literary groups underscores in the Greek context the close relationship between such a locale, literature, and politics.

Some of the chief figures in Athenian culture visited Mavros Gatos on a regular basis: the poets Palamas and Kariotakis, the author Tellos Agras, the critic Vutieridis, the prose writer Vutiras, the journalist Panos Tagopulos, and the scholar, translator, and novelist K. Theotokis. Language was the topic most hotly debated. Other areas of concern were literary movements such as futurism, the works of Oscar Wilde, as well as the literary achievement of the newly discovered Cavafy. The organization of the meetings and other activities was facilitated by a four-member committee, which announced in one of its bulletins that, in the absence of a "literary" (*filoloyiko*) center in Athens where intellectuals could "read their unpublished works among themselves and exchange opinions on literary topics," it would organize "Literary Saturday Evenings" (in Papakostas 1987).

Such activities are a good example of the collaborative enterprises referred to earlier, and of the relationship between social spaces in the public sphere. They generated innovative ideas, alternate literary practices, and sometimes other institutional spaces. The members of Mavros Gatos, for instance, organized an alliance called the Kallitehniki Sintrofia, to promote their work. The publishing house Ikaros was formed by individuals associated with the literary magazine *Nea Grammata* and the Café Brazilian, Lumidi, and Vizandion (Axelos 1984: 24).

Similar to the cafés, private salons were organized by leading intellectual figures between 1880 and 1910. The most influential, the salon of the poet Palamas, attracted not only the leading cultural personalities of the day (Xenopulos, Porfiras, Griparis, Mirtiotissa, Hatsopulos, Kambisis) but also foreigners such as Hesseling, Dietrich, and Pernot, who promoted Greek culture abroad. (Indeed, the culture they presented in their works was the one produced by this group of demoticists. In the same way, what westerners currently understand as modern Greek culture was shaped by the Generation of the 30s.) A result of their cooperation was the publication of *I Tehni,* the first major demotic journal.

The literary cafés and salons were specific points in the topographical network of the demotic public sphere. They sponsored cultural alliances of editors, poets, prose writers, professors, and journalists. As actual sites in the public sphere, the literary cafés demonstrate not only the social aspect of literature but also the practical work it presumes. The nature of these places makes plain the negotiations, struggles, arguments, and sheer labor implicated in the production of literature even before a text or work reaches a reader. Significantly, like nearly all institutions producing demotic culture, they were unofficial, public spaces for private individuals, sites on the border of the state infrastructure.

The literary societies (*filoloyiki silloyi*) also formed part of the demotic social and discursive network trying to reformulate Greek society through literary culture. The Heptanesian poet, disciple of Solomos, and scholar Andreas Laskaratos (1811–1901) referred to their involvement in social affairs in a passage concerning the society Viron with which he was associated and whose eponymous magazine often published his work:

> You have literary societies in Athens. Very good! What is even better is that you do not restrict yourselves to pretentious arguments, pointless discussions, and inert issues; but you serve in a practical way the divine mission of bringing universal agreement among peoples, and you intervene in the affairs of the Nation by providing free lessons for the poor children of your locality. (1959 III: 510)

Laskaratos well understood the role of literary discussions and schooling—the hallmarks of the Enlightenment project—in fabricating a cultural homogeneity among Greeks. Konstantinos Xenos, president of Viron, underscored the society's commitment to the edification of the nation by announcing the compilation of a "library of the people" and a collection of Greek popular traditions.

This sociopolitical orientation characterized the oldest of these associations, Parnassos, established in 1865 and still in existence today. What began as an insignificant club of young aristocratic students grew into an influential cultural organization, attracting many of the leading figures in the fields of letters, sciences, and arts, and came to be regarded, at least during the last three decades of the nineteenth century, as the equivalent of the Greek academy (Vovolinis 1951: 22). Parnassos acquired this cultural authority because it became a leading force in building an integrated demotic culture, its general goal being the "intellectual, moral, and social" improvement of the nation. The society arranged regular lectures on all matters of cultural interest, held poetry readings, put on theatrical productions, set up artistic exhibitions, published books, organized a drama competition (with Roidis as judge in 1877), as well as sponsoring classes on constitutional law on Sundays and running schools for the poor in Athens and Corfu. It was a literary association in the broadest meaning of the word. The society thus functioned as another site in the demotic public sphere, which, although detached from the state mechanisms, sought no less a social affect than the state.

The contents of the society's magazine, *Parnassos,* reflect the society's multifaceted orientation. While every issue contained a number of essays on works of literature, it ran even more articles on archaeology, history, the classics, law, and astronomy. Nevertheless, in regularly publishing literary and critical works, it provided an authoritative space for the development of a literature and criticism. In its inaugural volume of 1877 there appeared poetry, popular songs, and translations, as well as an article on the Greek theater by Alexandros Rangavis (January), one on the author Tertsetis by Angelos Vlahos (February), Roidis's adjudication of the drama competition (March), Vlahos's response to Roidis (May), Roidis's famous piece on the state of contemporaneous Greek criticism (October), and an essay on poetry and poetics by Laskaratos (December). Interestingly, all these texts were classified in the table of contents as "modern Greek *filoloyia,*" along with "ancient *filoloyia,*" and "modern *filoloyia,*" the latter concerned with modern European literature. The three subsections came under the major category of *filoloyia.* Although texts of literature and criticism were not sufficiently distinguished from each other, they were differentiated from articles with historical, archaeological, or legal themes.

Parnassos valorized literary practice but not as an end in itself. While it cleared a space for the literary, it did not endow it with an autonomous status. In its lectures, its public events, and taxonomical criteria *Parnassos* integrated literature with its other cultural practices. It ascribed to literature a major public function, the induction of people into a shared culture through the collective narration of stories. For this reason literature could not exist at this time as an autonomous institution, a phenomenon that would appear after the 1930s when literature began to assume a compensatory function. A differentiated literature, as I have suggested, is leading to the transformation of the demotic public sphere.

Book Trade

No social revolution, argues Elizabeth Eisenstein, is as fundamental as that which saw book learning (previously under the purview of old men and monks) gradually ingrain itself into daily life during childhood, adolescence, and early adulthood (1979: 432). The promotion of literacy was made possible by the availability of printed books and linked, as I demonstrated in the third chapter, to a new way of reading the Bible. The social penetration of literacy meant that people could study the Bible in the privacy of their homes instead of listening to the scriptures read in church. This solitary act involved the reader in a more active and interpretive relationship with the Bible, a relationship transferred eventually to secular texts.

During the medieval period book production was controlled by the church, a monopoly challenged during the sixteenth century by lay commoners who began in time to take over the book trade. The shift in book production was a blow to ecclesiastical authority, since the new print shops, which attracted scholars from the monasteries and places of learning, began to print secular material. The merchant-publishers found a ready market in the emergent bourgeoisie being trained in the new art of reading. The mass production of books also created the corporate fields of communication necessary for the creation of unified class consciousness and national culture.

In the Greek-speaking world the book trade was similarly appropriated by lay individuals in their mission to wrest cultural production away from clerical control and devise a shared realm of experience. The book trade contributed to this process by facilitating the transmission of Enlightenment ideas among diaspora communities and the expanding Greek centers in the Ottoman Empire. More important, it enabled a greater number of people to gain access to the new nationalist stories recited by the intellectual and mercantile elites. These narratives insinuated themselves in the daily practice, redirecting the way people imagined themselves and others; that is, no longer as coreligionists within an empire ruled by Muslims but as fellow citizens in an autonomous state.

Before the introduction of print shops in the Greek territories, Greek books were produced largely in the Greek communities of Europe and circulated, often by subscription, among readers residing in Venice, Trieste, Vienna, Bucharest, Odessa, Jasy, Moscow, Petropolis, Istanbul, Smyrna, Thessaloniki, Alexandria, and a host of other cities. Like many instruments of Greek culture, printing and publishing originated in the diaspora as the Greek speakers came into contact with western life. Subscription proved to be the most popular method for the circulation of scholarly books before the War of Independence and for some time afterward (Iliu 1975: 104).

Although popular in Europe since the beginning of the eighteenth century, this practice did not consolidate itself in the Greek world until the middle of the same century. Subscription afforded printers financial security, as they knew before the printing of a text the exact number of buyers. Owners of a press would advertise the appearance of a book in a newspaper or magazine such as *Ermis o Loyios* or *Ellinikos Tilegrafos,* to which readers would respond with expressions of interest by sending the appropriate payment. If the number of readers warranted the cost, the book would be printed with an appended list of subscribers. It is estimated that between the years 1749 and 1821 about 119,726 copies of books circulated among 22,891 subscribers (Iliu 1975: 164).[25] For much of the eighteenth century this was often the only way that a scholarly book could get into print.

This method was used to a certain extent by many printing presses to secure capital for their publishing projects. Glikis, the best-known press of the time, relied on it, as did Bortoli, Theodosiu (all in Venice), Vendotis, Baumeister, Schneirer (all in Vienna), Breitkopf (Leipzig), and the many others interspersed in the cities listed above. Of these, Glikis, which was founded in 1670 and continued to function till 1854, was the most productive, controling between 1670 and 1820 up to 33 percent of the book trade (Veloudis 1974: 85). Not all books were sold on subscription; primarily the scholarly ones were produced this way. Learned men, however, did not constitute the major consumers, as a vast number of books printed by these presses, especially in the first half of the eighteenth century, were of a theological or liturgical nature. The readership of the time consisted of two tiny groups out of the overall population (who remained anonymous to the printers): clerics and scholars (Veloudis 87). The market retained its largely scholarly and religious character until the late eighteenth and early nineteenth centuries, when, with the spread of education and an increase of wealth among the communities abroad and in Greece, readership grew as it absorbed new members from the merchant and professional classes.

Until that time most books were destined for churches and monasteries. As in Europe a few centuries earlier, the church had control over cultural affairs, including the manufacture and dissemination of manuscripts and books. Indeed, in the first half of the eighteenth century religious books constituted anywhere from 74.7 percent to 77.6 percent of the overall production; grammars of all sorts comprised 6.2 percent to 9.3 percent; all other subjects, including physics, mathematics, philosophy, geography, dictionaries, literature, practical handbooks (on health and lifestyle), and commercial studies ranged from 15.8 percent to 16.1 percent (Veloudis 1974: 86.) The predominance of religious and theological texts in the book trade began to erode, however, with the displacement of ecclesiastical influence in Greek life by the secular culture of the Enlightenment. The appropriation of the book trade by lay individuals was one struggle among many, showing microcosmically the more general conflict between secular and clerical forces for control of culture. In the period 1801–25 the percentage of religious books published dropped to 21.5, that of grammars to 2, while that for various other subjects rose to 76.5 of the overall book market. This period also witnessed a dramatic increase in the amount of books published: while from 1670 to 1750 about 874 volumes were printed, in the years between 1751 and 1820 the figure reached 3,180 (Veloudis 85), a testament no doubt to the expansion of both economy and culture.

Of this amount only an inconsiderable portion consisted of literary texts, as can be seen in the approximately 103 books published between 1749 and 1821 on the basis of subscription. An investigation of this subscription catalogue (in Iliu 1975) indicates that the vast number had scholarly and secular themes: editions of classical texts, grammars, books on history, rhetoric, philosophy, geography, mathematics, astronomy, and theology. In this list only one, the *Erotokritos,* was an edition of modern Greek literature. Of course other literary texts were published, as can be seen in the catalogues of Zaviras, Sathas, and Papadopulos-Vretos, which list a limited number of works of literature (see chapter 4). But when one considers that a sizeable proportion of books printed during the second half of the eighteenth century was still purchased by the church (anywhere from 52.7 percent to 69.9 percent), then the number of literary texts could not have been substantial. Some may argue that such texts were neither printed nor catalogued because only a few had actually been written. While this may of course be true, it cannot account for the significant number of "literary" texts available from the late Byzantine period and the Cretan Renaissance alone. It is fair to say that Greek scholars did not concern themselves with such works. Literature is not a fixed concept for scholars and readers to discover. It is a category produced partly by them. If we do not find many texts of Greek poetry and prose in the register of printed books from this period, it is because most were in the vernacular and scholars did not consider it worthwhile to edit, study, and analyze them. Their interest lay in the codification of all Greek writing instead of simply one genre.

This changed in the period after the War of Independence, as Greece itself became the chief cultural center of Hellenism. The liberated nation required books not just for political enlightenment but also for entertainment. To meet these demands, Athens quickly evolved into the publishing capital of the Greek world as printers arrived to establish presses there. Many such operations were founded by immigrating Greeks, but some also by enthusiastic philhellenes such as Byron, Stanhope, and Didot (Mazarakis-Enian 1970: 266). As early as 1827 the government press began operations in Egina, having started in Nafplion two years earlier. It transferred back to Nafplion in 1830 and moved to Athens a year later. In addition to official documents it printed literary and educational material (Filberg 1901: 149). From 1834 to 1838 eleven presses were in operation, and nineteen more were inaugurated by 1844. Even so, an organized book trade had not yet developed in Athens, as many of the printers had additional interests or professions. Konstantinos Rallis was a scholar and translator of classical literature;[26] Emmanuil Antoniadis ran two newspapers, *Ion* and *Athina;* Ioannis Filimon was a historian and for a time edited a newspaper in Nafplion. Their presses operated on a small scale. The printers themselves were responsible for production, advertising, and sales. Often the press served also as a bookstore, as was the case of Konstantinos Garpolas, who called his business a "bookstore, printing press, and bookbindery" (Papayeoryiu 1975: 68). For a long time the publishing business maintained this loose organization, as often newspapers and magazines, and later, literary societies published their own books. These print shops were not independent publishing houses but adjuncts to other institutions.

The growing number of printing presses indicates an increasing market for books. While press owners, not wishing to take undue risks, concentrated on educational works (classical editions, translations, grammars, dictionaries, medical treatises), histories of Greece, memoirs of military men, and practical books (on agriculture, health, cooking), they did venture into the publication of a noticeable number of literary texts. Significantly, the first book to be printed in Athens was a volume of poetry, *Ta Lirika ke Vakhika,* of Athanasios Hristopulos (1825). Many other literary texts followed. Andreas Koromilas's famous press went into operation in 1835 with his influential anthology—the first in Greek literature—of the poetry of Rigas, Solomos, Vilaras, and Hristopulos (see chapter 3).[27]

The expansion of the book trade should be seen as a sign of an emerging literary public sphere; but not, as was the case in contemporaneous Europe, of its dissolution. In Germany, for instance, the annual number of books published between 1868 and 1877 jumped from 10,653 to 13,925; in 1887 it rose to 17,000, having increased by 62 percent. The factors contributing to this growth were, according to Hohendahl, the formation of a postal system, the rise in the number of universities and schools, and the urbanization of the population (1989: 325). More important, the nature of book producers changed, from being small family enterprises to being commercial publishing houses. The popular book market continued to grow after 1870 following the near-elimination of illiteracy and the consequent emergence of a mass reading public. Conditions in Greece were not yet ripe for the emergence of a culture industry—neither the technological infrastructure nor a large enough market of potential readers existed. The task in Greece was still the creation of a national popular culture rather than a mass culture.

In Athens, at first books were available for purchase only in bookstores, which also came to serve as meeting places. Toward the end of the century it was possible to purchase them, along with magazines and pamphlets, on the streets. This practice began in 1876 when the magazine *Estia* reprinted an article by the critic Roidis and had it sold on the streets (Angelu 1987: 24). Since the kiosk—where much printed material is sold in Greece today—had not yet been introduced, the street and the square became spaces in the formation of literary culture. Boys often stood on street corners selling their wares, shouting out the titles to entice passersby. By 1880 *Estia* circulated six such pamphlets of thirty-two pages each on topics ranging from patriotism to the scholar Korais, the poet Valaoritis, and the novels of Zola. Novels in serialized form were also sold by these street vendors to consumers eagerly awaiting the next installment. Sometimes even works of scholarly criticism reached the street, blurring in this way any meaningful distinction between high and low culture. Indeed, the same street merchant would offer works of "light literature" as well as highbrow culture. The literary society Parnassos circulated in this manner Roidis's controversial and influential article "On the State of Criticism in Contemporary Greece," which he had read to the members of the society. The fact that such a scholarly and lengthy (sixty pages) article was hawked on the street suggests that a broad market existed for these cultural goods outside the walls of the university, literary society, and library (Angelu 27).[28]

The street with its fast pace and coarse tastes served for a certain time as a site in which texts were sold just like other commodities. In the street the scholarly and the popular, aesthetics and commerce, high and low, work and pleasure, appreciation and enjoyment coexisted. The invention of a national culture was a phenomenon of the agora. For nearly one hundred years, however, this public sphere was restricted to the unofficial spaces of the nation. Only by the 1980s was it possible to speak of an integration of culture and state, a development that of course enables the state to intervene in the cultural realm. Paradoxically, this realization of demoticism's goal is leading to the disintegration of the public sphere as constituted during the last hundred years. Culture, no longer contested, is becoming invisible, transformed into an ideology, floating in the air, diffusing itself through all patterns of life. Culture seems to be bifurcating into high/private and low/public realms. A "sophisticated" cosmopolitan discourse is surfacing that defines the popular as the low Other. This discourse demands the withdrawal from the street and the renunciation of noisy declamation in favor of silent interpretive intensity. To be sure, modernity entails a movement from the outdoors to indoors. It posits art as the absolute form of domestic space, a haven from the public, a compensation for the isolated individual in a fragmented order. Valorizing the practices within the interior, it rejects spectacle and ritual as forms of a lower order. But there are sites of opposition. The low can resist the imposed hierarchies. It violates the norms of aesthetic culture by celebrating the codes, values, and manners of the abandoned agora.

Afterword: The End of the Stories?

One of my aims in this study was to explore the key role played by literature in the construction of cultural identities. Literature was instrumental in the formation of class consciousness in the bourgeois public spheres of Germany, England, and France, as it was also privileged in the nationalist projects of European communities. Literary writing is a force even today in the struggles against colonialism and imperialism in the Middle East, Africa, and South America, as shown by Barbara Harlow in *Resistance Literature* (1987). Through didactic texts it participates in the resistance to foreign domination and the creation of shared communities. Land can be recovered in the imagination, Said observes, even before the colonizer is actually overthrown (in Eagleton et al. 1990: 77).

Literature enables individuals to experience a heightened sense of solidarity, and eventually national unity, before, as well as after, the achievement of territorial and political integration. Literary culture also permits groups to empower themselves, particularly when, in societies of belated modernization, they feel politically disenfranchised. In the ensuing conflict between state and civil realms, they invest in culture to gain political authority, transforming culture into a domain from which they can resist the authoritarian state. Excluded from state structures, the demoticists in Greece produced a national popular culture that eventually appropriated the state. Culture in such cases is not a reconciliatory agent; it does not compensate for absence of power, but serves as a domain for capturing it.

The tension between state and civil society enacted in peripheral countries is just another contradiction at the heart of nationalist discourse. The nationalist explosions inaugurating the 1990s indicate that the nation-state, the sociopolitical experiment in enforcing a coincidence between ethnicity and territory, a system of signification and a physical topography, is unstable. Such an overlap between culture and demography takes time to perfect, and often entails the expulsion, extermination, or suppression of communities unable to fit within the new political order. National culture is assigned the task of homogenizing differences, ultimately by aestheticizing them into a transcendental fraternity. The continuous revision of the world's map, necessitated by the disappearance and appearance of states, shows that the nationalist question has not lost its force since it first arose at the end of the eighteenth century. A paradox in this obsession with nationalism, however, is the inconclusive sense of what constitutes a nation. As with other ideological structures, people are willing to die for something they believe in but don't understand. It is disconcertingly difficult to define the nation, as Ernst Renan concluded in 1882. Not an objective entity, a nation cannot adequately be conceived of in racial, ethnic, or religious terms. It is rather a "daily plebiscite," by which Renan meant the "clearly expressed desire [of a people] to continue a common life" (1990: 19). Because the ideas constituting nationhood are shared, people have to be conditioned to identify with them. Consent is engineered. Herein lies the significance of literary culture.

Literature was conscripted into the service of nationalism because of the capacity of stories both to promote popular identification with territory and history and to instill national symbols into daily practice. Narratives, of course, can also conceal the illusory nature of the nation. Although the nation exists only insofar as it is imagined by its citizens, it represents itself in their experiences as a very concrete and real essence. It is the stories reciting the past, present, and future of the nation that occlude the mediating process of interpretation and production involved in its construction. Through their fiction they contrive "effects of truth" (Alonso 1988: 34). They depict the nation's history as a unitary process of unfolding expectations leading to ever-greater self-fulfillment. Its culture likewise is portrayed as a univocal, homogeneous organism inspired by national interest and common purpose. This collective vision is, of course, a fabrication. Literature's original role in the nationalist enterprise was to tell a new story, and then to relate personal and regional narratives to the national one. Only in this way could experiences of everyday life be linked to national events: People remember where they were and what they were doing at the outbreak of a revolution or the assassination of a leader. The national myth, a rhetorical construction replacing older tales (of empire, aristocracy, royalty, and religion) is naturalized, becoming as real and transparent as language.

This occurs when dissenting voices are effectively silenced, when counter-narratives are pushed to the margins (from where, of course, they can still demystify official representations and chronologies). The memory of struggles waged over the nation is suppressed by the winning discourse, giving thereby the impression that the nation was born rather than made. No nation has ever been immaculately conceived, and quite often its genesis has necessitated war. Often in the name of racial, linguistic, or ethnic purity, nationalist discourse can slide from the realm of signification to a brutish literalism. This of course is another paradox of nationalism. It patterns people's lives, providing them with a sense of meaning and solidarity as it also forges an identity in reaction to foreign domination. But this very productive impulse can turn destructive when threatened by historical contingency or bedeviled by feelings of superiority.

When literature ceases being a tool for constructing a national identity in order to become a means of orchestrating an ideological consensus, it has for all intents and purposes been aestheticized. Surprisingly this happens even in marginal nations such as Greece, where the strains of forced modernization, brought on by the anxiety of belatedness, necessitate a compensatory medium. (Comparative analyses from nonwestern societies will reveal the extent to which this has occurred in other traditions.) An aesthetic culture acts as an imaginary realm where enervating dichotomies are harmonized and past battles forgotten. Although culture constitutes both an arena and an instrument in the nation-building process, it begins to disappear behind the scenes once the major conflicts are resolved. No longer fought over, it is taken for granted, becoming a part of everyday common sense, invisibly linking people in an intimate cohesion and guiding them through the differentiated spaces of modernity. People consent to it daily because national ideology, composed of narratives and symbols, has insinuated itself in their very sentiments, beliefs, and rituals.

Benedict Anderson has pointed to the pivotal role of print capitalism in the sociocultural realignments of seventeenth- and eighteenth-century Europe, leading to the nation-state as the dominant order of political organization. By creating new reading publics and unified fields of exchange, print enabled "rapidly growing numbers of people to think about themselves, and to relate themselves to others, in profoundly new ways" (1983: 40). The proliferation and dissemination of national narratives, in the form of histories, geographies, poems, biographies, and novels, were made possible by the technology of print and the expanding markets for its products. Literature was the first art to be mass-produced and put in the service of nationalism. In a sense, literature was nothing more than the framing of these narratives, those designated as fiction, which were thought to represent the life and manners of the nation and its citizenry. It was endowed with the capacity to mirror both the individual and the general, binding in this way private moments with public truths.

Other technologies of information and communication have been substituted for print in the fabrication of collective identities. Not only the press but also the movie industry, radio, and television are involved in the production of shared values and in the articulation of national symbols and meanings. The mass media yield pleasure but also enable ideologies to implant themselves in everyday practice. They also promote the spread of nationalism, as well as counter-ideologies, throughout the world much faster than, say, schooling did in the past. Cassettes, for instance, were used as an effective means of communicating the message of the Ayatollah Khomeini while he was in exile and his printed texts were banned in Iran.

New disciplinary technologies have been deployed, as Foucault's work has explained, in classifying, recording, identifying, at first deviant groups, then the entire population. While Foucault's research on sexuality, the prison, the asylum, and the hospital did not address the nation-state per se, it has shown the extent of public intervention in the most intimate aspects of life through techniques of surveillance. "The state documentation project," Bernard Cohn and Nicholas Dirks argue, "is both totalizing and individualizing. It participates in the constitution of social categories and identities (educated, uneducated, rich, poor, male, female, young, old), it marks off religions, languages, customs, and ethnic groups, and it implies various forms of hierarchies which are officially recognized" (1988: 226).

Future research, applying Foucault's genealogical method to studies of nation building and the creation of public identities, will no doubt reveal the new relationship being formed between state and culture. For the state's penetration of civil society undoes the essential bourgeois distinction between the private and public domains. The validity of bourgeois society has rested on the concept of autonomy, itself so central to the experience of modernity. If postmodernism heralds the collapse or the conflation of the autonomous spheres organizing human activity, then the dissolution of the boundaries between state and culture provides proof of the twilight of modernity.

The internal relations constituting the nation-state have changed. There have also emerged entities such as multinational corporations, which, more powerful and self-sufficient than most nations, challenge or ignore their legitimacy and authority. Although recent international developments—the formation of unified common markets (e.g., the European Community) and the negotiation between states of tariff-free trade pacts (e.g., between Canada and the United States)—have undermined the economic usefulness of states, the nation as an imagined realm of signification has maintained its vitality. Nothing has yet arisen to replace national identity. The nation-state has shown a remarkably stubborn staying power, having been mechanically reproduced all over the globe ever since its invention in 1789. Although literature in western nations may no longer be important in the production and legitimation of cultural identities, the significance of stories to express a common destiny, to concoct shared memories, and to promote collective dreams has not diminished. National narratives as well as nations still seem necessary.

Why do people wish to regard themselves primarily as members of such a community and why do revolutions in the Third World continue to define themselves in national terms? Why is the appeal of nationalism so seemingly universal? The answer may lie ultimately in the metaphysics of nationalism, which has transformed it into the global theology of the modern age. Nationalist discourse, with its tales of progress, self-fulfillment, and manifest destiny, allows modern individuals to deny their mortality in the face of change. Nationalism recites not, as Seamus Deane claims, the fall of humankind from "bliss" into alienation (in Eagleton et al. 1990: 9) but quite the reverse, the hope of redemption. Though people are confronted with the achievements of other societies, past and present, nationalism allows them to forget contingency, to ignore that they are part of history, that their story is one among many and certainly not the greatest, and that their culture, the most intrinsic experience of themselves as social beings, is not natural but invented.

Notes

1. Criticism as National Culture

1. Pratt's observation is certainly valid for modern Greece, whose entire culture was, and often still is, regarded by classical philologists as a degenerate form of its classical precursors. Greece, as I argue throughout this study, is perhaps the country to have suffered the most from its "glorious past." Indeed, Greece may be unique, Michael Herzfeld contends, "in the degree to which the country has been forced to play the contrasted roles of *Ur-Europa* and humiliated oriental vassal at one and the same time" (1987: 19).

2. Paradoxically, as Tzvetan Todorov points out in *The Conquest of America,* it is the capacity of western civilization to understand the Other which has permitted it to conquer not only America but also much of the entire world. The task of this understanding, Todorov argues (extrapolating from Cortés's successful subjugation of the Aztecs), is not to come to terms with the Other but to assimilate it in western ideology. "The Europeans exhibit remarkable qualities of flexibility and improvization which permit them all the better to impose their own way of life" (1984: 248).

3. For an argument along similar lines see Jusdanis (1987c).

4. See also Hooks (1981) and Hull, Scott, and Smith (1982).

5. In his response to the articles in *Critical Inquiry* dealing with race and writing, Tzvetan Todorov voices this very complaint. Although, as he says, two-thirds of the volume is devoted to an analysis of the image of the Other in European literature, the choice field of study is English literature from the last two centuries (1986: 177). On the hegemony of this discipline see Reed Way Dasenbrock's "English Department Geography" in which he explains how English has appropriated a vast number of authors writing in the English language despite their nationality, ethnic origins, or current country of residence. "Place of birth is important if that happens to be English; place of residence all important if it happens to be English. Heads England wins; tails the rest of the world loses" (1987: 56). The criteria used to determine whether an author is "English" always work toward the advantage of this field.

6. For this reason he worked toward the abolition of the English department at the University of East Africa. Ngugi strongly disputes that the English tradition is the central root of African cultural heritage since, quite simply, Africa is not an extension of the West. If there is a need to study the historic continuity of a single culture, he contends, it should be an African one (1972: 146). The department was eventually dissolved and replaced by two autonomous entities, one for languages and the other for literatures. In both, African languages and literatures formed the core curriculum.

7. The functionality of the "aesthetic," its use in specific situations, is often juxtaposed by critics of minority and minor discourse with the aestheticist isolation of art in nineteenth-century western Europe. This contrasting conception of "art" is encapsulated in Larry Neal's pithy statement concerning the Black Arts Movement of the 1960s in the United States: "The Black Arts Movement believes that your ethics and aesthetic are one" (in Gayle 1971: 275). In such an ideological framework the question for black critics, according to Addison Gayle, is not how beautiful a melody, poem, or novel is but "how much more beautiful has the poem, melody, play, or novel made the life of a single black man?" (1971: xxiii). As Larry Neal argues, black art is the aesthetic of black power. Black art merges with black power; while the former is concerned with the relationship between art and politics, the latter articulates the art of politics (272). The task facing minority critics is to help construct an "aesthetic" not in abstract, essentialist terms, but one defined by a certain world view, position, use of language, and understanding of art which, due to social circumstances, departs from dominant aesthetics.

8. In his response to Joyce, Henry Louis Gates disclaims an extended political role for criticism and espouses instead an "epistemological politics": "I do not think that my task as a critic is to lead black people into 'freedom.' My task is to explicate black texts" (1987a: 357). Although Gates understands the implications of the use of theory in the study of African-American literature, he nevertheless concludes that the racism of the western tradition should not deter black critics from using contemporary theoretical innovations (349), since all students of literature share the art of interpretation even when they do not share the same texts (351).

This interpretive disposition prompts Gates to espouse the methodologies of close reading practiced by western scholars: "Close reading of any critical complexion is what this volume advocates; there can be no compromise" (1984: 13, 4). In an earlier essay he states that a black text is like any literary text and its explication must be an activity of "close textual analysis" (in Fisher 1979: 68). It is highly questionable, however, that literary interpretation, a practice rooted in western textual analysis (biblical and legal) is a universal act binding us all. In any case, when African-American critics exploit any "tool" helping them to elucidate the "complexities of figuration" peculiar to their tradition (1984: 4) they automatically convert texts of that tradition into aesthetic structures and objects of aestheticist interpretation. Gates's black texts end up performing the same structuralist and deconstructive moves of their white counterparts; they conceal their binary oppositions, parody other writing, and refer to their own intertextuality: "We the readers must exploit the oppositions and give them a place in a larger symbolic structure" (in Fisher 1979: 222). Gates finds, for instance, that "Reed's parodic use of intertextuality demonstrates that *Mumbo Jumbo* is a post-modern text" (1984: 302). The application to these texts of methodologies adopted from literary theory necessarily transplants them into an institution of literature, the autonomous entity—which is a western construct. This may not be an undesirable goal for Gates or any other critic, but it should be recognized. The pursuit of close readings, the search for intertextuality, and the exploration of figurative language in black (or any) texts carries with it specific ideological implications. While in her rejection of poststructuralism Joyce is wrong to state that black poetry—particularly that written during and after the 60s—defies the "poststructuralist sensibility," she at least acknowledges the political consequences of this approach.

9. In his *Blues, Ideology, and Afro-American Literature: A Vernacular Theory,* Baker offers a very useful survey of African-American criticism from the integrationist poetics of the 50s, the black aesthetic of the 60s, to the reconstructionists of the 70s. He is interested in explicating a form of thought that grounds African-American discourse in concrete, material situations (25). Although he criticizes his colleagues for their exclusively literary study of texts, he also provides just readings of texts, albeit ideological ones that take into account the vernacular. He says, for example, that the "ideological analysis of discursive structure that yields the foregoing interpretations of *The Life of Olaudah Equiano* [a slave narrative] is invaluable for practical criticism" (38). Baker too is working with a western notion of reading, text, and interpretation. His last chapter ultimately ends up illustrating another (though ideologically aware) method of reading.

10. On the importation of the novel in the Arabic context, see Beard (1987). Wlad Godzich and Jeffrey Kittay argue that when historians and ethnographers refer to the modern notion of prose for whatever is not versed they end up "fatally distorting" their object of study (1987: 193). They prefer the term "nonverse" as a more accurate description of narratives not composed in verse.

11. Baudrillard makes this observation in his critique of historical materialism. The analysis of the contradictions in western society, he adds, has not led to a comprehension of earlier societies but has succeeded in exporting these contradictions to them. Having failed to undertake a radical critique of political economy, historical materialism reactivates "its model at a world-wide level" and naturalizes earlier societies "under the sign of the mode of production" (89–91). Castoriadis makes a similar point when he says that in the ancient world the economy was not yet constituted as an autonomous moment of human activity. To assume, he argues further, that people have always sought the greatest possible development of productive forces and that societies have always been motivated by this tendency, is to extrapolate to the whole of history the motivations and values of present capitalist society. The idea that life consists in the accumulation of wealth is madness to the Kwakiutl Indians, who amass wealth only to destroy it (1987: 13, 24).

12. On the literary production of Greek Americans, see Giannaris (1985) and Alexander Karanikas's "Greek American Literature" in Di Pietro and Ifkovic (1983). Di Pietro and Ifkovic point to the difficulties experienced by "ethnic" authors in having their work recognized. In spite of the cultural pluralism of the American public, the authors argue, textbooks and anthologies favor texts of the "ethnically neutral mainstream" (1983: 1). In "I'm here: An Asian American Woman's Response" Amy Ling (1987) discusses the problems she has encountered in gaining acceptance for research on Asian American women writers.

13. Those minorities not corresponding to their definition can receive little attention. Considering that their topic is minor literature, the authors manifest a bias for European minorities (Czech Jews) and modernist texts (Kafka and to a certain extent Joyce). There is nothing wrong in investigating one community as an ethnographic base, but it is misleading to generalize conclusions that are specific to this group. Deleuze and Guattari's ideas, Renato Rosaldo insists, cannot be applied, for instance, to Chicano literature (1987: 65–66). "American minority history," he argues, "should neither be ignored nor reshaped according to Eurocentric models of minority literature" (67).

2. From Empire to Nation-State: Greek Expectations

1. A very interesting study could be made of how these two peoples exploited the position of their ethnic communities within the discourses of Hellenism and Hebraism respectively to equate with western interests their struggles for nationhood and their subsequent irredentist campaigns. Occupying privileged places in the imaginings of the West, they capitalized on

the familiarity of their cause against the oriental Otherness of their opponents. In both cases atrocities against the Greeks and Zionists received prominent coverage in western media, whereas those they committed were often ignored or played down. Both emergent nations made grandiose promises to an expectant and hopeful West: Greece undertook to become nothing less than a glorious Hellas while Israel claimed to teach a new morality. It seems they have failed both themselves and the world in the realization of their visions. See Lambropoulos's *Emancipation and Interpretation: Autonomy and the Aesthetic Turn in Modernity* (Forthcoming), a study that offers a genealogy of the Hebraic and Hellenic models and an account of their central role in the project of modernity.

2. In her study of the representations of Greece and Greeks in European painting Fani-Maria Tsigakou has observed that even those painters who had visited Greece in the early eighteenth century depicted not the actual Greek landscape but "the scenery of the imagined classical Greek world" (1981: 28). Temples were often portrayed in dense foliage; the Mycenaean citadel was shown surrounded by idyllic knolls rather than by barren rocks; the Attic hills were painted as volcanic mountains in order "to contribute a sense of sublimity to the 'Acropolis Rock' they encircle" (29). Later other artists took a more serious interest in modern Greece itself. In the works of a committed philhellene like Eugène Delacroix Greeks appeared in contemporary dress among the classical ruins. By the late nineteenth century, however, modern Greece had lost its appeal for European artists but classical Hellas still remained a compelling subject.

3. As Michael Herzfeld (1982: 130–35) points out, the "yours" is often replaced by "ours" whenever the line appears on its own or out of context. This substitution had enormous implications for Greek nationalism and the doctrine known as the *Megali Idea* (Great Idea) which I shall discuss later. The prophetic conclusion became political in the discourse of nationalism.

4. It was called the Rum or Roman millet because the Byzantines continued to regard themselves as the eastern half of the Roman Empire. This usage has been carried over in popular form as *Romios* to signify the local, indigenous, Orthodox, eastern element of Greek identity as opposed to the Hellenic, western, and classically oriented component. Herzfeld has examined the effect of the imposition of an official discourse upon Greeks that rejected many of the most familiar aspects of their indigenous culture as exotic or flawed (1982: 186).

5. Korais and most other Greek and European thinkers completely omitted Byzantium in their histories of Greece, demonstrating in this way their Enlightenment prejudice against the medieval period. Their message to Greeks, in the words of Cyril Mango, was to break with Byzantium, cast out the monks and the Phanariot aristocracy, and form an egalitarian democracy (1965: 37). The place of Byzantium in Greek culture was consolidated by philologists and historians in response to Fallmerayer's arguments against continuity. Most noteworthy in this enterprise was the five-volume history of the Greek nation by Konstantinos Paparigopulos (1815–91), a powerful expression of pan-Hellenism that presented the history of the Greek people as a dynamic unity of related periods.

6. This can be seen specifically in the realm of Greek art. The School of Arts was erected in Athens in 1836, two years before the founding of the university. In the beginning its professors were all foreigners; Greeks, educated mainly in Munich and Rome, were not hired until 1842. After graduating from the School of Arts Greek artists themselves were immediately dispatched to Munich for further study. A result of this close link between the School of Arts and the artistic institutions of Munich was that the Bavarian city continued to influence the taste of the Athenians well into the twentieth century. There is an irony here, as pointed out by Alexander Xydis, for in thinking that western art was superior, Greek artists and scholars ironically allied themselves with a secondary artistic center and thereby isolated themselves from such vital capitals of art as Paris or Berlin (1984: 145). Three generations of artists were

formed by the "School of Munich," so that even by the end of the nineteenth century Greek art retained its classical-academic and classical-realist character. This was what the artists had learned in Munich (and to a certain extent in Rome) and this was what the Athenian patrons demanded.

7. The effect of this policy was the patriarchate's suppression of the Serbian Patriarchate of Pec in 1766 and the Bulgarian Archbishopric of Ochrid in 1767.

8. Even in 1828, 90–95 percent of Greek men were illiterate; in 1840, 87.5 percent; in 1870, 71.38 percent; in 1907, the rate was reduced to 50.20 percent. Among women illiteracy remained at 82.55 percent. In 1830 only 10–15 percent of the population was urban; in 1879, 18 percent; in 1889, 21 percent; and in 1908, 24 percent (Tsoucalas 1977: 393, 165).

9. Like many other indigenous, preindependence institutions, it continued to wield considerable power in Greek society, frustrating in this way the plans of the westernizers for a modern, secular, and liberal nation. In the new secular system the church was to be subordinate to the state, responsible, as is typical in a functionally differentiated society, for only one sphere of identity—the spiritual life of citizens. But the Greek church, having inherited the dual (religious/civic) function of the post-Byzantine patriarchate, maintained its influence, if unofficially, in the temporal affairs of the state. Its authority, for instance, can be seen in the name of the ministry of education: The Ministry of Education and Religious Affairs. A clause (16) in the constitution of 1952 institutionalized this authority: "Instruction at all levels of primary and secondary schools aims at the moral and spiritual education and the development of a national consciousness in youth based on the ideological orientations of Hellenochristian civilization."

The patriarchate of Constantinople (I refer to this body as such because this is its ecclesiastical title, though it is located in Istanbul) recognized the Autocephalous Greek Church only in 1850. This was the first major fissure in its ecumenical authority. As the various ethnic communities of the Orthodox millet evolved into independent nations, they formed their own churches. Today the patriarchate has jurisdiction over the Orthodox of Turkey (where only a few thousand live after the mandatory exchange of populations in 1922), Crete and various other islands of the Aegean, North and South America, Mount Athos, and Finland (Ware 1963: 140–41).

10. In 1832 the superpowers and guarantors of Greece bestowed a monarchy upon the independent country, offering the "hereditary sovereignty" to Prince Frederick Otto of Wittelsbach, the seventeen-year-old son of King Ludwig of Bavaria.

11. In 1832 the three powers served as guarantors of a loan of sixty million francs, but demanded changes in economic policy. In 1854–57 England and France occupied the port of Pireas to enforce fiscal control. The rival Greek political parties, seeking the support of those powers, formed the English, French, and Russian parties. These organizations operated until 1856, acting as the powers' proxies in Greece. In the civil war (1831–32), for instance, following the assassination of Governor Ioannis Kapodistrias, France and Britain campaigned, through their respective parties, to secure strong monarchical principles in the constitution (Couloumbis, Petropulos, Psomiades 1976: 64).

12. Greece continued to be English until after World War II, when, with the declaration of the Truman Doctrine, it entered the American sphere of influence.

13. On the notion of the comprador bourgeoisie see Poulantzas 1976 and Hoogvelt 1978.

14. Note that in the late 1980s the party slogan of the conservative New Democracy party was "Greece belongs to the West" while for the socialist and populist PASOK it was "Greece belongs to the Greeks." Although in favor of further Greek integration into Europe, New Democracy also supports a strong Orthodox culture. Similarly, PASOK, despite its rhetoric of populism and xenophobia, embraces the modernization of Greek institutions.

15. In the encyclical letter the patriarch exhorted the Orthodox faithful not to be deceived by Catholicism and democracy, and denounced the christening of children with classical names. The text is found in K. Th. Dimaras (n.d.).

16. Margaret Alexiou (1982: 172–73) addresses the schizophrenic predicament of students at the University of Athens in the early 1970s. They would have learned demotic at home and at primary school but *katharevusa* at all higher levels. Under the reforms introduced by the Yeoryios Papandreou government in 1964, and by the time they were in high school, the language of instruction in school was demotic. But this was banned by the junta in 1967, so all textbooks had to be republished in *katharevusa*. At the university all lectures were held in the purist register. All formal work submitted at the universities had to be in that register as well. Yet there was an increasing amount of scholarly material written in demotic, largely by professors from the University of Thessaloniki. Students had to shift between these two codes, with the result that some mastered neither.

17. A new movement has been launched in the 1980s by some intellectuals who, fearing the importation of foreign words and the "vulgarization" of the language under the populist policies, wish to retain some form of *katharevusa* as a bulwark against further change.

3. The Making of a Canon: A Literature of Their Own

1. I refer here specifically to texts because this chapter deals with the literary canon. I do not intend in this way to reify the category of literature and separate the literary canon from other canons. The literary canon lends itself well to such an analysis, but it is possible to investigate canon formation in other text-based structures such as law, religion, and philosophy, and also in non-text-oriented fields such as music and fine art.

2. Its admission into the English language, and into literary criticism, remains obscure. The *Oxford English Dictionary,* published between 1884 and 1928, does not contain in its fifteen listings for the word any entries approximating the modern meaning of a catalogue of books. The closest is the fourth entry, in which *canon* is defined as a "collection or list of books of the Bible accepted by the Christian Church as genuine and inspired. Also any set of sacred books" (74). Only in the supplement, published in 1972, is this definition expanded to include "those writings of a secular author accepted as authentic" (427). Two sources are provided: the first comes from the *Encyclopaedia Britannica* of 1885, which refers to the "Platonic canon," and the second from C. J. Sisson's *Shakespeare: Complete Works* (1953), in which the heading "The canon and the texts" appears. The relatively late recognition of this particular meaning of the term by the *OED* suggests that, although it had been used as early as 1885, it was not considered worthy of recording. This holds true for more recent reference books as well. The *Princeton Encyclopedia of Poetry and Poetics* (1974) has no listing for *canon*. J. A. Cuddon's *A Dictionary of Literary Terms* (1976) contains an entry for the term but stresses its usage in biblical studies. Although it defines the word as a "body of writings established as authentic" it notes that the term "usually refers to biblical writings accepted as authorized" (99). It concludes, however, that the word can apply also to an author's works "accepted as genuine." The fact that such standard reference works either ignore or consider secondary the literary dimension of *canon* demonstrates that even as late as the last decade the canon was not regarded as an object of critical attention.

3. In his discussion of the works of Polyclitus, the Roman historian Pliny notes that he fashioned "what artists call a 'Canon' or Model Statue, as they draw their artistic outlines from it as from a sort of standard; and he alone of mankind is deemed by means of one work of art to have created the art itself" (*Natural History,* XXXIV, XIX, 55–57). The work that Pliny refers to is said to be the *Doryphoros,* which, as Pliny observes, embodied the principles of Polyclitus's art and came to be regarded as a classic work of sculpture. Galen

mentions Polyclitus's treatise, the *Canon,* in *de Placitis Hippocratis et Platonis:* "For having taught us in that text all the proportions of the body, Polyclitus supported his argument with a work; he fashioned a statue according to the principles of his argument, and called the statue, like the work, the 'Canon'" (Galen 1874: V, 449). Galen also refers specifically to this sculpture: "And a statue may be commended, the one called the 'Canon' of Polyclitus which derives its name from the precise symmetry that all its parts have to one another" (*Peri Kraseon,* I, 566). On Polyclitus's notion of the canon see Schulz 1955.

4. In book I of the *Institutio Oratoria* Quintilian writes that the old teachers of language and letters "were not content with obelizing lines or rejecting books whose titles they regarded as spurious . . . but also drew up a canon of authors from which some were omitted altogether" (I, iv, 3). These passages represent a major source for those trying to recover the composition of the Alexandrian canon. Quintilian himself provides a list of Greek and Roman authors arranged according to genre which a young orator might study to improve his vocabulary and style. See the discussion of this list in Zetzel (1984: 121–22). Zetzel notes that the *Pinakes* by Callimachus, which has not survived, was said to be a complete list of one hundred and twenty books of all earlier "literature" arranged according to genre (97). Similar lists were prepared by other scholars and poets of the Museum in Alexandria who were responsible for classifying by genre earlier Greek literature. Due to scanty evidence philologists have difficulty in determining the authors included in the Alexandrian canon. On the basis of the lists drawn by Quintilian and Dionysus of Halicarnassus, and of a tenth-century manuscript found in Mount Athos, it is possible to propose the following list (from Sandys 1915: 40): *Epic Poets:* Homer, Hesiod, Peisander, Panyasis, Antimachus; *Iambic Poets:* Semonides, Archilochus, Hipponax; *Tragic Poets:* Aeschylus, Sophocles, Euripides, Ion, Achaeus; *Comic Poets, Old:* Epicharmus, Cratinus, Eupolis, Aristophanes, Pherecrates, Crates, Plato; *Middle:* Antiphanes, Alexis; *New:* Menander, Philippides, Diphilus, Philemon, Apollodorus; *Elegiac Poets:* Callinus, Mimnermus, Philetas, Callimachus; *Lyric Poets:* Alcman, Alcaeus, Sappho, Stesichorus, Pindar, Bacchylides, Ibycus, Anacreon, Simonides; *Orators:* Demosthenes, Lysias, Hypereides, Isocrates, Aeschines, Lycurgus, Isaeus, Antiphon, Andocides, Deinarchus; *Historians:* Thucydides, Herodotus, Xenophon, Philistus, Theopompus, Ephorus, Anaximenes, Callisthenes, Hellanicus, Polybius.

5. It is assumed that Quintilian is referring to a catalogue of earlier poets compiled by Aristophanes of Byzantium, which contained in Aristophanes' view the best examples of classical "literature." Aristophanes' list was one of many catalogues of classical authors whose style was regarded as exemplary and thus suitable for emulation by students. To the lists of foremost poets were added in time those of orators, historians, and philosophers. Caecilius of Calacte (first century B.C.), for instance, wrote a treatise on the characteristics of the Ten Orators, a fact demonstrating that a canon of orators had already been recognized by that time. He may have derived his list, according to John Sandys (1915: 40), from Hermippus of Smyrna, a grammarian of the third century B.C. who wrote a work on famous poets, philosophers, and law-givers. Furthermore, Seneca refers to a catalogue of philosophers (Epistle, XXXIX, 2). By the second century A.D. a number of canons of representative rhetoricians had been formulated and were circulating in Alexandria and Pergamum. At this time, J. J. Pollitt believes, some grammarians even began comparing specific oratorical styles with those of painters and sculptors, thereby creating similar canons of artists (1974: 60).

6. It is believed that the word *classicus* was first used by the late antique author, Aulus Gellius (c. A.D. 130–180) in *Noctes Atticae.* In a passage concerning correctness of certain grammatical forms, Gellius advises readers to consult classic writers, that is, those writing for the upper classes: "So go now and inquire . . . whether any orator or poet, provided he be of that earlier band—that is to say, any classical [*classicus*] or authoritative writer, not one of the common herd [*proletarius*]—has used *quadriga* or *harenae*" (XIX, 8, 15). In

antiquity the idea of a model author had a linguistic basis, oriented by the grammatical criterion of correct speech (Curtius 1973: 250). The *classici* were those people possessing an income above a certain level. Gradually for the Romans the classic came to be used metaphorically to mean an author of first-class quality. The modern notion of the classic has retained this signification. It suggests a work of the highest order, the best, a standard of excellence worthy of emulation. (It also refers specifically to the art and literature of Greece and Rome, since in the history of western culture only these works were considered first class and thus suitable objects of study.) For Sainte-Beuve the classic is an index of civility and a product of individual genius; a classic author is one "who has enriched the human spirit, who has truly increased its treasure, who has caused it to take a step forward" ([1850] 1971: 86). T. S. Eliot discussed the meaning of this concept in his essay "What Is a Classic?" (1944) in which, referring primarily to Virgil and secondarily to Dante and Racine, he defined the classic as the realization of a language and of a history in one single author (1957: 54). This universal classic, which arises only when a civilization, a language, and a literature are mature, differs from the relative classic, which he saw as the outstanding work of one literature only. Frank Kermode expanded on Eliot's thoughts, seeing the classic, much like the Bible, as a work open to accommodation, remaining alive, meaningful, and contemporary under varying conditions (1983: 44). Whatever specific meaning is attached to this term it is obviously an integral part of canon formation. Classics are read, praised, and imitated. They are not only canonized but also create their own minor traditions, thereby ensuring their survival both as individual texts and as intertexts. From the perspective of canonicity, however, the relevant question is not the ontological "What is a classic?", as posed by Sainte-Beuve and Eliot, but rather the historical "Why and how was it established?"

7. On the survival and transmission of classical texts see Reynolds and Wilson 1974. It would be interesting to consider the politics behind the formation of the classical canon, that is, the reasons why grammarians chose one text for examination over another. Were their decisions taken strictly on linguistic and stylistic grounds, as is generally believed, or were there other factors? Surely, as stated earlier, it is not a coincidence that nearly all the works of a conservative philosophical figure such as Plato have survived while only fragments remain from the oeuvre of his opponents. Tradition has not only destroyed their texts but has also succeeded in branding them as enemies of truth and philosophy.

8. My source for the discussion of the Gnostic gospels is Pagels (1979).

9. With this in mind, it is worth asking whether canons can exist in the natural sciences, which, as Thomas Kuhn has argued, place no such value on the past. Science, Kuhn insists, willfully and necessarily destroys its genealogy. In order to establish itself, a new paradigm must successfully falsify the assumptions and truths of previous systems. "When it repudiates a past paradigm, a scientific community simultaneously renounces, as a fit subject for professional scrutiny, most of the books and articles in which that paradigm had been embodied" (1970: 167). Scientific education, Kuhn adds, has no equivalent of the art museum or of a collection of classics. This is quite at odds with the arts and the humanities, whose existence seems to depend on the proper maintenance of a library of masterpieces. This divergent attitude toward the past emphasizes the impossibility of a canon in science. Science has no use of canons since past solutions are regarded as mistakes. A new breakthrough necessitates the removal of the suddenly outdated material from the science library, since these books and journals have no more scientific value (Kuhn 1977: 345). They will become meaningful one day only to historians of science. In the canons of art and literature works may fall from the center of current interest but such "lost" texts may always one day be "rediscovered." For an attempt to relate Kuhn's notion of paradigm to the realm of aesthetics see Brown 1986.

10. Francis Haskell writes that our modern aesthetic sensibilities were formed largely between 1790 and 1870. This period witnessed a radical transformation of artistic values, a movement away from the baroque and away from the Hellenistic and Roman to the classical (1976: 5). In the obsession with taste common to the time, the eighteenth century set the direction and pattern for ages to follow. Although changes have taken place since 1870, they cannot be compared, in Haskell's opinion, with the upheavals in taste marking the eighteenth century. As we are on the topic of art history, it is interesting to note that reversals can easily occur in the fate of individual works within the artistic canon when the authorship of a particular painting or sculpture is challenged. Art historical or laboratory evidence can demonstrate that the work is a fake, that it was produced by an assistant instead of a master, or that it is of a later age. Such discoveries could result in the removal of the work in question from the museum or a shift in the hierarchy of great artists. A fascinating example is the case of an ancient bronze horse declared a forgery by an expert from the Metropolitan Museum when he discovered that an underseam on the belly of the horse showed evidence of a type of casting not invented until the fourteenth century. In the mid-70s, however, researchers concluded that the seams were in fact indigenous to the casting procedures of the Greeks, a finding verified by laboratory evidence. The horse is now back in the museum as a "masterpiece" of Hellenistic sculpture. For other such examples, see "Masterpieces Rise and Fall on a Tide of New Expertise," *New York Times,* December 7, 1986.

11. Therefore, if marginalized groups, such as, for instance, feminist critics, desire to undermine canonic practices and the canon itself, they must address the function of the canon, and not least the centrality of literature in contemporary culture. Otherwise only a revision would occur, the appropriation of neglected texts in the traditional hierarchy that would leave intact the process itself and the assumptions supporting it. It would be as elitist as its patriarchal predecessors, since it would by definition exclude, that is, it would separate the deserving from the undeserving, useful from nonuseful, good from bad. My caveat is not intended to belittle the feminist canon, since the construction of such a canon would in itself introduce significant changes through the imposition of a new hierarchy on textual production.

12. Fowler rightly stresses the crucial role played by genre in canon formation. Indeed, he considers it the most consequential factor in the transformations taking place within the hierarchy of texts (216). Changes in the literary canon, he argues, may often be understood as evaluation and devaluation of genres. Fowler thus shifts the emphasis away from the individual text to the formation it belongs to, since if the position of this grouping moves up or down the ladder, the fate of the texts characterized by it will probably (though not necessarily) be affected. Genre, however, cannot be considered the most decisive element in the formation of canons. In Greece, for example, the struggle between purism and demoticism posited the type of Greek used as the chief criterion for canonicity. The literary and the canonical were primarily determined not by the choice of genre—whether authors composed lyric, epic, or tragedy—but the form of language—whether they wrote in the archaizing register or the vernacular.

13. The *Odyssey* by Nikos Kazantzakis comes immediately to mind, an epic poem of 33,333 verses written in a seventeen-syllable unrhymed iambic measure of eight beats. Its publication in 1938 met first with bewilderment and indignation and then with neglect. Since then, although the poem has attracted a cult audience abroad, critics both in Greece and overseas have largely ignored it. One of the main reasons for this is the absence of a contemporary category in which it may be classified and discussed as literature. The epic in our day, despite the "qualities" of individual works, is not regarded as a relevant genre. In the future, however, if the hierarchy of genres changes, it may once again become a viable category and Kazantzakis's *Odyssey* may achieve a central place in the Greek canon. Although epic has fallen out of the repertoire of available genres for today's writers, classics such as the *Odyssey, Iliad,*

and *Aeneid* remain impervious to these fluctuations in taste. They have been endowed through the ages with such a degree of cultural meaning that they have entered an almost petrified canon of western masterpieces. Although Homer may have been ridiculed and assaulted during the "quarrel" of the Ancients and Moderns, and although some periods may have preferred Virgil to Homer, the value of these works in western culture seems to have been largely unaffected. In this and parallel cases the individual text has become more relevant than the genre in which it is classified.

14. Thompson points to the case of Chippendale chairs in England, which, as commonplace furniture, belonged to the transient category. Through dilapidation and change in fashion they lost even this value and disappeared into attics until some odd, though culturally powerful, individuals placed them in their drawing rooms and extolled their virtues. At a certain point, Thompson concludes, some eccentric aesthetic judgments become sufficiently centric to result in the emergence of a new fashion or style (27).

15. This is not always the case. As Jonathan Culler (1985) points out in a review of Thompson's book, contemporary culture takes pride in producing material that clearly is transient, if not rubbish. Television programs, replaced one after the other, and best sellers, whose authors are quickly forgotten, are two examples of commodities meant to be immediately consumed and discarded. Kitsch presents an interesting classification: it makes the rubbish of mass culture durable by converting it into high art.

16. Modernist abstract art is the most radical manifestation of this aestheticism. Its devaluation of mimetic representation and exclusion of narrative place a premium on form that baffles and silences all but the educated. Although, as W. J. T. Mitchell argues, ordinary consumers have very little to say about it, those versed in theory know its secrets and can discuss it endlessly (1989: 349). Theory, unavailable to the public at large, allows access to the world of modernist art. Consumption of this art is the most prestigious form of cultural capital.

17. Lamont and Lareau argue that cultural capital is not central to cultural and social reproduction in the United States, for instance. High-status cultural symbols are less stable in the United States than in France because the public for cultural goods changes more rapidly. Purchasable goods show greater status here than culturally acquired ones. Furthermore, the consensus necessary for high culture is negatively affected by race and ethnicity (1988: 161). On prestige see the special issue of *Cultural Critique* 12, 1989; on status see Turner (1988).

18. The task was undertaken by Greek intellectuals as well as enthusiastic philhellenes. A case in point is Theodor Kind's *Neugriechische Poesieen* (1833), a bilingual edition published in Leipzig that contains both popular poetry and the recognized Greek poets of the time: Hristopulos, Ipsilantis, Rizos-Nerulos, and A. Sutsos. The volume is probably the earliest in Greek or any other language to anthologize the work of Greek poets. What is most striking about Kind's book is the missionary zeal of the prologue (written in Greek). Kind declares his fervent hope to contribute to the rebirth of Greek culture with the book's publication. He exhorts his Greek readers to get to know their culture, study the civilization of their ancestors, and cultivate their vernacular. His own eagerness for things Greek led him in 1849 to publish a collection of Greek folk songs accompanied by a German translation (Kind 1849).

Kind's volume was not the earliest collection of popular poetry but it was probably the first volume to anthologize the works of poets. For the earliest (and very influential) collections of popular verse see Fauriel (1824) and Haxthausen (1935). Both Fauriel and von Haxthausen were motivated by the philhellenism sweeping Europe. Fauriel, in his introduction, speaks favorably of the Greeks, praising their spirit of independence, and characterizing the collected poems as an expression of "l'esprit national" (1824: xxv). His English translator, Charles B. Sheridan, shares similar sentiments. In the dedication to his *Songs of Greece* he refers to the translated poems as documents proving the heroism of Greece. This is a valuable collection, he reiterates in the preface, "not so much of beautiful poems, as of historical documents, which prove the capacity of the Greeks to defend and govern their country" (1825: xviii). The Greek collectors were also motivated by nationalism. One of the earliest anthologies published in Greece, the collection (1880) by Antonios Sigalas, brought to the fore the nationalist ideology informing such projects. Sigalas writes in his prologue that his main purpose in collecting and publishing these folk songs is their preservation. Thus he traveled to the outskirts of the provinces, beyond the reaches of "foreign influence," to gather songs of "authentic and true Greek character." He hoped that this work would subsequently prove useful in the "development and perfection of a national music."

19. Even Dionisios Solomos (eventually crowned the national poet of Greece) and his followers in the Heptanesian School, though profoundly influenced by the popular songs, took an interest in them as material for the creation of a national literature rather than as folk poetry (Beaton 1980: 8). The popular songs continue to have an ambiguous relationship with Greek literature. Although their existence has been fully accepted, their position within the canon is tenuous because their stories cannot easily be accommodated in the account of high literature. Anthologists and literary historians usually set a section aside, often in the beginnings of their books, for folk poetry and then proceed to the examination of other literary texts. This separation is of course inevitable, since the narration of literature is author-based while the songs are generally regarded as anonymous. Composed outside the paradigm of high literature, they do not lend themselves easily to the traditional study of literary texts.

20. Michael Herzfeld explores some of these problems with regard to the emergence of folklore studies. He investigates how the discipline of folklore was created to provide intellectual reinforcement to the process of nation building. Folklorists set out from the beginning to search for classical survivals in modern Greek culture. Folk songs were plundered for proofs of Hellenic identity, texts were purged of non-Greek (i.e., Turkish) elements, and the *klefts* (revolutionaries and brigands) were identified with classical heroes. The tenet of cultural continuity, Herzfeld argues, informed the discipline of folklore and provided the organizing principle for the collection, classification, and ranking of all ethnographic items (1982: 10). On the relationship among nationalism, politics, and folklore see also Alexiou (1984/85). Loring Danforth examines the ideological consequences of this theory in contemporary anthropology, which, in claiming that modern Greek rural culture preserves ancient Greek elements, denies that culture coevalness both with the anthropologists and with urban elites, thereby transforming it into an exotic anachronism (1984). Brian Joseph shows how the discipline of linguistics in the nineteenth and twentieth centuries constructed a linguistic continuity in defense of the Greek language, sometimes despite evidence disproving these conclusions. Greek linguists, Joseph argues, regularly sought in ancient Greek the etymologies of modern Greek words and often overlooked plausible evidence of linkage to neighboring non-Greek languages (1985: 90).

21. About twenty years later Mihalis Lelekos conducted the same form of emendation and revision on texts in his collection of folk songs (1852). In order to prove that the modern folk songs preserved both the language and thought of the ancient Greeks, he doctored the texts. Some songs, as Herzfeld argues (1982: 81), are forgeries, complete with references to Sophocles and Persian dogs. As a point of contrast, N. G. Politis, the "founder" of Greek folklore, refused to alter songs. In the prologue to his monumental *Ekloye apo ta Tragudia tu Elliniku Lau* (Selections from the songs of the Greek people, 1914) he stated categorically that his task was similar to that of an editor of a philological text. He thus limited himself only to *recensio* (restoration) and not *mendatio*. For this reason many of the songs were published with metrical errors and seem unfinished. Although, he acknowledged, emendation would have been simple, it would not have befitted a scholarly project.

22. Taste of course changed, and this school established its place in the Greek canon, eventually pushing the purist tradition into obscurity. Writing on the anthology of Hantseris, the demoticist Dimitris Margaris observed that in his day (1940) this collection was not read and resembled something like a "spiritual mold." But in its time, he asserted, it was representative of contemporary poetry in which society "found itself" (1940: 212).

23. See chapter 5 for further discussion of the magazine *Estia* and the role it played in gaining recognition for the short story as a legitimate literary genre.

24. This should be compared with those included in Mirambel (1950), which, having been published after the successful institutionalization of the demotic canon, includes none of these purist writers.

25. The poet Kostis Palamas integrated into the demotic canon the archaizing poet Andreas Kalvos (1792–1869), who until the publication of Palamas's essay (1889) was largely unknown. Because Kalvos's work could not easily be assimilated by either the demotic or the purist tradition, he faded without leaving any heirs (Dimaras 1975: 225). Although sometimes included in anthologies, Kalvos remained a minor figure until Palamas's intervention. As the leading living poet of his time, Palamas possessed sufficient cultural authority to introduce into the canon such a difficult, erudite, and archaizing poet and to do so, moreover, at a time of fervent demoticism. Eventually, as a result of other major interpretations of his work, not least two essays by Seferis and Elytis, Kalvos came to occupy a formidable place in literature.

26. Although Greek criticism of the twentieth century adopted many of its concepts and methods from western Europe, it had not developed, as I shall show, a professionalized discourse and ethic to enforce rules of conduct. We have seen how some anthologists felt quite free to edit passages in order to enhance the overall beauty of the text. Parashos and Lefkoparidis, in a move that would make the professional critic in western Europe or North America cringe, did not identify the author of each selection. Although they provided a register of names at the end of the book, they felt that to name the writer of each poem would cast a "personal and individual shadow" on something that should be impersonal. In contrast, Valetas did not permit anonymous texts to remain authorless; when he could not determine a text's author he simply provided a "symbolic" name, so that each text might take its rightful place in Greek grammatology.

27. On Cavafy's modernism and his relationship to European and modern Greek literature see Jusdanis (1987a). Palamas, Cavafy's contemporary and chief rival for the position of Greece's foremost modern poet, has been superseded by Cavafy. Although during his lifetime Palamas was generally recognized as the outstanding poet after Solomos, now Cavafy is considered the greatest Greek poet of this century. But Palamas's shift from the center to the periphery should be differentiated from the fate shared by purist authors. The latter do not belong to the current canon since their entire ideological and epistemological framework is no longer considered relevant; it does not correspond to the current definition of literature. While purist poetry is not regarded as literary, Palamas's texts have simply lost their authority in the writing of poetry and their prominence in critical discussions. There is no question (yet) as to the literariness of Palamas. Some may believe his work to be old-fashioned and romantic, others may view it as "bad" poetry, but it would be almost impossible for such critics under the demotic aesthetics of taste to expel his oeuvre outside the current boundaries of literature, the fate shared by the purists. Palamas is part of the present literary discourse and tradition, interwoven in its language. For Palamas and Solomos to be dismissed as nonliterary the entire system of evaluation would first have to be usurped.

28. Although critical schools differ in their foundational principles, they are all nevertheless committed to literature and devoted to its interpretation. Despite their radical rhetoric, even discourses such as Marxism and deconstruction have not really departed significantly from

the inherited paradigms. They have in fact been co-opted as innovative approaches to literature, with the result that we now have Marxist and deconstructive (and feminist) readings of texts. These readings are in fact different from those offered in the past but, insofar as these and other discourses remain faithful to the institution of literature, the notion of text, and the need for its explication, they will not undermine the enterprise of liberal humanism, an end to which they seem to aspire.

29. By the 1950s the Greek canon had been legitimated in the sites of culture. Anthologies of this decade and subsequent ones simply consolidate this gain; they maintain the received hierarchy. With the canon no longer under threat, editors can now step back to examine the entirety of the tradition, reflecting on its wealth. The most influential of these anthologies is the encyclopedic forty-eight volume *Vasiki Vivliothiki* (1951–57). Not an anthology in the usual sense, this work attempts to provide an official record of the development of modern Greek letters from the Byzantine period to the present. As a standard reference tool, it contains both literary and nonliterary texts: documents of criticism, letters, scholarly essays, travelogues, memoirs, philosophy, and folklore. Although heterogeneous in content, it has a unifying theme; it narrates the story of modern Greek literature on the way to itself. The *Vasiki Vivliothiki* has engendered a series of encyclopedic works that also set out to anthologize the whole course of modern Greek poetry, starting either from the Byzantine period or the fall of Constantinople to the present. All are multivolume sets and share the vision of one unbroken, pan-Hellenic tradition. In 1954 there appeared Mihalis Peranthis's collection. Four years later Markos Avyeris, M. Papaioannu, Vassilis Rotas, and Thrasivulos Stavru published their four-volume anthology (1958–59). This was followed in 1975 by the seven-volume *Piitiki Antholoyia* (Poetic anthology) edited by Linos Politis. For a brief look at Politis's and other poetic anthologies see the short irreverent review "Antholoyies Ellinikis Piisis," in *Pali* 5, 1965, 89–90. This journal appeared as a defense of the Greek avant-garde, and as such took a critical stance toward all cultural developments preceding it. Special issues of magazines and literary journals devoted to individual authors are a useful gauge of the composition of the literary canon insofar as they point to the authors receiving the most exposure and promotion. Martha Karpozilu has compiled a valuable sourcebook (1982) of these special issues.

4. The Emergence of Art and the Failures of Modernization

1. This of course differs substantially from the way we, post-Kantians, view beauty and art. Although the two positions are perhaps incommensurable, Aristotle's conception of *techne* as a purposive act is diametrically opposed to Kant's definition of the aesthetic judgment as a "purposefulness without a purpose" (*Zweckmässigkeit ohne Zweck*). See the discussion of Kant that follows.

2. This is why, as I noted above, it is nearly impossible to compare the two positions. If the ancients had no concept in any way approximating the modern notion of art, then on what basis can we draw parallels between Aristotle's view of art and, say, that of Kant? This problem, concerning not simply the translation of words (a process in itself fraught with hazards) but rather systems of thought, lies at the heart of the hermeneutic act—the conveyance of ideas from one time or society to another. Classical studies still seek the ancient equivalents of such modern notions as art, author, or sexuality. Yet the very act of conceptually isolating these categories leads to distortions. Writing on the topic of homosexuality, David Halperin stresses that the challenge confronting the cultural historian of the ancient world is first "how to recover the terms in which the experiences of individuals belonging to past societies were actually constituted and, second, how to measure and assess the difference between those terms and the ones we currently employ" (1986: 38). Cultural anthropology, a field of inquiry posited on the idea of difference and Otherness, has always had to face the challenge of

representing the informant's point of view and making this somehow relevant to its readership in western Europe and North America. Recent experimental ethnographies, using a self-reflexive manner reminiscent of literary modernism, have converted the idea of translation, representation, and interpretation into their central problematic. Through textual strategies these ethnographers, as George Marcus and Michael Fischer state, render the situation of the fieldworker disturbing to readers so as to explore the philosophical and political problems of cultural translation (1986: 48). On experimental ethnography see also Clifford and Marcus 1986.

3. For Derrida's critique of Kant see his "Economimesis" (1981).

4. The end of his deduction was written as an answer to British empiricists such as David Hume, who also claimed that beauty is not a quality in things themselves but exists in the mind contemplating them. But the conclusion that Hume drew from this is that each mind perceives a different beauty ([1757] 1937: 257). In Kant's view this beauty must be the same for all of humankind, since if an object is beautiful the pleasure afforded by it appeals to a universal human sense. Yet by apparently giving every person the right to make a judgment of taste Hume does not open the door to chaos, since later he qualifies his argument, adding that only those who know different types of beauty are entitled to an opinion on an object (65). By comparison we blame or praise. Though the principles of taste, Hume says, may be universal and nearly the same for everybody, only few are qualified to give judgment on any work of art "or establish their own sentiment as the standard of beauty." Only a strong sense, Hume insists, "united to delicate sentiment, improved by practice, perfected by comparison and cleared of all prejudice can entitle a critic to be a true judge of fine arts" (68-69). Although theoretically each person may pass an opinion on a beautiful object, it turns out that only the civilized, educated individual may be a "true standard of taste and beauty." The apparent subjectivism and relativism in Hume's argument is circumscribed, as it is in Fish's notion of interpretive community, by an appeal to interpretive authority.

5. The separation of these three spheres has created problems of mediation among them. In his work, particularly the *Theory of Communicative Action* (1984), Habermas has attempted to develop a theory of communicative rationality that would overcome the alienation produced by the autonomous status of the three fields. To this extent Habermas strives to preserve modernity and fortify the aesthetic, which would compensate for fragmentation and enable communication between the independent realms. He aspires to a consensus maintained through rational discussion. His critique of Foucault and Derrida stems from his contention that these writers want to destroy the boundaries between the autonomous spheres, and hence, the edifice of modernity.

6. Wellbery notes that with romanticism the representational theory gradually gave way to the expressive approach, which modeled the aesthetic on the expressive event. Since art was conceived as the expression of an author, the task for the subject was to try to decode the author's message. The audience understood art's meaning by communicating with the author. Its mode of operation was, and still is, hermeneutic. On the shift toward expressive theory see also Abrams 1953.

7. Zygmunt Bauman in *Legislators and Interpreters* provides a penetrating Foucaultian analysis of the Enlightenment project of social engineering. Building on the Frankfurt School's insights regarding the Enlightenment—namely, that instead of restoring light it legislated and regulated social practices—Bauman explains that one of the projects of the Enlightenment was to neutralize the threat of an expanding vagabond population. The sixteenth and seventeenth centuries witnessed in Europe the rise of a dangerous vagabond class, a product of urbanization and the increase in poverty (1987: 44). Since traditional means of surveillance were unsuccessful with such a rootless class, they were transplanted to supervised areas—prisons, workhouses, hospitals, insane asylums—where they could be monitored at all times.

These sites yielded specialized knowledge not only about their inmates but also about the modification of such inmates' behavior.

8. For an analysis of the current French art market see Moulin 1987.

9. Quintilian, in his treatise on the education of an orator, *Institutio Oratoria* (II, 1, 4), states explicitly that *litteratura* is the Latin equivalent of *grammatike*. See also Suetonius, *De Grammaticis et Rhetoribus Liber* (4).

10. This was true in the United States; according to Benjamin Spencer, *literature* in eighteenth-century America signified not only belles lettres but also philosophical, historical, scientific, and political writing (1957: 25). This meaning became progressively more exclusive when, in an attempt to liberate American writing from British domination, readers, editors, publishers, and scholars began to search for original American compositions, written in American idiom and portraying American manners.

11. Modern art, elitist in character, has widened this gap, José Ortega y Gasset contends, thereby completely shattering the "profound injustice of the assumption" that all people had similar access to art (1968: 7). For a century and a half, Ortega y Gasset argues, the masses were believed to constitute all of society. But Stravinsky's music and Pirandello's dramas compelled the masses to recognize themselves as a "secondary factor in the cosmos of spiritual life." Like politics, art had been divided into two ranks: the illustrious and the vulgar, those with finer senses and others who could not comprehend art at all.

12. The romantic theory of art as individual expression, according to Wartofsky, developed in this context of the commodification of art, when the artist, severed from the previous world of patronage, became an entrepreneur dependent on the conditions of the market—on buyers, their agents, critics' views, the politics of style and taste (1980: 245). No longer enjoying direct access to the patron and official art, the artist's involvement with the art world was determined by intermediaries. Although "freed" to fashion what they wanted, artists as creative individuals were also at the mercy of the market. The "alienation" of romantic artists was to a certain extent a product of their entry into the agora.

13. In *Distinction: A Social Critique of the Judgment of Taste* Bourdieu undertakes a socioeconomic analysis of both the judgment of taste and aesthetic value as posited by aesthetics. Not conceiving the aesthetic system as autonomous, Bourdieu unceasingly posits taste in the social context and demonstrates, often through historical and statistical techniques, how it operates at various social levels. Taste, Bourdieu argues, classifies objects as much as it classifies the classifier, insofar as individuals distinguish themselves in the distinctions they make between the beautiful and ugly (1984: 6). But far from being universally valid, these distinctions depend on the social group to which the individual belongs. In identifying the beautiful and the proper way of seeing it people are aided by their class and educational backgrounds. This can be seen by people's reactions to the body, "the most indisputable materialization of class taste" (190). What and how to feed it, how to clothe and exercise it is determined by the individual's social position.

14. On the specialization of the arts, particularly following the rise of modernism, see Clement Greenberg's "Modernist Painting" (1966) in Gregory Battcock (1973). Of further interest is Ingeborg Hoesterey's "Der Laokoon-Faktor in der Moderne: Zum Problem der Mediendifferenzierung in den Künsten" (1982), which discusses the topic of medium specificity in modernism and postmodernism.

15. The trade unions were also subjugated through co-option. Their incorporation in the body politic demonstrates, according to Mouzelis, that the postoligarchic broadening of political participation and the growth of industries after 1929 only reinforced authoritarian state features (73). Given the absence of a public sphere to limit state encroachment upon civil society, autonomous groups were inhibited from forming. The state apparatus remained strong with regard to these interests, though power was often maintained through the intervention

of the military. In addition to the clientelistic relationships, populism became indispensable for integrating the masses into the state and mobilizing them in support of nationalist causes. This feature, common to peripheral countries, took the form in Greece of the irredentist *Megali Idea.* See also Andreopoulos (1989).

16. An article "Politics, a Greek Passion" in the newspaper *To Vima* (11 June, 1989, 42) confirms the politicized nature of Greek society even today. Greeks, of all Europeans, according to statistics from the EEC, show the greatest interest in politics. Greece has also the largest number in Europe of daily newspaper readers and followers of radio and television programs on politics. They also consider themselves the least alienated from the political sphere.

17. Georg Veloudis notes that in the Greek Enlightenment the prevailing expression for literature was *grammatia* (1983: 545). Scholars may have indeed been translating with this term their understanding of "literature" but it is doubtful that such a realm of textuality had been isolated in Greek culture at this time. *Filoloyia,* on the other hand, as defined by the magazine *Ermis o Loyios,* was the study of the classical world and incorporated political history, archaeology, mythology, the arts, philosophy, and ancient texts (Oct. 1811, 352–53).

18. The absence of a consensus in the definition of these terms can be seen in the lecture "Logos Isitirios peri Filoloyias" (1899), delivered by Grigorios Vernardakis as his inaugural address at the University of Athens. As professor of Greek philology, he understands *filoloyia* in the context of the classics. For him it is not limited exclusively to the study of the classical language but extends to the Greek language as a whole, and to its textual production. Greek *filoloyia,* he observes, resembles a panorama in which we see the entire world from Homer till today (1899: 17). *Filoloyia* is not an object of study but a branch of learning (*epistimi*) (7).

19. His suggestions did not necessarily receive wide currency. Although *logotehnia* now means literature and *filoloyia* on the whole denotes the study of classical texts, there is still some confusion about the other two terms. Veloudis proposes that *grammatoloyia,* which he regards as a faithful translation of *Literaturwissenschaft,* refer to the study of all of modern Greek texts, and *grammatia* to this very body of Greek texts; *logotehnia* constitutes one part of this body (1987: 10).

20. The fact that Cavafy's work promoted and assumed an autonomous literature may be one of the reasons behind the rejection of his poetry by his contemporaries. For other factors see Jusdanis (1987a).

21. Even foreign scholars approached the area of Greek writing in this all-inclusive manner. In his *Researches in Greece* William Martin Leake wrote that the "progress of the literature of the modern Greeks, and its present state, will be best understood from a list of authors, and their publication" and then provided such a catalogue (1814: 76). Although he uses the term *literature* he too does not differentiate the literary from the nonliterary. The German Carl Iken also adopted this strategy (1825) and, indeed, based his list (*Verzeichnis neugriechischer Schriftsteller*) on Leake's. Iken arranged his catalogue according to author, title, and place and date of publication.

22. Iosif De-Kigallas's work (1846), published a decade earlier, is similar in scope. Its subtitle identifies the work as a catalogue of modern Greek writers and translators from 1550 to 1838. De-Kigallas records all the authors known to him without necessarily assigning a special place to poets or dramatists.

23. Andronikos Dimitrakopulos (1871) provides corrections and emendations to Sathas's catalogue.

24. The subject of Nicolai's *Geschichte der Neugriechischen Literatur* is neither belles lettres nor writing in general but rather fictional texts. Nicolai considers these texts literature and undertakes to outline their history. Yet, although his ostensible subject is literature, he begins to discuss this topic only halfway through the book. Up to that point his study concerns the works' cultural and historical background. He devotes much time, for instance, to an inves-

tigation of the Greek language, since he feels that questions of language are inseparably linked with those of literature. He introduces his examination of literary works with an extensive analysis of Greek education, language, and history. This lengthy section alters the direction of the work. For, although Nicolai promises to trace the history of Greek literature, his book tends to be as much about cultural as it is about literary history. Furthermore, while his conception of literature encompasses imaginative texts only, it has not been sufficiently defined to permit a rigorous examination of its history. It is difficult for the reader of Nicolai's book to imagine what constitutes the uniqueness of literature. The margins between literature, language, and history are still undefined. Despite its title the study is more a cultural history than a literary one.

M. A. C. Gidel's *Etudes sur la littérature grecque moderne* (1864) precedes Nicolai's work though it is not, strictly speaking, a literary history. It does, however, concentrate almost exclusively on literary texts, though they are not really modern Greek but rather late Byzantine poems and romances. Similarly Juliette Lamber, in *Poètes grecs contemporains* (1880), chooses poets as her subject and provides an overview of the leading, though largely demotic, Greek poets. She admits, however, that the "Greek spirit" is still in the first steps of its development and that Greece still does not possess a "truly national literature" (1880: 15).

25. Karl Dieterich, in *Geschichte der Byzantinischen und Neugriechischen Literatur,* took a very critical view of his predecessors. He dismissed early "literary historians" like Rangavis and Nicolai as dilettantes, interested more in compiling inventories of poets and scholars than in composing histories of literature (vii). (Commenting on the work of Zaviras and Rizos-Nerulos, Andreas Mustoxidis similarly noted the impossibility of a history of early Greek writing. Those authors, he writes, situated between the fall of Constantinople and the War of Independence constitute material not for a grammatological history [*grammatoloyiki istoria*] but for biographies of learned men [1843: 95].) Dieterich, on the other hand, claims to understand literature solely as imaginative, fictional, nondiscursive writing and traces its history from the Byzantine period down to the modern era. Dieterich embraces a more circumscribed concept of literature but, like Nicolai, he composes his volume less from the perspective of aesthetics than from that of cultural history. While Dieterich promises a true history of Greek literature, his approach is informed by orientalist ideology. He devotes a significant portion of his study to showing how the Greeks should emancipate themselves from their eastern tradition—to which the Byzantines first succumbed—and finally rejoin Europe, their authentic home and the product of their forefathers. A struggle, he warns, for the possession of the Greek people is taking place between the dark and backward Orient and the radiant and progressive Occident. Greek poetry, he contends, will flourish only when Europe triumphs over Asia in a conflict "of which the history of Byzantine and modern Greek literature represents a typical illustration" and when all orientalizing tendencies are finally overcome (224). His study, ostensibly of Greek literature, extends beyond the narrow limits of literary history. Dieterich writes literary history as propaganda. On the ideological role played by the East in the composition of histories of modern Greek literature see Jusdanis (1987b).

26. D. C. Hesseling's *Histoire de la littérature grecque moderne,* a translation by N. Pernot from the original Dutch text (1920), is perhaps the first historical account of the modern Greek literary tradition that pays exclusive attention to literature: poetry, drama, short stories, novels.

27. For a critical bibliography of all modern histories of Greek literature see Kehagioglou (1980).

28. Nikolaos Sofianos was a Renaissance humanist and polymath among whose many works is the first study of the modern Greek (demotic) language. Martin Crucius, one of the first European scholars to take an interest in modern Greece, sought manuscripts in the

modern language and collected information on Greece and its culture—largely through his correspondence with Greek clerics in Constantinople—which he published in his multivolume *Turcograecia* in 1584. Du Cange (1610–88) wrote a history of Byzantium but his most lasting contributions are the glossaries of classical Greek and Latin. Korais and Psiharis are difficult to classify because they wrote texts that are clearly scholarly, others that are considered literary, and still others that straddle both categories. Literary historians must always grapple to find the most appropriate category for both writers.

29. On the political implications of Gervinus's work see Werner Krauss's "Literaturgeschichte als Geschichtlicher Auftrag" in Krauss (1959). For an investigation of the theoretical problems involved in literary history see Gerhard Plumpe and Karl Conrady, "Probleme der Literaturgeschichtsschreibung" in Brackert and Stückruth (1981); and the special issues of *New Literary History* 3, Spring 1985 and of *Poetics* 14, 1985. Michael S. Butts's *A History of Histories of German Literature* (1987) offers a factual, though theoretically uninformed, investigation of German literary historiography.

5. Spaces of a Public Culture

1. This does not mean, as Fish repeatedly emphasizes, that meaning and texts are subjective, since they are products of public assumptions as opposed to individual whims. In introducing the notion of interpretive community Fish aims to overcome the object/subject, objectivity/subjectivity dichotomy. A true objectivity cannot arise, since what is normative for one community is not necessarily so for another. By the same token subjectivity and nihilism are impossible, since one's views are not one's exclusive property but are the function of social norms and rules existing beyond the individual's control. The second of the two points is of more consequence for Fish, and is the one that intimidates traditional scholars the most. Yet Fish works hard to allay the fears that his theory instills in some people, assuring this audience—the only one shocked by his iconoclastic gestures—not to worry (321). The stability (15) of the interpretive community remains intact; it is impossible to disrupt the game or throw a monkey wrench in it (357); a text cannot be overwhelmed by an irresponsible reader (336); we lose very little in recognizing that "we do persuasion and not demonstration" (367).

2. The anecdote recounted in the chapter entitled "How to Recognize a Poem When You See One" about a class that, after having been mischievously informed by Professor Fish that a list of five proper names on the board was a religious poem, followed his cue and proceeded to analyze the names as a literary text, simply indicates that reading is conventional (1980: 322–37). This story, like the idea of the interpretive community, is not really concerned with literature as institution but describes how readers operating within it apply interpretive strategies. It is one thing to say that any text can be considered literary and quite another to argue that literature is a social institution and product of modernity. In other words, the institution of literature is just as conventional as its norms.

3. On the promotion of a contemporary philosophical school see Michèle Lamont's provocatively titled article "How to Become a Dominant French Philosopher: The Case of Jacques Derrida" (1987). Lamont analyzes the intellectual, cultural, and institutional conditions that have legitimated Derrida's work, often resorting to graphs and charts to show the dissemination of his texts through professional networks. She demonstrates, for instance, that while in France, Derrida targeted his work to an educated public as a sophisticated way of dealing with the politics of the 1960s, in the United States his theories were reframed and distributed in departments of literature. Investigations such as Collins's and Lamont's are invaluable in revealing the institutional support and collaborative unions necessary for the legitimation of

knowledge. But in bringing attention to individuals, their friends, and ambitions, they also come close to resurrecting biographies and the subject in critical theory.

4. The knowledge of literary criticism was until recently available, if not to the general public, at least to educated middle-class readers. Empirical, positivistic, and content-oriented analysis enabled readers not directly associated with the university to gain access to it. The introduction of "theory" in the 1970s led to the rarefication of knowledge, with the result that it was understood only by practitioners of a particular school, and not even by all critics. Producers of this specialized criticism write for other producers, thereby limiting entry even more to what already is, according to Bourdieu, a "restricted field of production" (1985). Was theory an attempt by academic critics to monopolize critical production by delegitimizing certain forms of knowledge while simultaneously preserving the dominance of the exegetical method at a time of diminishing authority for the humanities?

5. Modernist art pushed this autonomy to its most rarefied form by creating works that referred either to themselves or to their tradition. In so doing, it severely restricted the number of consumers acquainted with this history to experts, who, because of their superior knowledge, were the only ones capable of talking about this art. The historical avant-garde, Peter Bürger (1984) has demonstrated, undertook a critique of art's autonomy by relentlessly pointing to its institutionalized nature. It tried to violate the boundaries between art and nonart by incorporating into the institutions objects of everyday use, unintended for aesthetic appreciation. These acts of transgression turned out to be, however, a form of institutional self-criticism; they were subsumed by the institution they sought to criticize and became art history.

6. The institutional theory of art, having emerged after the critique of art's status by the avant-garde, according to Marx Wartofsky, is a theory not of art in general but of the notion of status in contemporary art (1980: 247). It addresses the problem of an "art-violative" art, of art refusing to abide within the conventions of the art world. This trait first appeared in the late nineteenth and early twentieth centuries. Only after the avant-garde put the status of art into doubt and posed the question "Is it art?" was attention directed toward how status is achieved in art. Yet this does not necessarily mean that an institutional approach is only an ad hoc theory, as Wartofsky claims, and that it deals only with avant-garde art (244). An examination of the social character of art would be helpful in understanding not only modern (post-eighteenth-century) art but also the arts of other ages. It is a useful way of seeing "art" as a product of a given time and culture instead of a modern concept ethnocentrically and anachronistically imposed on other cultures and eras.

7. Jacques Dubois, whose study is based on Althusser and Bourdieu, uses the notion of institution to analyze both the ideological function of literature in society and the specific institutional sites involved in its production. He examines, for instance, the authority of certain magazines and publishing houses to promote specific authors and genres, pointing, for example, to the support given by Editions de Minuit to the nouveau roman (1978: 90–91). He also investigates literature's relationship to the education system and the role it plays in inculcating bourgeois values in the children of the middle classes (35). For Dubois, literature is an institution insofar as it is an autonomous organization, a socializing agent (système socialis-ateur), and an ideological apparatus (32–34). Though an independent system, it is connected with the press, the publishing house, education, and the entertainment industry.

8. Habermas states that the term *public* entered English discourse by the mid-seventeenth century to replace the words *world* or *mankind*. This happened later in the seventeenth century in France and in the eighteenth century in Germany, where *Publikum* was exchanged for *Lesewelt* (world of readers) (1989: 26).

9. The first newspaper to appear in the Greek mainland was *Salpinx Elliniki* (The Greek trumpet), printed in the city of Kalamata in 1821. After the revolution many papers came to press in a small, usually four-page format. For a good sourcebook on the early Greek press

see Koumarianou (1971), an anthology of relevant passages taken from newspapers that appeared first abroad and then in Greece. It also contains a useful introduction to the role played by the press in the War of Independence.

10. Much of the magazine was devoted to foreign cultural affairs. The first issue contained a higher proportion of non-Greek to Greek material, including an essay on Heine, translations from the work of de Musset, and a report on theater in Naples. In subsequent issues the magazine published both original texts of Greek poetry and prose and review articles, and works of criticism. For instance on January 15, 1863, there appeared a review by A. Vizantios of Ramfos's novel *E Teleftee Imere tu Ali Passa* (The final days of Ali Pasha) as well as poems by Ahilefs Parashos. On later dates the magazine included works of Vlahos, A. Rangavis, Tantalidis, Mavroyiannis, Karasutsas, and Vizantios. The texts by and about Greek writers were always fewer than the articles devoted to matters concerning European culture.

11. Its articles dealt with education, archaeology, geography, and social customs. It printed translations, reviews (such as Roidis's analysis of *To Taxidi mu* by Psiharis), poetry, and prose works such as the novel *Lukis Laras* by Vikelas. Many of the best-known writers and scholars of the period, including Roidis, N. Politis, Palamas, and Drosinis, collaborated with this periodical in some way or other. In its final years, under the editorship of the prose author Grigorios Xenopulos, *Estia* introduced to the Athenian readership the work of writers who would become dominant figures in the literary canon: Griparis, Papantoniu, Kambisis, and not least, Cavafy.

12. The subsequent appearance of *I Tehni* (1898-99), the first demotic periodical, *Dionisos* (1901-2), and later of *Numas* (1902-23), the main organ of demoticists, demonstrates demoticism's success in appropriating sites of discourse from purist control or in creating entirely new ones. The magazines of the twentieth century established the networks of the new demotic public sphere. Significantly, with the emergence of an autonomous literature, magazines were published with a decidedly literary bent. The *Nea Grammata* (1935-40), for instance, was started to promote the texts and theories of the Generation of the 30s. Although this aim was ideological, the magazine's politics, having been aestheticized, were restricted to literature. By this time political discourse was dissociating itself from critical and aesthetic practice.

13. The Akritic popular songs, dating probably from the ninth or tenth century, were woven into an epic cycle that celebrated the exploits of the *akrites,* the frontier guards defending the eastern borders of the Byzantine Empire. They had been preserved by oral tradition in the districts of Pontus and Cappadocia as well as in Cyprus and Crete. The famous epic *Diyenis Akritas,* produced around the end of the tenth and beginning of the eleventh century, is the culmination of this cycle. The demoticists posited this epic poem as the inaugural work of modern Greek literature. By heralding it as the Urtext of modern Greek they extended the demotic poetic tradition to the time of the Byzantines and thus endowed the demotic language with an illustrious genealogy. On the Akritic Cycle see Beck (1971) and on the *Diyenis Akritas* itself see Beaton (1981).

14. Other contemporaneous writers who could be considered critics were Grigorios Xenopulos, Tellos Agras (1899-1944), Kostas Varnalis (1884-1974), Aristos Kampanis (1883-1957), Markos Avyeris (1884-1973), Kleon Parashos (1894-1964), Timos Malanos (1896-1986), and Alkis Thrilos (pseudonym of Eleni Urani, 1896-1971).

15. The chair in modern Greek literature, originally founded at the University of Athens in 1925-26, was also responsible for Byzantine literature. Art history has faced similar problems in receiving recognition as an academic discipline. For a long time the history of art was taught by professors of archaeology; the first chair in the history of medieval and modern art was created in 1964 at the University of Thessaloniki.

16. The list of courses, as well as other useful information on the university, is provided by Ioannis Pantazidis in *Hronikon tis Protis Pentikontaetias tu Elliniku Panepistimiu* (1889),

an excellent study covering the first fifty years of the University of Athens. For course offerings and names of professors and lecturers see the university course bulletins: *Anagrafi ton epi to Akadimaikon Etos tu en Athines Ethniku Panepistimiu* (for the 1800s) and *Epetiris: Ethnikon ke Kapadistriakon Panepistimion* (for the 1900s). For the history of the University of Athens see Barth (1937).

17. I have not been able to determine whether the course *Istoria tis neoteras filoloyias* actually referred to the history of modern Greek philology or the history of modern Greek writing. If it means the latter, as is most likely the case, it probably took the form of the annalistic histories (examined in chapter 4), which set out to record the tradition of Greek writing.

18. In 1830 there were 71 schools; in 1840, 252; in 1869, 1,029; in 1889, 2,278; and in 1910, 3,551 (Tsoucalas 1977: 392). For an account of Greek education in earlier times see Polizoidis (1876, reprinted 1973). For an analysis of the ideological function performed by Greek education see Konstantellou (1991).

19. The first men bearing the title "professor of English literature," according to H. Bruce Franklin, appeared in the United States during the Civil War. Through instruction in rhetoric and literature they strived to cultivate collegiate men of the business classes (in Fiedler and Baker 1981: 97). By the 1880s and 1890s this task developed into a specialized professional activity that provided to men of lower classes the vocational skills to gain access to high (i.e., bourgeois) culture. The study of literature was the primary route for students to become acculturated in the class to which they aspired.

20. As in Germany, women were excluded from critical practice. Their inability to enroll in science and the classics left only one option for them, the "soft" study of English and foreign languages. The study of English literature was regarded as suitable education for women, even though there was opposition to it from conservative scholars who feared their influx into this area of study (and hence the university). Yet many women refused to study English, wishing instead to compete directly with men in the more privileged disciplines of classics and mathematics (Jardine 1986: 210). Women were not the only group targeted for literature's civilizing mission. This "woman's subject" was also being promoted in the ever-expanding area of extension programs for adults of the lower classes. It also proved itself essential in the teaching of linguistic and rhetorical skills to the businessmen and bureaucrats engaged in the expanding area of overseas trade. English was recognized as an academic subject in Cambridge only when the children of the lower middle class, on entering that elitist university, challenged the established assumptions of literary study. Influenced by Arnold's writings on the function of literature and criticism, teachers and professors of English literature aspired through the study of literature to establish social harmony, pacify radical movements, and consolidate social control. The civilizing power of literature was thought to counter the evils of anarchy (Baldick 1983: 66).

21. Kriaras (1964) enumerates these scholars and provides a list of the texts they worked on and the critical editions they published.

22. Sikutris was regarded as a brilliant classical philologist. Trained in Germany by the formidable philologist Wilamowitz, he returned to Greece out of patriotism, to help in the development of classical philology and literary criticism. In this task he clearly was applying European standards, as he wished to bring Greek literary scholarship to a European level. His designs met with hostility. When in 1937 he published an edition of the *Symposium,* in the introduction to which he discussed the question of homosexuality in the text, a furor arose in academic circles and characteristically among lay people as well. In a move that underscores the public nature of discussions over tradition, language, and literature, even the association of *kuluria* (small ring-shaped bread) vendors of Patra protested against the introduction. The

politics of identity and of the past made itself felt in what otherwise was the specialized publication of a classical text. The controversy pushed Sikutris to suicide.

23. On the poetry competitions the following sources are useful: Valetas (1937), Papapanu (1973), Mulas (1981).

24. This period also witnessed the appearance of other associations whose concern was the transmission of information about Greek culture and history. In 1882, for instance, the Historical and Folkloric Society was founded to collect and preserve the monuments of popular life. In addition to acquiring a museum to house such relics, it sponsored a periodical in which demotic songs, tales, proverbs, and narratives were published. Not unrelated to the interests of the society in contemporary culture was the passage of the bill in 1884 prescribing the teaching of modern Greek (*katharevusa*) in school. In 1884 a society for the study of Greece's Christian heritage was organized. The association for the preservation of antiquities, the Filomuson Eteria, was launched in Athens in 1813, much earlier than the declaration of the new state. The archaeological society, which directed the first excavations, was formed in 1837, the year of the founding of the university and of the school of fine arts in Athens. The establishment of both societies at such a relatively early date indicates once more the significance Greeks attached to cultural institutions in the modernization of society. On the concern for ancient monuments see Skoku (1977).

25. Filippos Iliu provides useful catalogues of the books financed with subscriptions, their place of publication, and the number of subscribers. See also Papacostea-Danielopolu (1970).

26. In 1834 he published his demotic translation of Aeschylus's *Eumenides* and expressed the intention in the prologue to print other translations if warranted by public demand. It seems that at the time there was little interest in demotic translations of classical texts, and although his shop was in operation until 1847 he did not publish any other translations.

27. In that year Koromilas also published the comedy *O Tihodioktis* (The adventurer) by M. Hurmuzis, whose other comedy *O Ipallilos* (The employee) was printed by Antoniadis in 1836. This press also published Moliére's comedy *Amphitryon* that year. In 1837 two comedies of I. Rizos-Nerulos also appeared. In addition, a considerable number of translations of novels, primarily French, were being printed. A few Greek novels appeared in serial form. The practice of subscription continued, but principally for scholarly works.

28. In Greece public libraries were set up immediately after the revolution, though others existed in monasteries and schools. The national library was founded in 1834 while one in Parliament was built in 1845. Alongside the official libraries there are many private collections and archives open to general readers. The existence of these private (though public) sites illustrates again the significance of nonstate institutions in cultural production. For an informative source on the history and present state of libraries see Kokkinis (1969) and Kakuris (1971–72).

References

Abrams, M. H. 1953. *The Mirror and the Lamp*. Oxford: Oxford University Press.

Adhikari, Guatam. 1988. "Yes, Mr. Buckley, There's an Indian Lit." *New York Times,* June 10.

Agras, Tellos (ed.). 1922. *I Nei. Ekloyi apo to Ergo ton Neon Ellinon Piiton*. Athens: Eleftherudakis.

Aldridge, Owen A. (ed.). 1969. *Comparative Literature: Matter and Method*. Urbana: University of Illinois Press.

Alexiou, Margaret. 1982. "Diglossia in Greece." *Standard Languages: Spoken and Written*. W. Haas, ed. Manchester: Manchester University Press.

———. 1984–85. "Folklore: An Obituary?" *Byzantine and Modern Greek Studies* 9, 1–28.

Alonso, Ana Maria. 1988. "The Effects of Truth: Re-Presentations of the Past and the Imagining of Community." *Journal of Historical Sociology* 1, 1, 33–57.

Alsop, Joseph. 1982. *The Rare Art Traditions*. New York: Harper and Row.

Anderson, Benedict. 1983. *Imagined Communities*. London: Verso.

Andreopoulos, George J. 1989. "Liberalism and the Formation of the Nation-State." *Journal of Modern Greek Studies* 7, 2, 193–224.

Angelomatis-Tsougarakis, Helen. 1990. *The Eve of the Greek Revival: British Travellers' Perceptions of Early Nineteenth-Century Greece*. London: Routledge.

Angelu, Alkis. 1987. "Polithisomen Simeron en tes Odis." *Tetarto*, November, 22–27.

Anonymous. 1873. *Neos Parnassos: Diafora Lirika Temahia ek tis Singhronu Ellinikis Piisis*. Athens: Peristeras.

———. 1913. *Nea Elliniki Antholoyia*. New York: "Atlantis."

———. 1920. *Antholoyia ton Neon Piiton mas 1900–20*. Athens: "Politismos."

———. 1925. *Antholoyia ton Neoteron Piiton*. Athens: Melissa.

———. 1957. *Elliniki Nomarhia*. Athens: Vivlioekdotiki.

Apostolidis, Iraklis N. (ed.). 1953–54. *To Diiyima Antholoyimeno*. 2 vols. Athens: n.p.

———. 1954. *Antholoyia*. 5th ed. Athens: Estia.

189

Appiah, Anthony. 1984. "Strictures on Structures: The Prospects for a Structuralist Poetics of African Literature." In *Black Literary Theory.* H. L. Gates, ed. New York: Methuen.

Aristotle. 1984. *The Complete Works of Aristotle I.* Jonathan Barnes, ed. Princeton: Princeton University Press.

Arnold, Matthew. [1864] 1962. *Lectures and Essays in Criticism III.* Ann Arbor: University of Michigan Press.

Asante, Molefi Kete. 1987. *The Afrocentric Idea.* Philadelphia: Temple University Press.

Ashcroft, Bill, Gareth Griffiths, and Helen Tiffin. 1989. *The Empire Writes Back: Theory and Practice in Post-Colonial Literatures.* London: Routledge.

Atlas, James. 1987. "Chicago's Grumpy Guru: Best-Selling Professor Allan Bloom." *New York Times Magazine,* January 31.

Attali, Jacques. 1985. *Noise: The Political Economy of Music.* Brian Massumi, trans. Minneapolis: University of Minnesota Press.

Atwood, Margaret. 1972. *Survival: A Thematic Guide to Canadian Literature.* Toronto: Anansi.

Auerbach, Erich. 1953. *Mimesis: The Representation of Reality in Western Literature.* Willard R. Trask, trans. Princeton: Princeton University Press.

Avlonitis, Yeoryios (ed.). 1924. *Ekloyi Neoteron Piimaton.* Athens: Zografidis.

Avyeris, Markos, M. M. Papaioannu, Vassilis Rotas, Thrasivulos Stavrou (eds.). 1958–59. *I Elliniki Piisis Antholoyimeni.* 4 vols. Athens: Kipseli.

Axelos, Loukas. 1984. "Publishing Activity and the Movement of Ideas in Greece." *Journal of the Hellenic Diaspora* 11, 2, 5–46.

Babiniotis, G. 1979. "A Linguistic Approach to the 'Language Question' in Greece." *Byzantine and Modern Greek Studies* 5, 1–16.

Baker, Houston A., Jr. 1984. *Blues, Ideology, and Afro-American Literature: A Vernacular Theory.* Chicago: University of Chicago Press.

Baldick, Chris. 1983. *The Social Mission of English Criticism 1848–1932.* Oxford: Oxford University Press.

Barasch, Moshe. 1985. *Theories of Art from Plato to Wincklemann.* New York: New York University Press.

Barman, Roderick J. 1988. *Brazil: The Forging of a Nation, 1798–1852.* Stanford: Stanford University Press.

Barth, W. 1937. "Zur Geschichte der Athener Universität." *Hellas-Jahrbuch,* 25–40.

Battcock, Gregory (ed.). 1973. *The New Art.* New York: Dutton.

Batteux, Charles. 1746. *Principes de la littérature I.* 5th ed. Paris: n.p.

Baudrillard, Jean. 1975. *The Mirror of Production.* Mark Poster, trans. St. Louis: Telos Press.

————. 1981. *For a Critique of the Political Economy of the Sign.* Charles Levin, trans. St. Louis: Telos Press.

Bauman, Zygmunt. 1987. *Legislators and Interpreters: On Modernity, Post-Modernity, and Intellectuals.* Cambridge: Polity Press.

Baumgarten, Alexander Gottlieb. 1954. *Reflections on Poetry.* Karl Aschenbrenner and William Holther, trans. Berkeley: University of California Press.

Beard, Michael. 1987. "Loose Canons: The Pursuit of Middle Eastern Identities." *Critical Exchange* 22, 43–51.

Beaton, Roderick. 1980. *Folk Poetry of Modern Greece.* Cambridge: Cambridge University Press.

————. 1981. "Was *Digenes Akrites* an Oral Poem?" *Byzantine and Modern Greek Studies* 7, 7–28.

Beck, Hans-Georg. 1971. *Geschichte der byzantinischen Volksliteratur.* Munich: Beck.

Becker, Howard S. 1982. *Art Worlds.* Berkeley: University of California Press.

Belinsky, Vissarion. 1976. "Thoughts and Notes on Russian Literature." In *Belinsky, Chernyshevsky, and Dobrolyubov: Selected Criticism*. Ralph E. Matlaw, ed. Bloomington: Indiana University Press.

Bernal, Martin. 1987. *Black Athena: The Afroasiatic Roots of Classical Civilization*. London: Free Association Books.

Blackall, Eric A. 1959. *The Emergence of German as a Literary Language*. Cambridge: Cambridge University Press.

Bourdieu, Pierre. 1984. *Distinction: A Social Critique of the Judgement of Taste*. Richard Nice, trans. London: Routledge and Kegan Paul.

———. 1985. "The Market of Symbolic Goods." *Poetics* 14, 13–44.

Brackert, H., and J. Stückruth (eds.). 1981. *Literaturwissenschaft Grundkurs 2*. Hamburg: Rowohlt.

Braude, Benjamin, and Bernard Lewis (eds.). 1983. *Christians and Jews in the Ottoman Empire*. Vols. I and II. New York: Holmes and Meier.

Brennan, Timothy. 1990. "The National Longing for Form." In *Nation and Narration*. Homi K. Bhabha, ed. London: Routledge.

Brown, Richard H. 1986. "Toward a Sociology of Aesthetic Forms." *New Literary History* 17, 2, 223–28.

Browning, Robert. 1983. *Medieval and Modern Greek*. 2d ed. Cambridge: Cambridge University Press.

Brunetière, Ferdinand. 1904. *Variétés Littéraires*. Paris: Calmann-Lévy.

Bruns, Gerald L. 1984. "Canon and Power in the Hebrew Scriptures." In *Canons*. Robert von Hallberg, ed. Chicago: University of Chicago Press.

Bürger, Christa. 1977. *Die Ursprung der bürgerlicher Institution Kunst im hofischen Weimar*. Frankfurt: Suhrkamp.

Bürger, Christa, Peter Bürger, and Jochen Schulte-Sasse. 1980. *Aufklärung und literarische Offentlichkeit*. Frankfurt: Suhrkamp.

———. 1982. *Zur Dichotomisierung von hoher und niederer Literatur*. Frankfurt: Suhrkamp.

Bürger, Peter. 1979. *Vermittlung—Rezeption—Funktion*. Frankfurt: Suhrkamp.

———. 1984. *Theory of the Avant-Garde*. Michael Shaw, trans. Minneapolis: University of Minnesota Press.

Butts, Michael S. 1987. *A History of Histories of German Literature*. New York: Peter Lang.

Campenhausen, Hans von. 1972. *The Formation of the Christian Bible*. J. A. Baker, trans. Philadelphia: Fortress Press.

Carby, Hazel V. 1982. "White Woman Listen! Black Feminism and the Boundaries of Sisterhood." In *The Empire Strikes Back: Race, Racism in 70s Britain*. London: Centre for Contemporary Studies.

Carlson, Marvin. 1989. *Places of Performance: The Semiotics of Theater Architecture*. Ithaca, N.Y.: Cornell University Press.

Castoriadis, Cornelius. 1987. *The Imaginary Institution of Society*. Kathleen Blamey, trans. Cambridge: Polity Press.

Chaitin, Gilbert. Forthcoming. "Otherness." In *Comparative Literature*. Clifford Flanigan and Claus Clüver, eds. Carbondale: Southern Illinois University Press.

Chassiotis, Georges. 1881. *L'Instruction publique chez les grecs*. Paris: Ernest Leroux.

Chinweizu, J. Onwuchekya, and M. Imechukwu. 1983. *Toward the Decolonization of African Literature*. Washington, D.C.: Howard University Press.

Chow, Rey. 1986–87. "Rereading Mandarin Ducks and Butterflies: A Response to the 'Postmodern' Condition." *Cultural Critique* 5, 86–93.

Clemens of Alexandria. 1906. *Stromata I–VI*. Otto Stählin, ed. Leipzig: Hinrichs Buchhandlung.

Clements, Robert J. 1978. *Comparative Literature as Academic Discipline*. New York: MLA.

Clifford, James, and George Marcus (eds.). 1986. *Writing Culture: The Poetics and Politics of Ethnography*. Berkeley: University of California Press.

Clogg, Richard. 1969. "The 'Didaskalia Patriki' (1798): An Orthodox Reaction to French Revolutionary Propaganda." *Middle Eastern Studies* 5, 87–115.

———. 1972. "Two Accounts of the Academy of Ayvalik (Kydonies) in 1818–1819." *Revue des études sud-est européennes* 10, 4, 633–67.

———. 1973. "Aspects of the Movement for Greek Independence." In *The Struggle for Greek Independence*. London: Macmillan Press.

———. 1976. "Anticlericalism in Pre-Independence Greece c.1750–1821." In *The Orthodox Churches and the West*. Derek Baker, ed. Oxford: Basil Blackwell.

———. 1979. *A Short History of Modern Greece*. Cambridge: Cambridge University Press.

Cohn, Bernard S., and Nicholas B. Dirks. 1988. "Beyond the Fringe: The Nation State, Colonialism, and the Technologies of Power." *Journal of Historical Sociology* 1, 2, 224–29.

Collins, Randall. 1987. "A Micro-Macro Theory of Intellectual Creativity: The Case of German Idealist Philosophy." *Sociological Theory* 5, 47–69.

Couloumbis, Theodore A., John Petropoulos, and Harry A. Psomiades. 1976. *Foreign Interference in Greek Politics: An Historical Perspective*. New York: Pella.

Crow, Thomas E. 1985. *Painters and Public Life in Eighteenth-Century Paris*. New Haven: Yale University Press.

Cuddon, J. A. 1979. *A Dictionary of Literary Terms*. Harmondsworth: Penguin.

Culler, Jonathan. 1985. "Junk and Rubbish: A Semiotic Approach." *Diacritics* 15, 3, 2–12.

———. 1986. "Comparative Literature and Its Pieties." *Profession 86*. New York: MLA.

Curtius, Ernst Robert. 1973. *European Literature and the Latin Middle Ages*. Willard R. Trask, trans. Princeton: Princeton University Press.

Danforth, Loring M. 1984. "The Ideological Context of the Search for Continuities in Greek Culture." *Journal of Modern Greek Studies* 2, 1, 53–86.

Dasenbrock, Reed Way. 1987. "English Department Geography." In *Profession 87*. New York: MLA.

Dautis, Zisis. 1818. *Diafora Ithika ke Astia Stihuryimata*. Vienna: n.p.

De-Kigallas, Iosif. 1846. *Shediasma Katoptru tis Neoellinikis Filoloyias*. Hermoupolis: Yeoryios Polimeris.

Deleuze, Gilles, and Félix Guattari. 1986. *Kafka: Toward a Minor Literature*. Dana Polan, trans. Minneapolis: University of Minnesota Press.

Derrida, Jacques. 1979. "Living On—Border Lines." In *Deconstruction and Criticism*. New York: Seabury Press.

———. 1981. "Economimesis." *Diacritics* 2, 3–25.

Dertilis, Yiorgos. 1977. *Kinonikos Metashimatismos ke Stratiotiki Epemvasi 1889–1903*. Athens: Exantas.

Diamandouros, P. Nikiforos. 1983. "Greek Political Culture in Transition: Historical Origins, Evolution, Current Trends." In *Greece in the 1980s*. Richard Clogg, ed. London: Macmillan.

Dieterich, Karl. 1909. *Geschichte der Byzantinischen und Neugriechischen Literatur*. Leipzig: C. F. Amelangs.

Dikteos, Aris, and Fedros Barlas (eds.). 1961. *Antholoyia Singhronu Ellinikis Piiseos 1930–60*. Athens: Fexis.

Dimaras, Alexis (ed.). 1973. *I Metarithmisi pu den Eyine*. 2 vols. Athens: Ermis.

Dimaras, K. Th. n.d. *Adamantios Korais ke i Epohi tu*. Athens: Zaharopulos.

———. 1939. "Dimotikismos ke Kritiki." *Nea Estia* 26, 1498–1511.

————. 1975. *Istoria tis Neoellinikis Logotehnias.* 6th ed. Athens: Ikaros.

Dimiroulis, Dimitris. 1984. *I Kritiki ke i Piisi.* Ph.D. diss., University of Thessaloniki.

Dimitrakopulos, Andronikos. 1871. *Prosthike ke Diorthosis is tin Neoelliniki Fililoyia tu Konstantinu Satha.* Leipzig: Metzger & Gittig.

Dionysus of Halicarnassus. 1978. *Opuscules rhétoriques.* Germaine Aujuc, ed. Paris: Les Belles Lettres.

Di Pietro, Robert J., and Edward Ifkovic. 1983. *Ethnic Perspectives in American Literature.* New York: MLA.

Ditsa, Marianna. 1988. *Neoloyia ke Kritiki.* Athens: Ermis.

Doyle, Brian. 1982. "The Hidden History of English Studies." In *Re-Reading English.* Peter Widdowson, ed. New York: Methuen.

Dragumis, Ion. 1976. *O Ellinismos mu ke i Ellines.* Athens: n.p.

————. 1978. *Ellinikos Politismos.* 3d ed. Athens: Eleftheri Skepsis.

Drakoules, Platon E. 1897. *Neohellenic Language and Literature.* Oxford: Blackwell.

Dubois, Jacques. 1978. *L'Institution de la littérature.* Brussels: Editions Labor.

Eagleton, Terry. 1983. *Literary Theory: An Introduction.* Oxford: Basil Blackwell.

————. 1984. *The Function of Criticism: From the Spectator to Post-Structuralism.* London: Verso.

————. 1990. *The Ideology of the Aesthetic.* Oxford: Basil Blackwell.

Eagleton, Terry, Fredric Jameson, and Edward Said. 1990. *Nationalism, Colonialism, and Literature.* Minneapolis: University of Minnesota Press.

Eisenstein, Elizabeth L. 1979. *The Printing Press as an Agent of Change.* 2 vols. Cambridge: Cambridge University Press.

Eliot, T. S. 1957. *On Poetry and Poets.* New York: Farrar, Straus, and Cudahy.

Elytis, Odisseas. 1974. *Anihta Hartia.* Athens: Asterias.

Eusebius. 1889. *The Ecclesiastical History of Eusebius Pamphilus.* E. F. Crusé, trans. London: George Bell and Sons.

Fabian, Johannes. 1983. *Time and the Other: How Anthropology Makes Its Object.* New York: Columbia University Press.

Fallmerayer, Jakob Philipp. 1845. *Fragmente aus dem Orient II.* Stuttgart & Tübingen: J. G. Cotta.

Fauriel, Claude. 1824. *Chants populaires de la Grèce moderne.* 2 vols. Paris: n.p.

Fiedler, Leslie A., and Houston A. Baker (eds.). 1981. *English Literature: Opening the Canon.* Baltimore: Johns Hopkins University Press.

Filberg, F. 1901. "To Ethnikon Tipografion." *Armonia* 2, 135–59.

Filias, Vasilis. 1974. *Kinonia ke Exusia stin Ellada.* Athens: Makrionitis.

Filippidis, Daniil, and Grigorios Konstantas. 1988. *Yeografia Neoteriki.* Athens: Ermis.

Fish, Stanley. 1980. *Is There a Text in This Class? The Authority of Interpretive Communities.* Cambridge, Mass.: Harvard University Press.

Fisher, Dexter, and Robert B. Stepto (eds.). 1979. *Afro-American Literature: The Reconstruction of Instruction.* New York: MLA.

Fontius, Martin. 1977. "Productivkraftentfaltung und Autonomie der Kunst zur Ablösung ständischer Voraussetzungen in der Literaturtheorie." In *Literatur im Epochenumbruch.* Günther Klotz et al., eds. Berlin: Aufbau.

Forgacs, David. 1990. *Italian Culture in the Industrial Era: Cultural Industries, Politics and the Public.* Manchester: Manchester University Press.

Fowler, Alistair. 1982. *Kinds of Literature: An Introduction to the Theory of Genres and Modes.* Cambridge, Mass.: Harvard University Press.

Fritz, K. von. 1939. [Review of Oppel 1937]. *American Journal of Philology* 60, 112–15.

Frangos, George D. 1973. "The Philiki Etairia: A Premature National Coalition." In *The Struggle for Greek Independence.* Richard Clogg, ed. London: Macmillan.

Frangudaki, Anna. 1977. *Ekpedeftiki Metarrithmisi ke Fileleftheri Dianoumeni.* Athens: Kedros.

Galen. 1874. *De Placitis Hippocratis et Platonis I.* Müller, ed. Leipzig: Teubner.

———. 1969. *De Temperamentis III.* Georg Hermreich, ed. Stuttgart: Teubner.

Gates, Henry Louis, Jr. 1979. "Preface to Blackness: Text and Pretext." In *Afro-American Literature: The Reconstruction of Instruction.* Dexter Fisher and Robert B. Stepto, eds. New York: MLA.

———. 1984. "Criticism in the Jungle." In *Black Literary Theory.* H. L. Gates, Jr., ed. New York: Methuen.

———. 1987a. "What's Love Got to Do with It? Critical Theory, Integrity, and the Black Idiom." *New Literary History* 18, 2, 344–62.

———. 1987b. "Authority, (White) Power and the (Black) Critic." *Cultural Critique* 7, Fall, 19–46.

Gayle, Addison. 1971. *The Black Aesthetic.* Garden City, N.Y.: Doubleday.

Gellius, Aulus. 1927. *The Attic Nights of Aulus Gellius.* John Rolfe, trans. New York: Putnam's Sons.

Gervinus, Georg G. 1840. *Geschichte der poetischen National-Literatur der Deutschen.* Leipzig: Wilhelm Engelmann.

Giannaris, George. 1985. *I Ellines Metanastes ke to Ellinoamerikaniko Mithistorima.* Athens: Filipoti.

Gidel, M. A. C. 1864. *Etudes sur la littérature grecque moderne.* Paris: n.p.

Godzich, Wlad, and Jeffrey Kittay. 1987. *The Emergence of Prose: An Essay in Prosaics.* Minneapolis: University of Minnesota Press.

Godzich, Wlad, and Nicholas Spadaccini (eds.). 1986. *Literature among Discourses: The Spanish Golden Age.* Minneapolis: University of Minnesota Press.

Gourgouris, Stathis. 1989. "Writing the National Imaginary: The Memory of Makriyiannis and the Miracles of Neohellenism." *Emergences* 1, 95–130.

Graff, Gerald. 1987. *Professing Literature: An Institutional History.* Chicago: University of Chicago Press.

Gramsci, Antonio. 1985. *Selections from Cultural Writings.* William Boelhower, trans. Cambridge, Mass.: Harvard University Press.

Guyer, Paul. 1979. *Kant and the Claims of Taste.* Cambridge, Mass.: Harvard University Press.

Habermas, Jürgen. 1989. *The Structural Transformation of the Public Sphere: An Inquiry into a Category of Bourgeois Society.* Thomas Burger, trans. Cambridge, Mass.: MIT Press.

Halperin, David M. 1986. "One Hundred Years of Homosexuality." *Diacritics* 16, 2, 34–45.

Hantseris, Konstantinos A. (ed.), 1845. *Ellinikos Neos Parnassos, i, Apanthisma ton eklektoteron Piiseon tis Anayenithisis Ellados.* Athens: Garpodas.

Harlow, Barbara. 1987. *Resistance Literature.* New York: Methuen.

Haskell, Francis. 1976. *Rediscoveries in Art: Some Aspects of Taste, Fashion, and Collecting in England and France.* London: Phaidon.

Haxthausen, Werner von. 1935. *Neugriechische Volkslieder.* Münster: n.p.

Herder, Johann Gottfried. 1877. *Sämtliche Werke I.* B. Supham, ed. Berlin: Weidmann.

Herrnstein Smith, Barbara. 1984. "Contingencies of Value." In *Canons.* Robert von Hallberg, ed. Chicago: University of Chicago Press.

Herzfeld, Michael. 1982. *Ours Once More: Folklore, Ideology, and the Making of Modern Greece.* Austin: University of Texas Press.

————. 1987. *Anthropology through the Looking-Glass: Critical Ethnography in the Margins of Europe*. Cambridge: Cambridge University Press.

Hesseling, D. C. 1924. *Histoire de la littérature grecque moderne*. N. Pernot, trans. Paris: Les Belles Lettres.

Hoesterey, Ingeborg. 1982. "Der Laokoon-Faktor in der Moderne: Zum Problem der Medien-differenzierung in den Künsten." *Komparatistische Hefte* 5/6, 169–80.

Hohendahl, Peter Uwe. 1982. *The Institution of Criticism*. Ithaca, N.Y.: Cornell University Press.

————. 1983. "Beyond Reception Aesthetics." *New German Critique* 28, 108–46.

————. 1989. *Building a National Literature: The Case of Germany 1830–1870*. Renate Baron Franciscono, trans. Ithaca, N.Y.: Cornell University Press.

Holden, David. 1972. *Greece without Columns*. London: Faber & Faber.

Holland, Henry. 1815. *Travels in the Ionian Isles, Albania, Thessaly, Macedonia during the Years 1812 and 1813*. London: Longman.

Honnecke, Edgar. 1963. *New Testament Apocrypha*. Philadelphia: Westminster Press.

Hoogvelt, Ankie M. M. 1978. *The Sociology of Developing Societies*. London: Macmillan.

Hooks, Bell. 1981. *Ain't I a Woman? Black Women and Feminism*. Boston: South End Press.

Hrisanthopulos, E. P. (ed.). 1937. *Neoelliniki Antholoyia 800–1936*. Athens: Hrisanthopulos.

Hristopulos, Athanasios. 1847. *Antholoyia, iti, Diafora Asmata tu Athanasiu Hristopulu*. Athens: N. Angeliou.

Hull, Gloria T., P. Scott, and B. Smith (eds.). 1982. *All the Women Are White, All the Blacks Are Men but Some of Us Are Brave*. Old Westbury, N.Y.: Feminist Press.

Hume, David. 1937. *Principles and Practice of Teaching English*. New York: Prentice Hall.

Hunter, J. Paul. 1988. "News and New Things: Contemporaneity and the Early English Novel." *Critical Inquiry* 14, 3, 493–515.

Iken Carl. 1825. *Leukothea: Eine Sammlung von Briefen eines geborenen Griechen über Staatswesen, Literatur, und Dichtkunst der neueren Griechenlands*. Leipzig: Hartmann.

Ikonomu, M. H. (ed.). 1951. *Diiyimata Megalon Ellinon Diiyimatografon*. Athens: Papadimitrios.

————. 1952. *Antholoyia Ellinon Piiton*. Athens: Papadimitrios.

Iliu, Filippos. 1975. "Vivlia me Sindromites." *O Eranistis* 12, 69/70, 101–79.

————. 1989. *Ideoloyikes Hrisis tu Koraismu ston 20 eona*. Athens: Politis.

Issawi, Charles. 1983. "The Transformation of the Economic Position of the Millets in the 19th Century." In *Christians and Jews in the Ottoman Empire*. B. Braude and B. Lewis, eds. New York: Holmes and Meier.

Jameson, Fredric. 1972. *The Prison-House of Language: A Critical Account of Structuralism and Russian Formalism*. Princeton: Princeton University Press.

JanMohamed, Abdul, and David Lloyd. 1987. "Introduction: Toward a Theory of Minority Discourse." *Cultural Critique* 6, 5–12.

Jardine, Lisa. 1986. "'Girl Talk' (for Boys on the Left); or, Marginalizing Feminist Critical Praxis." *Oxford Literary Review* 8, 208–17.

Jauss, Hans Robert. 1982. *Toward an Aesthetic of Reception*. Timothy Bahti, trans. Minneapolis: University of Minnesota Press.

Jelavich, Barbara. 1983. *History of the Balkans: 18th and 19th Centuries*. Vol. 1. Cambridge: Cambridge University Press.

Jenkyns, Richard. 1980. *The Victorians and Ancient Greece*. Cambridge, Mass.: Harvard University Press.

Joseph, Brian. 1985. "European Hellenism and Greek Nationalism: Some Effects of Ethnocentrism on Greek Linguistic Scholarship." *Journal of Modern Greek Studies* 3, 1, 87–96.

Joyce, Joyce A. 1987a. "The Black Canon: Reconstructing Black American Literature." *New Literary History* 2, 18, 335–45.

———. 1987b "'Who the Cap Fit.' Unconsciousness and Unconscionableness in the Criticism of Houston A. Baker Jr. and Henry Louis Gates Jr." *New Literary History* 18, 2, 371–84.

Jusdanis, Gregory. 1987a. *The Poetics of Cavafy: Textuality, Eroticism, History.* Princeton: Princeton University Press.

———. 1987b. "East Is East—West Is West: It's a Matter of Greek Literary History." *Journal of Modern Greek Studies* 5, 1, 1–14.

———. 1987c. "Is Postmodernism Possible Outside the 'West'? The Case of Greece." *Byzantine and Modern Greek Studies* 11, 69–92.

Kaklamanis, Yerasimos. 1989. *Analisi tis Neoellinikis Astikis Ideoloyias.* 2d ed. Athens: Roes.

Kakuris, Yeoryios. 1971–72. "I Vivliothikes stin Ellada." *Kritika Filla* A, 326–32.

Kampanis, Aristos. 1925. *Istoria tis Neas Ellinikis Logotehnias.* 2d ed. Athens: Katsigonis.

———. 1935. *Istoria tis Neas Ellinikis Kritikis.* Athens: Nea Estia.

Kant, Immanuel. 1952. *The Critique of Judgement.* James Creed Meredith, trans. Oxford: Oxford University Press.

Karandonis, Andreas. 1976. *O Piitis Yiorgos Seferis.* 4th ed. Athens: Papadimas.

Karasutsas, Ioannis. 1860. *I Varvitos.* Athens: Sutsos.

Karpat, Kemal. 1973. *An Inquiry into the Social Foundations of Nationalism in the Ottoman State: From Social Estates to Classes, from Millets to Nations.* Princeton: Center for International Studies, Princeton University.

———. 1983. "Millets and Nationality." In *Christians and Jews in the Ottoman Empire.* B. Braude and B. Lewis, eds. New York: Holmes and Meier.

Karpozilu, Martha. 1982. *Afieromata Periodikon.* Athens: E.L.I.A.

Kasdonis, Yeoryios (ed.). 1896. *Ellinika Diiyimata.* Athens: Estia.

Katartzis, Dimitrios. 1970. *Ta Evriskomena.* Athens: Ermis.

Kedourie, Elie (ed.). 1970. *Nationalism in Asia and Africa.* New York: World.

Kehagioglou, Giorgios. 1980. "I Istories tis Neoellinikis Logotehnias." *Mantatoforos* 15, March, 5–66.

Kermode, Frank. 1979. "Institutional Control of Interpretation." *Salmagundi* 43, 72–86.

———. 1983. *The Classic.* Cambridge, Mass.: Harvard University Press.

———. 1985. *Forms of Attention.* Chicago: University of Chicago Press.

Kiklos 4. 1934. (special edition).

Kind, Theodor (ed.). 1833. *Neugriechische Poesieen.* Leipzig: n.p.

———. 1849. *Neugriechische Volkslieder.* Leipzig: n.p.

Kitroeff, Alexander. 1989. *The Greeks in Egypt, 1919–1937: Ethnicity and Class.* London: Ithaca Press.

Kitromilides, Paschalis M. 1985. "The Last Battle of the Ancients and Moderns: Ancient Greece and Modern Europe in the Neohellenic Revival." *Modern Greek Studies Yearbook* I. Minneapolis: University of Minnesota Press.

———. 1989. "'Imagined Communities' and the Origins of the National Question in the Balkans." *European History Quarterly* 19, 149–94.

Kitsos-Milonas, Andreas Th. (ed.). 1980. *Solomos: Prolegomena Kritika—Stai—Polila—Zambeliu.* Athens: E.L.I.A.

Kittler, Friedrich A. 1980. "Autorshaft und Liebe." In *Austreibung des Geistes aus den Geisteswissenschaften.* Friedrich A. Kittler, ed., Paderborn: Ferdinand Schöningh.

Knös, Börje. 1962. *L'Histoire de la littérature néo-Grecque.* Stockholm: Almqvist & Wiksell.

Kokkinakis, Dimitrios (ed.). 1902. *Panellinios Antholoyia, iti, Apanthisma ton Eklekteron Ellinikon Piimaton.* Athens: Kokkinakis.

Kokkinis, Spiros. 1969. *Vivliothikes ke Arhia stin Ellada.* Athens: n.p.

Kondilis, Panayiotis. 1988. *O Neoellinikos Diafotismos*. Athens: Themelio.

Konstantellou, Eva. 1991. "Beyond the Limits of Humanistic and Technocratic Ideologies in Education: A Critique of the Greek and American Models." Ph. D. diss., Ohio State University.

Konstantinidis, Anestis (ed.). 1884. *O Eros, iti, Silloyi Erotikon Asmaton*. Athens: Korais.

———. 1904. *Antholoyia, iti, Silloyi ton Ellinikon Asmaton*. Athens: Konstantinidis

Korais, Adamantios. 1949. *Adelfiki Didaskalia*. G. Valetas, ed. Athens: Piyis.

———. [1803] 1970. "Report on the Present State of Civilization in Greece." In *Nationalism in Asia and Africa*. E. Kedourie, ed. New York: World.

Kordatos, Yiannis. 1962. *Istoria tis Neoellinikis Logotehnias 1453–1962*. Athens: Epikerotita.

Koromilas, Andreas (ed.). 1835. *Antholoyia, i, Silloyi Asmaton, Iroikon ke Erotikon*. Athens: Koromilas.

Koumarianou, Ekaterini. 1964. "'Loyios Ermis.' Kosmopolitismos ke Ethnikos Haraktiras." *Epohes*, October, 3–7.

———. 1971. *O Tipos ston Agona*. Athens: Ermis.

Kourvetaris, Yorgos A., and Betty A. Dobratz. 1987. *A Profile of Modern Greece: In Search of Identity*. Oxford: Oxford University Press.

Krauss, Werner. 1959. *Studien und Aufsätze*. Berlin: Rütten & Loening.

Kriaras, Emmanuil. 1964. "I Filoloyiki Yenea tu 30." *Epohes*, January, 11–16.

Kristeller, Paul Oscar. 1965. *Renaissance Thought II*. New York: Harper and Row.

Kuhn, Thomas S. 1970. *The Structure of Scientific Revolutions*. 2d ed. Chicago: University of Chicago Press.

———. 1977. *The Essential Tension*. Chicago: University of Chicago Press.

Kumanudis, Stefanos. 1900. *Sinagoyi Neon Lexeon*. 2 vols. Athens: n.p.

Lamber, Juliette. 1880. Poètes Grecs contemporains. In *La Nouvelle Revue*, March.

Lambikis, Dimitris. 1936. *Ellinides Piitries*. Athens: n.p.

Lambropoulos, Vassilis. 1988. *Literature as National Institution: Studies in the Politics of Greek Criticism*. Princeton: Princeton University Press.

———. Forthcoming. *Emancipation and Interpretation: Autonomy and the Aesthetic Turn in Modernity*. Princeton: Princeton University Press.

Lamont, Michèle, 1987. "How to Become a Dominant French Philosopher: The Case of Jacques Derrida." *American Journal of Sociology*, 93, 3, 584–622.

Lamont, Michèle, and Annette Lareau. 1988. "Cultural Capital: Allusions, Gaps and Glissandos in Recent Theoretical Developments." *Sociological Theory* 6, 153–68.

Larson, Charles R. 1972–73. "Heroic Ethnocentrism: The Idea of Universality in Literature." *American Scholar* 42, 463–75.

Larson, Magali S. 1977. *The Rise of Professionalism: A Sociological Analysis*. Berkeley: University of California Press.

Laskaratos, Andreas. 1959. *Apanta III*. Athens: Atlas.

Lavagnini, Bruno. 1969. *La letteratura neoellenica*. Florence: Sansoni/Accademia.

Leake, William Martin. 1814. *Researches in Greece*. London: John Booth.

———. 1935. *Travels in Northern Greece IV*. London: Jay Rodwell.

Legg, Keith R. 1977. "The Nature of the Modern Greek State." In *Greece in Transition*. John T. A. Koumoulides, ed. London: Zeno.

Legrand, Emile (ed.). 1903. *Morceaux choisis en grec savant du XIXᵉ siècle*. Paris: Ernest Leroux.

———. 1907. *Collection de monuments pour servir à l'étude de la langue moderne*. Paris: n.p.

Lelekos, Mihalis (ed.). 1852. *Dimotiki Antholoyia*. Athens: Angelidu.

Leontis, Artemis. 1987. "'The Lost Center' and the Promised Land of Greek Criticism." *Journal of Modern Greek Studies* 5, 2, 175–90.

———. 1990. "Minor Fields, Major Territories: Dilemmas in Modernizing Hellenism." *Journal of Modern Greek Studies* 8, 1, 35–63.

———. 1991. "Territories of Hellenism: Modernism, Nationalism, and Tradition." Ph. D. diss., Ohio State University.

Leppert, Richard. 1989. "Music, Representation, and Social Order in Early-Modern Europe." *Cultural Critique* 12, 25–55.

Ling, Amy. 1987. "I'm Here: An Asian American Woman's Response." *New Literary History* 19, 1, 151–60.

Lloyd, David. 1986. "Arnold, Ferguson, Schiller: Aesthetic Culture and the Politics of Aesthetics." *Cultural Critique* 2, Winter, 137–69.

———. 1987. *Nationalism and Minor Literature.* Berkeley: University of California Press.

Loliée, Frédéric. 1904. *A Short History of Comparative Literature.* M. D. Power, trans. New York: G. P. Putman's Sons.

Lorentzatos, Zissimos. 1980. *The Lost Center and Other Essays on Greek Poetry.* Kay Cicellis, trans. Princeton: Princeton University Press.

Lovell, Terry. 1987. *Consuming Fiction.* London: Verso.

Luhmann, Niklas. 1982. *The Differentiation of Society.* Stephen Holmes and Charles Larmore, trans. New York: Columbia University Press.

Mackridge, Peter. 1985. *The Modern Greek Language.* Oxford: Oxford University Press.

Mainardi, Patricia. 1987. *Art and Politics of the Second Empire: The Universal Expositions of 1855 and 1867.* New Haven: Yale University Press.

Mango, Cyril. 1965. "Byzantinism and Romantic Hellenism." *Journal of the Warburg and Courtauld Institutes* 28, 29–43.

Mantran, Robert. 1983. "Foreign Merchants and the Minorities in Istanbul during the 16th and 17th Centuries." In *Christians and Jews in the Ottoman Empire.* B. Braude and B. Lewis, eds. New York: Holmes and Meier.

Marcus, George E., and Michael M. J. Fischer. 1986. *Anthropology as Cultural Critique.* Chicago: University of Chicago Press.

Margaris, Dimitris. n.d. *Ta Palia Periodika: I Istoria tus ke i Epohi tus.* Athens: Sideris.

———. 1940. "I Protes Neoellinikes Antholoyies." *Nea Estia* 27, 211–15.

Mariátegui, José Carlos. 1971. *Seven Interpretive Essays.* M. Urquidi, trans. Austin: University of Texas Press.

Matarangas, Panayiotis (ed.). 1880. *Parnassos: Anthodesmi, iti, Piitiki Silloyi pros Hrisis ton Pedion.* Athens: Mavrommatis.

Mazarakis-Enian, Ioannis K. 1970. "Ta Ellinika Tipografia tu Agonos." *Nea Estia* 88, 266–85.

Melas, Spiros. 1962. *Neoelliniki Logotehnia.* Athens: Fexis.

Mendelssohn, Moses. 1929. *Schriften zur Philosophie und Asthetik I.* Berlin: Akademie Verlag.

Mihalopulos, N. (ed.). 1888. *Antholoyia Piitiki, iti, Silloyi Eklekton Asmaton.* Athens: n.p.

Miller, William. 1905. *Greek Life in Town and Country.* London: G. Newnes.

Mirambel, André. 1950. *Anthologie de la prose néohellénique 1884–1948.* Paris: Libraire Klincksieck.

———. 1953. *La littérature grecque moderne.* Paris: Presses Universitaires de France.

Mitchell, W. J. T. 1989. "*Ut Pictura Theoria:* Abstract Painting and the Repression of Language." *Critical Inquiry* 15, 2, 348–71.

Moritz, Karl Philipp. 1962. *Schriften zur Asthetik und Poetik.* Tübingen: Max Niemeyer.

Moulin, Raymond. 1987. *The French Art Market: A Sociological View.* Arthur Goldhammer, trans. New Brunswick, N.J.: Rutgers University Press.

Mouzelis, Nicos P. 1978. *Modern Greece: Facets of Underdevelopment.* London: Macmillan.
———. 1986. *Politics in the Semi-Periphery.* London: Macmillan.
Mulas, Panayiotis. 1981. "I Athinaiki Panepistimiaki Kritiki ke o Roidis." In *I Kritiki sti Neoteri Ellada.* G. Dallas et al. Athens: Eteria Spudon.
Mustoxidis, Andreas. 1843–53. *Ellinomnimon i Simmikta Ellinika* [series of 12 pamphlets]. Athens: n.p.
Nelson, Cary. 1987. "Against English: Theory and the Limits of the Discipline." *Profession 87.* New York: MLA.
Ngugi Wa Thiong'o. 1972. *Homecoming: Essays on African and Caribbean Literature, Culture and Politics.* London: Heinemann
———. 1981. *Writers in Politics.* London: Heinemann.
Nicolai, Rudolf. 1876. *Geschichte der Neugriechischen Literatur.* Leipzig: Brodhaus.
Ohmann, Richard. 1976. *English in America: A Radical Critique of the Profession.* New York: Oxford University Press.
Oppel, H. 1937. "*Kanon.* Zur Bedeutungsgeschichte des Wortes und seiner lateinischen Ent-sprechungen." *Philologus,* Suppl. 30, 4, xiv-108.
Ortega y Gasset, José. 1968. *The Dehumanization of Art, and Other Essays on Art, Culture, and Literature.* Princeton: Princeton University Press.
Pagels, Elaine. 1979. *The Gnostic Gospels.* New York: Random House.
Panayiotopulos, I. M. 1936 [Review of Apostolidis's *Antholoyia*] *Kiklos,* 351–52.
Panayiotopulos, I. M., D. Zakithimos, and E. Papanutsos. 1956. *Neoelliniki Kritiki.* Athens: Aetos.
Pantazidis, I. 1886. "Filoloyia, Grammatoloyia, Logotehnia." *Estia,* KB' 545–48.
———. 1889. *Hronikon tis Protis Pentikontaetias tu Elliniku Panepistimiu.* Athens: n.p.
Pantazis, Yeoryios (ed.). 1850. *Silloyi Erotikon, Iroikon ke Simmikton Piimaton.* Zakinthos: K. Rosomilos.
Papacostea-Danielopolu, Cornelia. 1970. "Les lectures grecque dan les principautés roumaines après 1821 (1821–1866)." *Balkan Studies* 11, 157–68.
Papadimas, Adamantios D. 1923. *I Nei Diiyimatografi.* Athens: Athena.
———. 1976. *Logotehnia ke Zoi.* Athens: Th. Dimakarakos.
Papadopulos-Vretos, Andreas. 1854–57. *Neoelliniki Filoloyia.* 2 vols. Athens: Vilaras & Piumis.
Papakostas, Yiannis. 1982. *To Periodiko Estia ke to Diiyima.* Athens: Ekpedeftiria Kostea-Yitona.
———. 1987. "Ta Filoloyika Kafenia." *To Vima,* July 12.
Papapanu, Kostas. 1973. *I Piitiki Diagonismi ke i Dimotiki Glossa.* Athens: Idrima Evropis Dragan.
Papayeoryiu, Sofi. 1975. "I Tipografia stin Athina sta prota Othonika Hronia." *O Eranistis* 12, 68, 53–72.
Parashos, Kleon, and Xenofon Lefkoparidis (eds.). 1931. *Ekloyi apo ta Oreotera Ellinika Lirika Piimata.* Athens: Flammas.
Peranthis, Mihalis (ed.). 1954. *Megali Elliniki Piitiki Antholoyia 1453–1954.* Athens: Dimitrakos.
Petropulos, John A. 1968. *Politics and Statecraft in the Kingdom of Greece 1833–43.* Princeton: Princeton University Press.
Pfeiffer, Rudolph. 1968. *History of Classical Scholarship I.* Oxford: Oxford University Press.
Pliny. 1952. *Natural History.* H. Rackham, trans. Cambridge, Mass.: Harvard University Press.
Polemis, Ioannis (ed.). 1910. *Lira: Antholoyia tis Neoteras Ellinikis Piiseos.* Athens: Elliniki Ekdotiki Eteria.

Politis, Fotos. 1938. *Ekloyi apo to Ergo tu.* Athens: Estia.

Politis, Linos. 1973. *A History of Modern Greek Literature.* Oxford: Oxford University Press.

———. 1975. *Piitiki Antholoyia.* 7 vols. Athens: Dodoni.

Politis, N. G. 1914. *Ekloge apo ta Tragudia tu Elliniku Lau.* Athens: Estia.

Polizoidis, Anastasios. 1973. *Katastasis tis Ellinikis Pedias ipo to Kratos ton Othomanon.* Athens: Byron.

Pollis, Adamantia. 1987. "Notes on Nationalism and Human Rights in Greece." *Journal of Modern Hellenism* 4, 147–60.

Pollitt, J. J. 1974. *The Ancient View of Greek Art: Criticism, History, and Terminology.* New Haven: Yale University Press.

Poulantzas, Nikos. 1976. *The Crisis of the Dictatorships.* David Fernbach, trans. London: NLB.

Pratt, Mary Louise. 1986. "Comparative Literature as Cultural Practice." *Profession 86.* New York: MLA.

Prawer, S. S. 1973. *Comparative Literary Studies.* London: Duckworth.

Pringos, Ioannis. 1931. "To Hroniko tu Amsterdam." *Nea Estia* 10, 846–53.

Psiharis, Yiannis. 1935. *To Taxidi mu.* 4th ed. Athens: Vivlioekdodiki.

Quintilian, Marcus Fabius. 1922. *Institutio Oratoria.* H. E. Butler, trans. Cambridge, Mass.: Harvard University Press.

Rangavis, Alexandros (A. Rangabé). 1877. *Histoire littéraire de le Grèce moderne.* Paris: Michel Lévy Frères.

———. 1887. *Perilipsis Istorias tis Neoellinikis Filoloyias.* Athens: Bart.

Raptarhis, Ioannis (ed.). 1868. *Parnassos, i, Apanthisma ton Eklektoteron Temahion tis Neas Ellinikis Piiseos.* Athens: Tefarikis.

Remak, Henry H. 1961. "Comparative Literature, Its Definition and Function." In *Comparative Literature: Method and Perspective.* Newton Stallknecht and Horst Frenz, eds. Carbondale: Southern Illinois University Press.

Renan, Ernst. 1990. "What Is a Nation." In *Nation and Narration.* Homi Bhabha, ed. London: Routledge.

Retamar, Roberto Fernández. 1989. *Caliban and Other Essays.* Edward Baker, trans. Minneapolis: University of Minnesota Press.

Reynolds, L. D., and N. G. Wilson. 1974. *Scribes and Scholars: A Guide to the Transmission of Greek and Latin Literature.* 2d. ed. Oxford: Oxford University Press.

Rizos-Nerulos, Iakovos. 1827. *Cours de littérature grecque moderne.* Geneva: Abraham Cherbuliez.

———. 1870. *Istoria ton Grammaton para tis Neoteris Ellisi.* Olympia Abbot, trans. Athens: n.p.

Roidis, Emmanuil. 1978. *Apanta.* Athens: Ermis.

Rosaldo, Renato. 1987. "Politics, Patriarchs, and Laughter." *Cultural Critique* 6, 65–86.

Roxborough, Ian. 1979. *Theories of Underdevelopment.* London: Macmillan.

Rudolph, Lloyd I., and Susanne Hoeber Rudolph. 1967. *The Modernity of Tradition: Political Development in India.* Chicago: University of Chicago Press.

Ruhnken, David. 1823. "Historia Critica Oratorum Graecorum." *Opuscula I.*

Runciman, Steven. 1968. *The Great Church in Captivity.* Cambridge: Cambridge University Press.

Sahinis, Apostolos. 1964. *Simvoli stin Istoria tis Pandoras ke ton Palion Periodikon.* Athens: n.p.

Sainte-Beuve. 1971. *Literary Criticism of Sainte-Beuve.* Lincoln: University of Nebraska Press.

Saliveros, Mihalis (ed.). 1911. *Nea Elliniki Antholoyia, iti, Silloyi Eklekton ke Neoteron Ellinikon Piimaton.* Athens: Saliveros.

Sanders, Ivan. 1987. "The Other Europeans." *The Nation,* September 19.

Sanders, James A. 1972. *Torah and Canon.* Philadelphia: Fortress Press.

Sandys, John Edwin. 1915. *A Short History of Classical Scholarship.* Cambridge: Cambridge University Press.

Sangari, Kumkum. 1987. "The Politics of the Possible." *Cultural Critique* 7, 157–86.

Sathas, Konstantinos. 1868. *Neoelliniki Filoloyia: Viografie ton en tis Grammasi Dialampsanton Ellinon 1453–1821.* Athens: Koromilas.

Schenda, Rudolf. 1976. *Die Lesestoffe der kleinen Leute: Studien zur popularen Literatur im 19 und 20 Jahrhundert.* Munich: C. H. Beck.

Schiller, Friedrich. 1967. *On the Aesthetic Education of Man.* E. Wilkinson and L. Willoughby, trans. Oxford: Oxford University Press.

Schlegel, Friedrich. 1947. *Uber das Studium der Griechischen Poesie.* Godesberg: Helmut Küpper.

Schulte-Sasse, Jochen. 1985. "Afterword." In Jay Caplan, *Framed Narratives: Diderot's Genealogy of the Beholder.* Minneapolis: University of Minnesota Press.

———. 1986–87. "Imagination and Modernity; or, The Taming of the Human Mind." *Cultural Critique* 5, Winter, 23–48.

———. 1989. "The Prestige of the Artist under Conditions of Modernity." *Cultural Critique* 12, Spring, 83–100.

Schulz, Dieterich. 1955. "Zum Kanon Polyklets." *Hermes* 83, 200–220.

Seferis, George. 1966. *On the Greek Style.* Rex Warner and Th. Frangopoulos, trans. Boston: Little Brown & Co.

Seneca. 1917. *The Epistles of Seneca.* Richard Grummere, trans. New York: Putnam's Sons.

Shafer, Boyd D. 1972. *Faces of Nationalism: New Realities and Old Myths.* New York: Harcourt Brace Jovanovich.

Shaw, Stanford. 1976. *History of the Ottoman Empire and Modern Turkey.* Vol. 1. Cambridge: Cambridge University Press.

Sheridan, Charles Brinsley. 1825. *The Songs of Greece* [translation of Fauriel 1824]. London: Longman.

Shils, Edward. 1981. *Tradition.* Chicago: University of Chicago Press.

Sideris, Ioannis N. (ed.). 1921. *Neoelliniki Antholoyia.* 2d ed. Athens: Sideris.

Sigalas, Antonios N. (ed.). 1880. *Silloyi Ethnikon Asmaton.* Athens: H. N. Filadelfeos.

Sikutris, Ioannis. 1956. *Melete ke Arthra.* Athens: Ekdosis tu Egeu.

Simiriotis, Yioryis (ed.). 1952. *Nea Elliniki Antholoyia 1870–1950.* Athens: Hrisis Dafnis.

Skliros, G. 1976. *To Kinoniko mas Zitima.* Athens: Epikerotita.

Skokos, Konstantinos (ed.). 1920–28. *To Ellinikon Diiyima, iti, Apanthisma Eklekton Diiyimaton tis Neoellinikis Logotehnias.* 2 vols. Athens: Estia.

Skoku, Angeliki. 1977. *I Merimna yia tis Arheotites stin Ellada ke ta prota Musia.* Athens: Ermis.

Skopetea, Elli. 1988. *To "Protipo Vasilio" ke i Megali Idea.* Athens: n.p.

Sokolis, K. S. 1916. *Aftokratoria.* Athens: Angira.

de Souza, Anthony R., and Philip W. Porter. 1974. *Underdevelopment and Modernization of the Third World.* Washington, D.C.: Association of American Geographers.

Spencer, Benjamin T. 1957. *The Quest for Nationality.* Syracuse, N.Y.: Syracuse University Press.

St. Clair, William. 1972. *That Greece Might Still Be Free: The Philhellene in the War of Independence.* London: Oxford University Press.

Stallknecht, Newton P., and Horst Frenz (eds.). 1961. *Comparative Literature: Method and Perspective.* Carbondale: Southern Illinois University Press.

Stallybrass, Peter, and Allon White. 1986. *The Politics and Poetics of Transgression*. Ithaca, N.Y.: Cornell University Press.

Stavrianos, L. S. 1963. *The Balkans 1815–1914*. New York: Holt, Rinehart, and Winston.

———. 1974. "The Influence of the West on the Balkans." In *The Balkans in Transition*. Charles and Barbara Jelavich, eds. Hamden, Conn.: Archon.

Suetonius. n.d. *De Grammaticis et Rhetoribus Liber*. Cesare Bione, ed. Palermo: G. B. Palumbo Editore.

Sugar, Peter E. 1972. *Southeastern Europe under Ottoman Rule 1354–1804*. Seattle: University of Washington Press.

Sundberg, Albert C. 1971. "The Making of the New Testament Canon." In *The Interpreter's One-Volume Commentary on the Bible*. Charles Laymon, ed. New York: Abingdon Press.

———. 1975. "The Bible Canon and the Christian Doctrine of Inspiration." *Interpretation* 29, 4, 352–71.

Svoronos, Nikos. 1976. *Episkotisi tis Neoellinikis Istorias*. Ekaterini Asdraha, trans. Athens: Themelio.

Tagopulos, Dimitrios (ed.). 1899. *I Nea Laiki Antholoyia*. Athens: Papadimitrios.

Theotokas, Yiorgos. 1979. *Eleisthero Pnevma*. Athens: Nea Elliniki Vivliothiki.

Thompson, Michael. 1979. *Rubbish Theory: The Creation and Destruction of Value*. Oxford: Oxford University Press.

Tignor, Robert L. 1966. *Modernization and British Colonial Rule in Egypt, 1882–1914*. Princeton: Princeton University Press.

Tipps, Dean C. 1973. "Modernization Theory and the Comparative Study of Societies: A Critical Perspective." *Comparative Studies in Society and History* 15, 1, 199–226.

Todorov, Tzvetan. 1984. *The Conquest of America: The Question of the Other*. Richard Howard, trans. New York: Harper and Row.

———. 1986. "Critical Response." *Critical Inquiry* 13, 171–81.

Tompkins, Jane. 1986. *Sensational Designs: The Cultural Work of American Fiction*. Oxford: Oxford University Press.

Trypanis, C. A. 1981. *Greek Poetry from Homer to Seferis*. Chicago: University of Chicago Press.

Tsigakou, Fani-Maria. 1981. *The Rediscovery of Greece: Travellers and Painters in the Romantic Era*. New Rochelle, N.Y.: Caratzas Brothers.

Tsoucalas, Constantinos. 1977. *Exartisi ke Anaparagoyi: O Kinonikos Rolos ton Ekpedeftikon Mihanismon stin Ellada*. Athens: Themelio.

———. 1978. "On the Problem of Political Clientelism in Greece in the 19th Century." *Journal of the Hellenic Diaspora* 1, 5–15; 2, 5–17.

———. 1981. *Kinoniki Anaptixi ke Kratos: I Singrotisi tu Dimosiu Horu stin Ellada*. Athens: Themelio.

———. 1981. "Some Aspects of 'Over-Education' in Greece." *Journal of the Hellenic Diaspora* 8, 1 and 2, 109–21.

———. 1983. "Paradosi ke Eksinghronismo: Merika Yenikotera Erotimata." In *Ellinismos—Ellinikotita*. D. G. Tsausis, ed. Athens: Estia.

Turner, Bryan S. 1988. *Status*. Milton Keynes: Open University Press.

Turro, James, and Raymond Brown. 1968. "Canonicity." In *The Jerome Biblical Commentary I & II*. R. Brown, J. Fitzmyer, and R. Murphy, eds. Engelwood Cliffs, N.J.: Prentice Hall.

Tziovas, Dimitris. 1986. *The Nationism of the Demoticists and Its Impact on Their Literary Theory (1888–1930)*. Amsterdam: Adolf M. Hakkert.

———. 1987. *Meta tin Esthitiki*. Athens: Gnosi.

————. 1989. *I Metamorfosis tu Ethnismu ke to Ideoloyima tis Ellinikotitas sto Mesapolemo.* Athens: Odisseas.

Vakalo, Eleni. 1983. *O Mithos tis Ellinikotitas.* Athens: Kedros.

Valetas, G. 1937. "I Panepistimiaki Kritiki ke i Epidrasi tis sti Neoelliniki Piisi." *Nea Estia* 263, 1819–44.

————. 1947–49. *Antholoyia tis Dimotikis Pezografias.* Athens: Petros Panos.

Vayenas, Nasos. 1986. "Neoelliniki Logotehnia ke Elliniko Panepistimio." *Andi* 309, 50–52.

Velimirovic, Milos. 1986. "Changing Interpretations of Music." *New Literary History* 17, 2, 365–80.

Veloudis, Georg. 1974. *Das griechische Druck- und Verlagshaus "Glikis" in Venedig (1670–1854).* Wiesbaden: Otta Harrassowitz.

————. 1983. *Germanograecia: Deutsche Einflüsse auf die neugriechischen Literatur (1750–1944).* 2 vols. Amsterdam: Adolf M. Hakkert.

————. 1987 "Grammatoloyia, Grammatia, Logotehnia." *Diavazo* 175, 9–10.

Vernardakis, Dimitrios. 1884. *O Psevdattikismu Elenghos.* Trieste: n.p.

Vernardakis, Grigorios N. 1899. *Logos Isitirios peri Filoloyias.* Trieste: n.p.

Vikelas, Dimitrios. 1871. *Peri Neoellinikis Filoloyias.* London: Taylor and Francis.

Vilaras, Ioannis. 1935. *Apanta.* Athens: Pella.

Vitti, Mario. 1978. *Istoria tis Neoellinikis Logotehnias.* Mirsini Zorba, trans. Athens: Odisseas.

Voutieridis, Ilias. 1924–27. *Istoria tis Neoellinikis Logotehnias.* Athens: Mihalis Zikanis.

Vovolinis, Konstantinos, A. 1951. *To Hronikon tu "Parnassu" 1865–1950.* Athens: Parnassos.

Vranusis, L. I. 1971–72. "Neoellinikes Filoloyikes Spudes." *Kritika Filla* A. 39–50.

Walker, Christopher J. 1980. *Armenia: The Survival of a Nation.* London: Croom Helm.

Wallerstein, Immanuel. 1974. *The Modern World-System: Capitalist Agriculture and the Origins of the European World-Economy in the 16th Century.* New York: Academic Press.

————. 1979. *The Capitalist World-Economy.* Cambridge: Cambridge University Press.

Ware, Timothy. 1963. *The Orthodox Church.* London: Penguin.

Wartofsky, Marx W. 1980. "Art, Artworlds, and Ideology." *Journal of Aesthetics and Art Criticism* 38, 239–47.

Weisstein, Ulrich. 1973. *Comparative Literature and Literary Theory.* William Riggan, trans. Bloomington: Indiana University Press.

Wellbery, David E. 1984. *Lessing's Laocoon: Semiotics and Aesthetics in the Age of Reason.* Cambridge: Cambridge University Press.

Wellek, René. 1953. "The Concept of Comparative Literature." *Yearbook of Comparative and General Literature II,* 1–5.

————. 1970. *Discriminations.* New Haven: Yale University Press.

————. 1978. "What Is Literature?" In *What Is Literature?* Paul Hernadi, ed. Bloomington: Indiana University Press.

Wellek, René, and Austin Warren. 1963. *Theory of Literature.* Harmondsworth: Penguin.

Werblowsky, R. J. Zwi. 1976. *Beyond Tradition and Modernity: Changing Religions in a Changing World.* London: Athlone Press.

Williams, Raymond. 1977. *Marxism and Literature.* Oxford: Oxford University Press.

Wimsatt, William K., and Cleanth Brooks. 1957. *Literary Criticism: A Short History.* Vols. 1 & 2. Chicago: University of Chicago Press.

Woodmansee, Martha. 1984. "The Interest in Disinterestedness: Karl Philipp Moritz and the Emergence of the Theory of Aesthetic Autonomy in Eighteenth-Century Germany." *Modern Language Quarterly* 17, 3, 22–47.

————. 1988–89. "Toward a Geneology of the Aesthetic: The German Reading Debate of the 1790s." *Cultural Critique* 11, 203–221.

Xydis, Alexander. 1984. "Greek Art in the European Context." *Journal of Modern Greek Studies* 2, 141–62.

Xydis, Stephen. 1969. "Modern Greek Nationalism." In *Nationalism in Eastern Europe.* Peter Sugar and Ivo Lederer, eds. Seattle: University of Washington Press.

Yemeniz, Eugène. 1862. *La Grèce moderne héros et poètes.* Paris: Michel Lévy Frères.

Yerasimos, Stéphane. 1988. "Les Rapports Gréco-Turcs Mythes et Réalités." In *Le Différend Gréco-Turc.* Semih Vaner, ed. Paris: Editions L'Harmattan.

Yiannopulos, Periklis. 1963. *Apanta.* Athens: n.p.

Zambelios, Spiridon. 1852. *Asmata Dimotika tis Ellados.* Athens: n.p.

Zaviras, Yeoryios. 1872. *Nea Ellas, i, Ellinikon Theatron.* Athens: G. Kremos.

Zetzel, James E. G. 1984. "Re-creating the Canon: Augustan Poetry and the Alexandrian Past." In *Canons.* Robert von Hallberg, ed. Chicago: University of Chicago Press.

Index

Aesthetics of autonomy, 78–84; compensatory function of, 78
African-American culture, 9–10, 47, 168n
Alexiou, Margaret, 41, 172n
Anderson, Benedict, 26, 41, 163
Anthologies, 66–68; Hantseris, Konstantinos, 68–69; Kasdonis, Yeoryios, 75–76; Konstantinidis, Anestis, 75; Koromilas, Andreas, 6; Matarangas, Panayiotis, 70; Parashos, Kleon, and Xenofon Lefkoparidis, 83; Raptarhis, Ioannis, 69–70
Apostolakis, Yiannis, 137
Art: classical, 15, 89–90; courtly, 95–96; emergence of, 91–95; function of, 103; modern Greek, 170n; and public sphere, 96–100
Asante, Molefi Kete, 9–10
Auerbach, Erich, 59

Balkans, the, 18–19
Batteux, Charles, 91
Baudrillard, Jean, 10, 169n
Baumgarten, Alexander Gottlieb, 91
Becker, Howard S., 125
Bergk, Johann Adam, 61–62
Book trade, 154–59; controlled by church, 155; and printing presses, 156–58; and secularism, 156; by subscription, 154–55

Bourdieu, Pierre, 65, 181n
Bourgeois public sphere, 96–100; dissolution of, 100–102; and literature, 99–100; and music, 98; and painting, 99. *See also* Magazines; Press
Browning, Robert, 41
Bürger, Christa, 95–96
Bürger, Peter, 126–28

Canada, xvi, xviii, 47
Canons: and aesthetic consumption, 65; and anthologies, 75; and Christian Bible, 55–59; classical, 49–52; consolidation of Greek canon, 84–87; and cultural capital, 65–66; definition of, 61; emergence of, 61; etymology of, 53, 172n; function of, 59–62; and genre, 175n; and Hebrew Bible, 55; Hellenistic, 54, 173n; and modernity, 61–62; and natural sciences, 174n; and taste, 60–61; theories of, 49–52. *See also* Value
Cavafy, Constantine, 139, 178n
Classic, the, 174n
Clientelistic networks, 106–7
Comparative literature, 2–5; critique of, 3–4, 6; and nationalism, 4
Cultural capital, 65–66, 176n

Theory and History of Literature

Gregory Jusdanis is associate professor of modern Greek at the Ohio State University and the author of *The Poetics of Cavafy: Textuality, Eroticism, History* (1987).